UNDERSTANDING FAMILY CARE

0335195741

UNDERSTANDING FAMILY CARE
A Multidimensional Model of Caring and Coping

Mike Nolan
Gordon Grant
John Keady

Open University Press
Buckingham · Philadelphia

Open University Press
Celtic Court
22 Ballmoor
Buckingham
MK18 1XW

and
1900 Frost Road, Suite 101
Bristol, PA 19007, USA

First Published 1996

A catalogue record of this book is available from the British Library

ISBN   0 335 19574 1 (hb)   0 335 19573 3 (pb)

Library of Congress Cataloging-in-Publication Data
Nolan, Mike, 1953–
    Understanding family care : a multidimensional model of caring
and coping / Mike Nolan, Gordon Grant, and John Keady.
        p.   cm.
    Includes bibliographical references and index.
    ISBN 0–335–19574–1 (hardcover). — ISBN 0–335–19573–3 (pbk.)
    1. Aged—Home care.   2. Handicapped—Home care.   3. Caregivers.
4. Home care services.   I. Grant, Gordon, 1946– .   II. Keady,
John, 1961– .   III. Title.
HV1451.N66   1996
362'.0425—dc20   96–20513
                                                                CIP

Typeset by Graphicraft Typesetters Ltd, Hong Kong
Printed in Great Britain by St Edmundsbury Press, Bury St Edmunds, Suffolk

To *Janet Nolan, Margaret Grant and Claire, Jessica and Christopher Keady*

CONTENTS

ACKNOWLEDGEMENTS

It is impossible to thank on an individual basis all those people who, in one way or another, have contributed to the production of this book. It would certainly not have been possible without those family carers who so willingly shared their experiences with us and who provided the insights on which this book is based. We would like to offer them our sincere appreciation.

Thanks are also due to colleagues who commented on various drafts and to Joan Malherbe and Jacinta Evans of Open University Press for their patience and understanding.

We are however particularly indebted to one individual, Helen Shaw, who responded with unfailing good humour to the most dreaded of phrases, 'just one more minor amendment'. The brief recognition accorded her here in no way reflects the level of energy, commitment and skill that she brought to bear in producing this manuscript. Diolwch yn Fawr, Helen.

Introduction

FAMILY CAREGIVING – THE NEED FOR A MULTIDIMENSIONAL APPROACH

According to Arber and Ginn (1990), the term 'caring', at least in so far as it is currently applied to the interactions between families and cared-for persons, is very much a product of the 1980s. They suggest that prior to this, caring or caregiving did not even merit an entry in a dictionary. Yet by the middle of that decade it was confidently asserted that 'caring is news' (Ungerson 1987). Certainly, as George (1994) has noted, the academic literature on caregiving has grown significantly in both volume and sophistication in the last ten years, but despite what she describes as a 'decade of fertile effort', she is still of the opinion that there remains much to learn about caregiving at both conceptual and empirical levels. This perceived deficit exists despite the fact that the literature on caregiving is now so extensive that it is considered impossible to make sense of it 'within a coherent scheme of understanding' (Gubrium 1995: 267).

Herein lies both a conundrum and a paradox: how can such a voluminous literature still only cover a 'small corner' of the potential field of study (Kahana et al. 1994)? We seek to address such issues. In writing this book we are conscious that there will be those who may consider that such a volume is unnecessary, that the field of family caregiving has already been 'done to death'! Nothing could be further from the truth, for in reality much of what has been written has been dominated by either a particular methodological or theoretical stance, and is limited as a consequence. Such a partial consideration is perhaps inevitable in a relatively new and still-emerging field of study, but the inherent risk is that because the literature on caregiving is so extensive it will be thought that there is little left to learn. We would agree with Gubrium (1995) that it is time to take stock, to question the value of overly simplified causal models and to return to such basic questions as: 'What is this thing some call caregiving?' 'How does it relate to the way everyday life is practised in relation to it?' (p. 268).

This is necessary because the term 'caring', despite extensive usage, remains poorly defined irrespective of whether it is applied to family (Arber and Ginn 1990) or professional carers (Radsma 1994; Kyle 1995; Scott 1995). As we shall illustrate, current definitions and models of caring are essentially limited to task-based conceptualizations. Indeed even those models which purport to offer a more 'sophisticated understanding' (Parker and Lawton 1994) seem unable to move beyond the physical dimensions of caring. Yet it has been apparent for some time that a primarily instrumental approach fails to capture the dynamic nature of family caregiving (Given and Given 1991), and there is now a growing recognition that we need to widen conceptual horizons (Greene and Coleman 1995) and to seek to understand caregiving by purpose and aspect rather than task (Wenger *et al.* 1996).

Kahana and Young (1990) suggested that the challenge for the future was to build more theoretically rigorous and empirically relevant models of care which would account for its multidimensional and dynamic nature. Such a plea has been reiterated a number of times (Schulz and Williamson 1993; Kahana *et al.* 1994; Opie 1994), highlighting the need to understand the interactive, contextual and temporal nature of caring. However, Tara-borrelli (1993) argues that such an approach is conspicuous by its absence and that much of the current literature fails to address the way in which experiences, orientations and social relationships change over time.

In summarizing the current literature it is possible to discern a number of major themes which encapsulate much of what we know about family caregiving. Although we will consider these in far greater detail later, they may be characterized in a number of ways:

- The predominant focus has been on the burdens or difficulties of caring which constitute a 'unifying theme' underpinning a substantial proportion of previous work (Kahana and Young 1990).
- Mirroring the focus on burden, there has been a concentration on the tasks or physical aspects of caring, particularly in the way that caring has been defined.
- Despite the fact that caregiver burden is considered to be one of the most studied topics in the gerontological literature (Kane and Penrod 1995), methodologically most work has adopted a quantitative approach using cross-sectional designs. This has tended to result in a static view of what is generally regarded as a fluid process (Langer 1993).
- The majority of studies have focused primarily on the caregiver, with far less attention having been given to the cared-for person. This has produced a somewhat partial and asymmetrical picture (Kahana and Young 1990; Brody 1995; Scott 1995).

- Because of the emphasis on the burdens or difficulties of caring, the potential for satisfactions or uplifts has been relatively neglected. There is, however, growing evidence that the majority of caregivers identify some positive aspects to their situation and that the presence of satisfactions may serve as an important coping mechanism. As yet we know little about the sources, types and frequency of caregiver satisfaction.
- The way in which carers cope with or manage their situations is similarly poorly understood. As with the burdens of caring this is attributable, in no small measure, to the use of theoretical models and methodological approaches that are 'too deterministic' (Burr *et al.* 1994).
- Despite the extensive literature there is evidence within much of the published work of a mildly parochial tendency to focus only on studies from a particular country (usually either the US or the UK), a limitation which is further compounded by a somewhat inadequate consideration of the relative contribution made by different theoretical approaches and cultural traditions.

Although it is important to recognize the contribution of earlier work, there needs to be a shift towards approaches which better capture the complexity and uniqueness of family caregiving. In part this is already occurring with a move away from carefully constructed quantitative studies (Langer 1993), even amongst those who started from an explicitly causal standpoint (Thompson *et al.* 1993), towards models which capture the lived and particularistic experience of carers (Opie 1994; Gubrium 1995). This reflects a re-emergence of the qualitative study (Opie 1994; Brody 1995) which more adequately illuminates carers' subjective experiences. In concert with this there is recognition of the need to develop a temporal understanding of the caring process, with a particular focus on key transition points (Given and Given 1991; Thompson *et al.* 1993; McLaughlin and Ritchie 1994; Brody 1995; Greene and Coleman 1995). If a more balanced view is to emerge, models need also to include the views of the cared-for person, again from a temporal perspective which allows a consideration of change over time (Corbin and Strauss 1988; Rolland 1994).

Although this focus on the uniqueness of each caregiving relationship is to be welcomed and will underpin much of what follows, there is a danger of going too far and totally neglecting any form of more generalized account. We believe that this would be a mistake. The absence of a coherent policy for caregivers is apparent both in the UK (Twigg and Atkin 1994) and the US (Kane and Penrod 1995), yet a policy cannot be constructed solely from an individualistic perspective. What is required is an empirically generated set of theoretical concepts which can help shape policy on a macro level whilst being sufficiently sensitive to inform interventions for individual carers and cared-for persons. It is this balance that we seek to attain in building a more complete picture of family caregiving.

As we have already noted, the literature on caregiving is now so extensive that it is not possible to fit it within a particular 'scheme of under-standing' (Gubrium 1995). However, we believe that it is necessary to have at least a broad theoretical framework to provide an element of cohesion in what might otherwise become a formless mass. In achieving some cohesion we will draw on, but not be constrained by, a stress-coping paradigm. We do this not because we wish to focus primarily on the 'pathologizing' aspects of care (Twigg and Atkin 1994), but since one of the major aims of this book is to present a more complete understanding of the satisfactions of care, we believe that a stress-coping paradigm, if interpreted in its broadest sense, provides the most fruitful avenue of exploration. First, as much of the pre-vious work in the field has adopted such a theoretical stance, to ignore this would be to fail to learn the lessons of the past. Second, we firmly believe that a stress-coping framework has the most promise for devising interven-tions that can be tailored to carers' individual needs. However, we will not be applying this framework in a causal or deterministic way, but instead will follow Lazarus's (1993) advice and focus on the role of personal meanings to achieve an understanding of how people cope with life events. Further-more, although we will be presenting a typology of caregiving and a longi-tudinal model of the caregiving process, like Pearlin *et al.* (1990), we would not wish these to be seen as literal representations of reality, but rather as providing heuristic devices to enhance understanding.

The primary aim of this book is therefore to present a multidimen-sional view of family caregiving which recognizes the difficulties and satisfactions of care and the delicate balance between them. We will outline a typology of care that challenges the currently prevalent task-based con-ceptualizations and will link this to a longitudinal model of the caregiving experience. Although the main emphasis will be on the family carer, the perspective of the cared-for person will also be considered. In order to allow for an integration of disparate and potentially conflicting perspectives, Rolland's therapeutic quadrangle (Rolland 1988, 1994) will be used. It is our hope that in this way a more sophisticated and holistic understanding will emerge that will add to theoretical and methodological debate, and to policy and practice in family caregiving.

A word about language

We are conscious that the use of language with respect to carers and the people for whom they care is a delicate and contested area. Experience has taught us that carers do not like the word 'informal', and that the people they are caring for do not like the word 'dependant'. Throughout this book therefore the term 'family carer' will be used instead of 'informal carer', and 'cared-for person' instead of 'dependant'. We recognize that this represents a less than ideal solution, for example not all carers are family members and 'cared-for person' does not fully capture the reciprocal nature of the caring relationship. Nevertheless, we feel that these terms are less pejorative than most and will adopt them in this book.

A word about methods and data

The data upon which this book draws are not the product of a single discrete study but have emerged from several studies spanning a number of years. Data have been collected from different groups of carers including those providing care for individuals with learning disabilities and older people with both physical and cognitive frailty. It is this extensive pool of data that informs the contents of this book.

Methodologically the studies have utilized a variety of methods of data collection and analysis, including several hundred semi-structured interviews, three large-scale postal surveys and periods of both participant and non-participant observation. Data have been analysed using qualitative techniques, especially content analysis, in addition to descriptive and multivariate statistics. Detailed methodological accounts of some of the previous studies that are drawn upon have already been published (Nolan and Grant 1992a; Grant et al. 1994, 1995), but our conclusions have also been informed by a considerable volume of previously unpublished data, particularly those relating to the satisfactions of caring and the coping strategies carers employ. We do not intend to go into detail about these studies here but brief mention will be made in the relevant sections of the text.

In keeping with our emphasis on the relative uniqueness of caring circumstances, we will draw primarily on the qualitative data to lay the foundations of our argument but will include, where appropriate, descriptive statistics. Therefore although we will describe and discuss a number of indices which can be used to appraise the difficulties, satisfactions and coping strategies of carers, detailed statistical properties of these indices will not be reported here.

The shape of the book

The book begins with an opening chapter that provides a context for what follows. It will highlight the current emphasis placed on family carers and outline a number of key themes necessary for a meaningful debate. It is not the intention to present a comprehensive consideration of these themes but to acknowledge that a number of issues such as gender, race and ethnicity and policy objectives are important to a complete picture.

The first substantive chapter of the book will address the question, cited by Gubrium (1995: 268) 'What is this thing some call caregiving?'. It will trace in particular the present preoccupation with the instrumental and physical aspects of caring, and the consequent relative neglect of the more subtle and less visible components. Building on the work of Bowers (1987, 1988), a more comprehensive typology of caring will be outlined which, rather than being based on the tasks of caring, explores the purposes underpinning care. The emphasis is not primarily on the motivational aspects of care in terms of love, duty or obligation but on a number of conceptually discrete but empirically overlapping *types* of care. An extension and reconceptualization of Bowers's original model will be presented (Nolan *et al.* 1995a) and its implications for the interface between family and professional (paid) care considered.

The following three chapters address different but related topics and will follow a similar format. Each begins with a review of the literature in a given field, prior to the presentation of new data and results from recent studies that we have undertaken. The focus of these chapters is, sequentially: coping strategies in family caregiving; the satisfactions of caring; and the development of a longitudinal model of the caring experience. Taken together these three chapters constitute the heart of the book and provide, we hope, the foundation for a more complete and holistic understanding of family caregiving.

Using the longitudinal model as a springboard, the following chapter will address the perspectives of the carer and the cared-for person using the biopsychosocial model of illness and disability first described by Rolland (1988, 1994). Termed the 'therapeutic quadrangle', this approach provides a mechanism to integrate disparate viewpoints, including those of carers, cared-for persons and service providers, whilst also accounting for the diversity and heterogeneity of chronic illness and disability.

The implications of our findings for service delivery and interventions with caregivers and cared-for persons are considered throughout the book, but are addressed in more detail in the concluding chapter, which also makes reference to further theoretical and methodological debates and policy advances.

1

Caring in Context

Suppose everybody cared enough, everybody shared enough,
wouldn't everybody have enough? There is enough in the world
for everyone's need, but not enough for everyone's greed.
(Frank Buchman 1947: 56)

This quote from one of Buchman's essays captures very well some of the themes and dilemmas about contemporary care. If only we all cared enough, life's problems, if not solved, would at least be considerably eased. 'Caring about' is something we all like to profess; if that reservoir of goodwill could be shared, surely there would be enough to go around? If only life were so simple.

We now know that 'caring about' another person, though a precondition for 'good' care, is not a guarantee that all the necessary tasks of 'caring for' a person will materialize. 'Caring about' and 'caring for' moreover are not universal commodities (Dalley 1988); there appear to be many constraints, political, economic and cultural, which affect the likelihood of care being available, let alone a shared concern; and if the rules for engagement are constantly shifting between the individual, the family and the state then questions about rights to and responsibilities for care may easily become confused. As governments around the world have striven to control public spending on welfare, 'family care' has been 'rediscovered', providing an impetus for a policy agenda linking families more closely into collective caring efforts. This raises some fundamental questions about how family and informal carers are perceived and how far their efforts can be recognized and supported (Litwak *et al.* 1994; Twigg and Atkin 1994).

In setting the scene for what is to follow we limit ourselves in this chapter to a brief review of four related questions: Why family caring and why now? How is such care distributed? What is policy doing to support carers? And how can useful questions be framed about carers' needs and circumstances?

Before proceeding it is necessary to add a brief caveat about the definition of caring. It will be apparent from the opening paragraphs of this chapter that there are some fundamental questions to be answered about the nature and definition of 'care' itself. The terms 'caring for' and 'caring about' have already been used; it is therefore necessary to achieve some clarity, or at least to explore further, the way that care is construed. For if caring is seen to consist of many facets which, if any, has hegemony? This important topic forms the substance of the next chapter. For the present purposes caring will be taken to refer to the range of primarily instrumental tasks that underpin policy definitions of caring, for as Twigg and Atkin (1994: 31) note, physical tending is often 'regarded as the defining feature of informal care'. The inadequacy of this approach, particularly from a carer's perspective, will be highlighted throughout the rest of the book, but such an explicitly instrumental focus is treated as unproblematic for the time being. However, it is felt important at this stage to consider briefly the differences and similarities between caring and support networks.

Care and support networks

This is not the place for a thoroughgoing review of the enormous literature on support networks though some of the more salient findings about the relationship between support networks and care are worth recording here.

To avoid possible confusion, support networks need to be distinguished from social networks. Mitchell (1969) considers a social network to comprise of all one's social contacts. Early attempts to study social or 'total' networks involved asking individuals to list all the people known to them. Inevitably these studies tended to be based on small samples because each network could lead to an exhaustive list of social contacts. Measuring social or total networks is time-consuming and not very effective if the primary purpose is to identify the scope of care provision within a social network. This has led to studies of partial or purposive networks, that is, those directed towards the fulfilment of specified purposes such as the provision of care. Wenger (1996) describes the range of methodologies involved.

On the whole, studies have concentrated on the structural properties of networks like size, density, membership and linkages perhaps because these are the most amenable to study. In more recent years there has been more interest in the function or content of relationships embedded within social networks. This has been described as the most important item of information about networks because it indicates something about the goods and services exchanged, the closeness and intimacy between members, the intensity of their interactions and the exchange of information involved (Bulmer 1987).

The structural properties of networks nevertheless can be construed as potential pathways for transmitting forms of care and support. In this sense they can be regarded as an 'opportunity framework'. The framework, or constellation of relationships, allows for support and care but does not guarantee it. The opportunity framework therefore of a person's network is merely a short-hand way of defining the human resources that may be available to individuals and the way these resources are interconnected. An analysis of support network structures can be particularly helpful in understanding the availability of support, its stability and dynamics, and the capacity for substitutability (Wenger and Shahtahmasebi 1991; Grant and Wenger 1993).

Support networks have been described as serving four principal functions: as a source of physical and emotional support to individuals; as a stress buffer for carers; as a screening and referral agent to formal services, and as a context in which attitudes, values and norms can be transmitted (Gourash 1978). Consequently there are alternative theoretical approaches to studying the functions of informal support. Human ecology theory, deriving from the early work of Bronfenbrenner (1979), has concentrated on understanding the direct and indirect impact on human development of a wide variety of ecologically conceived systems such as families, neighbourhoods and formal organizations. Social support and social network theory is more concerned with understanding relationships between different social units and how these impede the flow and exchange of social support and other resources (Gottlieb 1981). Finally help-seeking and help-giving theory, which appears to have its roots in American community psychology, is based largely on an analysis of the interdependencies between help-seekers and help-givers (Fisher et al. 1983).

However, at a general level it is by no means clear what it is about social relationships and networks that affects health or well-being and, equally importantly, how these effects occur. House et al. (1988) contend that three aspects of social relationships – their existence and quantity, their formal structure, and their functional content – must be conceptually and empirically distinguished if progress is to be made in this connection. This is not an easy task. Depicting the qualities of interpersonal ties is difficult enough but charting (in conceptually compelling ways) the relevant features of support networks in the aggregate is a major developmental challenge.

Rook (1992) provides a timely reminder about false assumptions that can be made about support and supportiveness. Carers and cared-for persons may hold very different views about what constitutes support, and how beneficial and enduring its effects are. Ell (1996) offers a critique of literature on social support, which she claims has overemphasized its beneficial effects. Her review suggests that social support research has often implied that an individual's recovery and adaptation following chronic illness will be negatively affected when family support is absent, or when such support is perceived as inadequate, misinformed, misguided, excessive or unwanted.

However, families are not 'static resource banks' from which disabled or chronically ill people obtain the support and care they need or want. Families are also potential sources of stress, and negative social exchanges can occur between members. More importantly, Ell claims that family members collectively experience stresses associated with illness and engage in interdependent coping among members. Hence studies aimed at discovering how support or care works for individuals need to take account of the opportunity structure of support, the characteristics of the support itself and how this is in turn construed by both providers and recipients. This is rarely done. Even in the best traditions of ethnographic study of family care, accounts about care have often been rendered solely from the perspective of the dominant provider of care.

It has been shown that strong ties give more support but that weak ties may provide more diverse support. Strong ties on the whole link people who are similar whereas weak ties link those who are less alike. High density networks tend to be cohesive groupings whereas low density networks are more fragmented and uncoordinated. Hence, dense networks may be able to rally help quickly but loose networks may be in a better position to identify additional help and resources. Put another way, members of loose-knit networks may be better able to shop around for help but this does not mean that the resulting help will necessarily prove reliable; members of dense networks may have fewer options in identifying sources of help but when found it is more likely to be reliable (Wellman 1981; Wenger 1996).

Unfortunately it has been shown that more stigmatized or vulnerable groups may be disadvantaged in support network terms. Dementia sufferers and people with mental illnesses appear to be amongst those with the smallest support networks (Pattison *et al.* 1975; Tolsdorf 1976; Thornicroft and Breakey 1991). Although support network shrinkage does not necessarily follow the life course for all vulnerable groups, the capacity for replacement of support from members lost through death, incapacity or moves can leave carers and cared-for persons with limited options (Grant and Wenger 1993).

Studies suggest that supportive and intimate personal relationships can guard against social isolation and stress. This has been shown amongst vulnerable groups like severely mentally ill people (Dunn *et al.* 1990; Thornicroft and Breakey 1991; Dayson 1992) as well as family and informal carers (Grant *et al.* 1990; Nolan *et al.* 1990). Moreover, Dayson (1992) has argued that good social relationships are associated with, and may even be causes of, good outcomes in chronic schizophrenia. Cotterill's (1994) study of people with schizophrenia suggests that adjustment, measured largely in terms of social contacts and social integration, is affected by age, gender and marital status.

The orientations and expectations of close associates within informal support networks appear to be quite influential in shaping patterns of adjustment for people with disabilities and other vulnerable groups. For example, kinship networks reflecting different orientations to involvement with adult relatives with learning disabilities have been reported to be related to levels of achievement in terms of independent living and employment (Winik *et al.* 1985), and support network types based on orientations to child-rearing appear to be related to patterns of child abuse and neglect (Crittenden 1985). Wenger's (1994) work has characterized the support networks of elderly people in terms of the proximity of close kin, the proportions of family, friends and neighbours involved, and the level of interaction between elderly people and their associates. Derived in this way, support network types have been shown to be related to the use of statutory domiciliary services and community or neighbourhood type. This being the case, we can expect care to be geographically uneven as well as linked with demands upon formal services.

To summarize, family caring takes place in an informally organized context; the structural properties of a person's support network may provide an initial guide about who may be available as a resource for care but the existence of such human supports should not be immediately equated with the actual provision of care; neither must care or support be presumed to be necessarily beneficial; in any case it may be that carers and cared-for persons have different ideas about both the nature of care and its effects. We are still at an early stage in understanding what aspects of the structural and relational aspects of support networks are conducive to the provision of reliable and effective care.

Why family caring: why now?

As has recently been noted, the world is currently facing the challenges posed by the 'first fully aged societies in human existence' at a time when policy developments and service initiatives are underpinned by a new vocabulary of individual autonomy (Johnson 1995). The response of virtually all developed countries to their changing demographic profiles has been to institute a policy of community care in an effort to achieve more cost-effective use of scarce resources (Dooghe 1992; Walker *et al.* 1993). In achieving this aim increasing emphasis has been placed on the role of the family (informal) system as the mainstay of care provision, often with inadequate support from more formal agencies (Alber 1993).

Whilst those in need of care are not of course exclusively the older members of a society – and certainly not all older people are in need of care, indeed many are care providers themselves – there is little doubt that in numerical terms it is amongst the older population that the greatest need for care exists. Dooghe (1992) contends that across Europe there will be a 213 per cent increase amongst those aged 80+ between 1980–2025; in the UK the British Medical Association (BMA 1995) cite figures that indicate a rise in the population aged 85+ from 897,000 in 1991 to 3,105,000 in 2051. Similar trends are apparent in the US (Kane and Penrod 1995) and indeed throughout the world (Davies 1995). Given the established link between increased longevity and relative dependency (Henwood 1992), the challenges posed by the ageing population are inescapable.

As Davies (1995) contends, there are complex issues in supporting older people which cannot necessarily be transposed across national contexts. Nevertheless, he considers that despite this apparent diversity, policies are characterized more by what they have in common than by how they differ. In framing their responses to an ageing population, policymakers throughout the world 'seem to be working hard to express the same sentiments, sometimes using almost the same words' (p. 22).

In his analysis of the current situation, Davies discerns three common trends:

- wherever possible to keep older people in their own homes or a homely environment within the community;
- an increased reliance on family and other informal sources of support and care;
- an emphasis on reducing the costs to 'public funds'.

It is now recognized that if the first and third of these aims are to be achieved then systems better able to support family carers must be instituted (Evers 1995). Herein lies a considerable tension. For as Evers (1995) argues, whilst there is no evidence to support the belief that by and large families are less *willing* to care than they used to be, there are considerable pressures on the *capacity* and *ability* of family carers, which threaten future supply. This situation has been summarized in the following way:

> A common objective in nearly all European countries is to maintain elderly peoples' dignity and independence in their own homes as long as possible. Informal care exceeds professional care but at the same time is under pressure from demographic and social changes. In this respect the support of the family seems essential to maintain the informal care systems.
>
> (Dooghe 1992: 381)

This observation highlights the primarily instrumental motivation behind the current emphasis on increased support for family carers, and falls very much into the 'carers as resources' model described by Twigg and Atkin (1994).

This was explicitly reinforced in a recent publication by the British Medical Association (BMA 1995) which charted the potential financial consequences of a reduction in what they termed 'unpaid' care, and stressed the importance of encouraging people to continue caring. Although the BMA recognizes that the figures they present (based on those supplied by the Institute of Actuaries and William Laing) are at best 'guestimates', such calculations nevertheless give an indication of the relative financial contribution of family and other informal care. It is estimated therefore that the total cost to the state of all institutional care is approximately £7 billion, the cost of all professional care provided in the community is £3.1 billion and the cost of replacing family care somewhere between £33.9 billion and £39.1 billion. On this basis the family currently provides 77 per cent to 80 per cent of all the care needed. Clearly there are compelling financial incentives for maintaining present levels of family care.

Herein lies a second tension, for even in those countries with the best-developed welfare systems, for example the Nordic countries, it is now appreciated that a largely public and professional solution to care needs cannot be provided (Evers 1995). However, well-developed systems for supporting family carers do not currently exist. Although recognizing the need for a more adequate financial recompense to carers would be a major development (BMA 1995), this is only part of the solution. In a wide-ranging analysis of the limitations and aspirations of current policies for family care across Europe, Evers (1995) contends that the emphasis must shift away from services and interventions that seek to replace or supersede family carers (Twigg and Atkin 1994) towards a system of complementary and supplementary interventions. This does not mean that practical support for carers has no value or that carers should be maintained in their roles beyond their willingness or capacity to care (Nolan *et al.* 1994). Rather it recognizes that most family carers wish to continue to care. Indeed, as will be discussed in greater detail later, many see themselves as having considerable expertise which is often overlooked or ignored by those professionals who either assess or deliver services (Nolan and Grant 1992a; Nolan *et al.* 1995a). Evers's (1995) argument indicates that interventions should seek to build on this wealth of knowledge rather than replace it.

The inadequacy of current services for carers in the UK has been documented for some time (Webb 1987) and has recently been reaffirmed quite unequivocally (Twigg and Atkin 1994; BMA 1995). Moreover, it is apparent that some carers, notably the vocal and articulate, get a disproportionate share of the limited services that are available (Nolan and Grant 1992a; Ellis 1993; Twigg and Atkin 1994). Such 'inequalities' have also been identified throughout Europe, a situation which is likely to be exacerbated as systems become more complex and fragmented (Evers 1995). Evers contends that if such inequalities are to be countered then the social competence of carers must be improved. As laudable as such an aim may seem, it is likely to remain at the level of rhetoric unless the current received wisdom is challenged. At the heart of this lies the necessity of extending definitions of care beyond the instrumental. For construing care primarily in such terms not only maligns the less visible aspects of care but, because dependency criteria are often used to indicate eligibility for services, it also has the pernicious effect of denying services to those potentially in most need (Levesque *et al.* 1995). Therefore if, as Evers (1995) suggests, we are to move towards a system that is complementary and supplementary rather than simply substitutive, we must develop a greater understanding of the dynamics of caring.

To develop such a better understanding it is necessary to have some appreciation of the current situation in terms of the numbers of family carers, the potential influence of factors such as gender and race/ethnicity, as well as an appreciation of current policy towards carers. These are considered next.

Care and stratification

Having begun this discussion by highlighting the importance of family caregiving in an international context, the focus now narrows to a consideration of the UK scene. In this section we are primarily concerned with who provides informal care, how responsibilities for care are divided, and with identifying important gaps in knowledge. Given different conceptualizations of care we may anticipate that there are varying estimates of the number and distribution of carers throughout the country.

This point is noted by Arber and Ginn (1990), who contend that the definition of caregiving used in recent national surveys such as that reported by Green (1988) 'is very inclusive' and is an approach which potentially inflates the numbers of carers. Adopting a different definition of a carer based upon the number of hours of care provided per week, Arber and Ginn acknowledge that this approach nevertheless has its limitations. As they point out, the search for a 'single ideal dichotomous definition' of a carer which differentiates a carer from a non-carer is likely to prove fruitless given the diverse nature of caring (even when it is considered mainly in instrumental terms). In interpreting the following figures therefore the limitations imposed by the definition used have to be acknowledged.

The first attempt to survey nationally the extent of informal care in Britain was provided by Green's (1988) analysis of the 1985 General Household Survey. In terms of the definition of a carer used, it adopted the broadly instrumental approach outlined above and also unfortunately excluded young children as carers. Adult respondents were asked whether they looked after or gave special help to anyone 'sick, handicapped or elderly' living in the same household or if they provided 'some regular service or help' to anyone 'sick, handicapped or elderly' living in a different household. On the one hand therefore this inclusive definition may have overestimated the number of total carers, but the exclusion of children as carers undoubtedly neglected a small but important group.

The findings suggested that one adult in seven (14 per cent) was providing informal care and that nearly one in five households (19 per cent) contained a carer. This represents approximately 6 million carers in Britain as a whole, 3.5 million women and 2.5 million men, or 15 per cent of women in the population and 12 per cent of men. The extent of involvement in care by families came as a surprise to many, flying in the face of a considerable amount of already published work. However, reanalysis of the data helped to put matters into perspective, demonstrating that less than a quarter of this number, 1.29 million people, were involved in the more personalized forms of care associated with working at the 'heavy end' of the caring spectrum (Parker and Lawton 1994). This also helped to quell some of the worst fears about the claims of carers on social security entitlements.

'Heavily involved' carers were likely to be: providing long hours of help; carrying out a wide range of activities, including both personal and physical assistance; looking after someone from the same household; caring for someone with some sort of mental impairment; and caring with little or no help from others. At one level there is an intuitive appeal in suggesting that such carers are the natural targets of service interventions, as fairly clear-cut criteria can be applied. On the other hand, it is now quite apparent that the simplistic assumption that 'giving care equals need for support' is not consistent with the way that carers experience burden; this will be explored in greater detail.

In terms of the total numbers of carers, Evandrou's (1993) analysis of the 1990 GHS data suggests a 2 per cent increase between 1985 and 1990, this being accounted for by those caring outside the home environment. Taking a slightly different perspective, Evandrou contends that there are 3.7 million sole carers in the UK and 1.7 million providing care in their own home. In reporting the same survey data, the BMA (1995) indicate that 17 per cent of women and 15 per cent of men are carers, and on this basis there are 3.9 million female carers and 2.9 male carers. Of those in receipt of care almost eight out of ten (79 per cent) are over the age of 65 and two out of ten (20 per cent) are over the age of 85. This is consistent with the assertion made earlier that many of those in need of care are elderly people.

Given these broad statistics, what are the influences of such variables as the gender, age, race and ethnicity of carers?

Gender is clearly a crucial factor mediating the experience of caring; its importance owes much to a strong tradition of feminist writing and critique about gender relations and care (Finch and Groves 1983; Ungerson 1987; Dalley 1988; Lewis and Meredith 1988a; Finch and Mason 1993). To some extent therefore the results of the 1985 GHS survey (Green 1988) came as something of a surprise, as they appear to suggest that gender differences are not as great as previously thought. Indeed recently there has been re-cognition that the focus on caregiving as a women's issue and a mainly feminist concern may have resulted in male caregivers being relatively ignored (Arber and Ginn 1995). What is needed therefore is a balanced consideration. For instance in their reanalysis of Green's survey data, Parker and Lawton (1994) demonstrated that men were far less likely to be the 'main' carer, more likely to be caring less than 20 hours per week and less likely to be involved in personal caring, thus reinforcing the findings of many previous survey studies. Though both male and female carers were less likely than their age peers to be in full-time paid work, this pattern was more striking among men. On the other hand, female carers were much more likely to be classified as permanently unable to work, principally because of being tied to homemaking. There was substantial variation in receipt of formal services depending on the gender of the carer and the gender of the cared-for person. Where women were caring for men, service receipt was at its lowest in relation to almost all services. However, Parker and Lawton suggest that there is little evidence of systematic discrimination against women.

Broadening the debate, Twigg and Atkin (1994) have reported evidence suggesting that men and women have rather different approaches to caring. Men appeared to find it easier to separate themselves from the caring situation, to set limits on their involvement and to see themselves as 'professional' carers who had a legitimate need for support. By contrast, women were more likely to subordinate their interests to those of the cared-for person, to be less detached, and to regard the acceptance of help as a sign of failure. The authors observed that the attitudes and behaviour of male carers conformed to an instrumental model which was bound more by rules than relationships and by an association with the values of paid employment. It was also noted that sexist practices were still in evidence amongst professionals, particularly GPs. Virtuous behaviour noted in a male carer could easily be passed over as merely an accepted part of the female carer's domestic role.

On the other hand, such findings are equivocal; Harris (1993) argues that relatively little is known about the qualitative experience of male caregivers and that many of the quantitative studies have produced conflicting results. On the basis of in-depth interviews with male carers she identifies four 'types': 'the worker'; 'the labour of love'; 'the sense of duty' and 'at the cross-roads'. One of these, 'the worker', is consistent with the arguments presented by Twigg and Atkin (1994), that male caregivers are more likely to see caring as an extension of paid employment. The other types however portray a differing picture and suggest that love and concern represent a major component of male caregiving, as identified in earlier work on male caregivers using respite services (Motenko 1988). Other studies have also failed to find significant differences between male and female caregivers (Beach 1993; Thompson *et al.* 1993), with Beach (1993) for example finding no variation between men and women in either their willingness to care or the sense of duty or obligation that they felt.

Fisher (1994), writing about the care of older people, takes up a related but rather different position. He points out that a considerable amount of care in this context is spouse care, drawing attention to Parker and Lawton's (1994) findings that coresident carers bear the brunt of caring to make the point that men can and do contribute to care 'at the heavy end' of the spectrum. He is critical of the easy assumptions made about the way women are described as assuming caring roles. Like Wenger (1990), he suggests that many older women as recipients of care prefer hands-on care to be undertaken by women. It is not that men are reluctant to undertake such care. He describes evidence where men accept the obligation to care, undertake intimate personal care, derive a sense of identity and reward from their work, and on the whole experience similar struggles, much as suggested by Motenko (1988). What is called for is a closer examination of caring by men, and how it can be understood and developed.

What therefore seems to emerge from this is that gender, though significant, is only one factor in the hierarchy of obligations about caring. Marital relationship and coresidency have powerful influences, as others studies attest (Qureshi and Walker 1989; Finch and Mason 1993). Whilst there can be no denying that gender is, and will remain, a significant theme within the caregiving literature as evidenced by the publication of a major new text on the subject (Hooyman and Gonyea 1995), there have been recent calls to adopt a more open mind. Opie (1994), writing from a feminist perspective, believes that a more 'finely tuned' understanding of caregiving will not emerge until there is a move away from seeing gender simply in terms of the sex of an individual. She believes that the affective elements or the emotional attitudes that influence caring are more significant. She outlines four of these: commitment, obligation, dissociation and repudiation; she considers that such positions are fluid and dynamic and not circumscribed by 'givens' such as gender. Opie sees caring as being strongly influenced by individual life histories irrespective of gender. She states:

> defining the characteristics of affective caring positions represents the activity of caring much more complexly than defining it in relation to care by wives, husbands, sons and daughters. Defining affective positions allows attention to be given to the process of caring, to its fluidity, to the potentiality of substantive movement within time and between positions, and offers a much more complex account of gendered behaviour.
> (Opie 1994: 47)

Similarly Farran *et al.* (1991) suggest that acknowledging the individual nature of caring means that factors such as race, gender and relationships, may be less important than previously thought. With respect to gender, the point was reiterated by Kane and Penrod (1995) when they cautioned against 'dismissing large ranges of human behaviour' as being attributable mainly to the oppression of women. They argue that holding this position has the tendency to inhibit rather than facilitate informed debate and the advancement of knowledge. Clearly gender will remain an important topic but it should not be allowed to dominate the debate and deny the diversity of caregiving.

Age by implication also becomes a significant factor in the provision of care. Parker and Lawton (1994) report that the oldest carers are overrepresented in personal and physical caring, that is, within the category of care deemed in their opinion to be the most demanding. Wenger (1990) describes older carers as more likely to care for shorter periods, to provide intimate personal care and heavy nursing tasks associated with terminal care, and typically to be caring for their spouse. Arber and Ginn (1990) have also demonstrated through their study that older people represent a considerable resource for care, and that 47 per cent of care to elderly people in their own homes is provided by older people. Coupled with the way many elderly people strive to assert their independence for as long as possible, the evidence points to an image of older people far removed from that of being a burden on society. Therefore as O'Neill and Sorenson (1991) argue, there is a need to consider caring from a family perspective that recognizes both the role older people play as providers of care and the contribution that older cared-for people can make to the family. Within this context caregiving is best viewed as a social process rather than primarily as an individual experience (Brody 1995). As others assert (Kahana and Young 1990), this signals the need to develop dynamic and relational models of caregiving.

Exploring further the importance of age, Twigg and Atkin (1994) provide some illustrations of age-related expectations held by carers. They conclude that older carers do not draw such sharp distinctions as younger carers about the way caring has impacted upon their social lives. Older people appear to view many of the restrictions they face as unexceptional and little different from other limitations of old age.

Age is also difficult to separate from stage in the life-cycle; an impressive stream of research in North America is beginning to change our conceptualizations of caring across the lifespan as a whole. It is giving rise to questions about caring 'careers', the cumulative effects of caring, the relationship between caring responsibilities, life-cycle stage and the course of chronic illness and disability, and patterns of reciprocity across the lifespan (Kahana *et al.* 1994; Midlarsky and Kahana 1994; Seltzer *et al.* 1994). Possibly because the contract culture seems to be fostering an even greater commitment to short-term research funding, there are real dangers that the potential for exploiting exciting approaches to lifespan research will be blighted. It is hoped that this can be avoided. We will be developing further some of the implications of a temporal model of caregiving in Chapter 5.

As literature reviews have shown (Atkin and Rollings 1992, 1993), there are many gaps in the present understanding of the structure and dynamics of informal care within different ethnic communities. Even one of the most recent attempts to gauge the prevalence of informal care in Britain (Green 1988) failed to provide information about either the number or circumstances of informal carers from black and ethnic minority groups. What we know is therefore dependent very largely upon local or small-scale studies or anecdotal evidence. Atkin and Rollings (1992, 1993) suggest in particular that there is very little information about the basic nature as well as the experience of informal care amongst black communities. Hence what it means to be an informal carer within an ethnic minority community in Britain is still a question to be explored empirically.

To compound matters, misplaced myths and stereotypes about different ethnic groups prevail. Foremost amongst these is a common perception that black and ethnic minority groups live within a predominantly extended family system. Another perception is that each ethnic group is homogeneous in terms of family organization and culture. Frequently overlooked is the important question of migration and the associated patterns of settlement and adaptation. Families from different racial and ethnic backgrounds have been settling in Britain for many years with the result that cultural norms will be susceptible to change. The beliefs, values and experiences of first-generation immigrant families are likely to differ significantly from those born here and the generations that follow. Yet we know next to nothing about the relationship between race, ethnicity and intergenerational differences in approaches to care. Differences in lifestyle preferences between the generations have however led to a range of comments and observations about the emergence of intergenerational role conflicts in this connection (Atkin and Rollings 1993).

Commenting on aspects of family organization, Brown (1984) and Westwood and Bachau (1988) have reported a 'high' proportion of Asian extended family households although these are far from being in the majority (18–21 per cent of the families surveyed). Bhalla and Blakemore (1981), in their study of 400 European, Afro-Caribbean and Asian elderly people, found that whilst far more Asian elderly people received support from relatives following hospital discharge, a large proportion in fact had no close relatives living in Britain. This is supported by Atkin et al. (1989), who describe a significant proportion of Asian people as living alone and with few relatives in this country. The British government's immigration policy is considered to have had exacerbating effects here (Fenton 1987; Atkin and Rollings 1992).

Continuing with the Asian community as an example, Gunaratnam (1993) bemoans the clumsiness of simplistic categories based on ethnic identity. She points out that Asian people in Britain come from a variety of countries and cultures and represent different languages, dialects, religions, histories and customs. This is well illustrated in her own small-scale study of 33 Asian carers in which linguistic representation included Bengali, Gujarati, Punjabi, Urdu, Hindi and Sindhi. An overemphasis on language can be highly misleading, however. Woollett et al. (1994) have further demonstrated in a small-scale qualitative study of Asian women in east London that their constructions of ethnicity and ethnic identity are fluid and can be linked to gender and developmental changes associated with motherhood. The use therefore of linguistic tags is clearly insufficient as a basis for comprehending perspectives. It is merely a starting point.

In support of this, Gunaratnam (1993) identified patterns of social and economic relations connected with the gender, age and country of origin of the carer which directly affected the experience of care. The cases she describes underline the particular importance of the carer's identity and perceptions in determining the distinction between the simple presence of family networks, the actual practical help available and how it was received. In one case she describes the carer's reluctance to trouble her son for help, whilst in the second the carer's feelings of isolation and frustration with lack of support from the wider family comes through strongly.

The results of several US studies point in the same direction. Cox (1995) examined black and white carers of dementia patients and found that a perceived lack of informal support and a sense of incompetence exacerbated stress among black carers but these had no effect on white carers. White carers were more affected by the impairment of their relatives. The findings, she concluded, were due to cultural differences in carers' expectations. In their study of caregiving among people with Alzheimer's' disease, Lawton *et al.* (1992) report that support network structures and caregiving attitudes and ideology were important differences between black and white carers. Wood and Parham (1990), in another study of carers of people with Alzheimer's' disease, found that black carers in particular used cognitive reframing strategies in positive terms whilst also expressing a strong determination to survive. Once more this points to the importance of having a framework for needs assessment which encapsulates the key dimensions of people's belief systems and values, whatever ethnic or cultural background people are from. A failure to deliver this is likely to result in black and ethnic minority service users and their families being viewed from a white or Eurocentric perspective (Begum 1992; Thanki 1994).

Well-grounded comparative research between ethnic groups would appear to have enormous potential in demonstrating what constitutes acceptable or workable coping strategies in different cultural contexts. Some of the lessons learned may turn out to have more general applications. For example, a study of ethnic differences in infant care practices (Farooqi 1994) reports that sudden infant death syndrome (SIDS) is lower amongst the Asian community. Asian families were much more likely to place their children in a prone sleeping position or sleep in the same room as their child, practices which afforded the child greater protection against SIDS. This also illustrates that what is accepted cultural behaviour for one group is different from another. Further examples from the fields of child care and psychiatry respectively can be found in Hackett and Hackett (1993) and Perkins and Moodley (1993). An important message for professionals here is to avoid pathologizing behaviours that are culturally normative for different ethnic groups.

Disentangling socio-economic from cultural factors in understanding the experience of informal care is not straightforward. Studies by Blakemore and Boneham (1993), Brown (1984) and Norman (1985) provide evidence about the overrepresentation of black people in terms of low income, poor-quality housing and unemployment, all of which impinge upon ill-health. These same factors are also signs of potential resources for care, and as such they are likely to affect coping strategies of families.

Studies have repeatedly shown that linguistic, economic and cultural factors can adversely affect both knowledge about and take-up of services among ethnic communities (Bhalla and Blakemore 1981; McCalman 1990; Gunaratnam 1993; Fatimilehin and Nadirshaw 1994). This is seen less as a manifestation of the allegedly insular and self-servicing characteristics of these communities than a failure of policy and formal services to find appropriate, non-discriminatory means of informing and supporting individuals.

Despite these difficulties, reports have begun to show that meaningful service level contracts can be secured to the benefit of carers from ethnic minority groups, resulting from particularly carefully considered methods of consultation (Anwar and Hill 1994a,b). The recruitment and training of more people from different ethnic communities into services is seen as one of the long-term ways of securing a meaningful dialogue with users and carers from the same communities (Carlisle 1994). More intelligible, culturally sensitive information for these carers is gradually appearing following attempts to research their needs. Eribo (1991) presents just such a package for Afro-Caribbean carers. There is little room for complacency, however, as there are signs that policy has so far tackled only part of the problem.

What is policy doing to support carers?

The new pattern of community care following the implementation of the NHS and Community Care Act (1990) offers unprecedented opportunities for both users and carers. Potentially it provides for their involvement in 'needs-led' assessment and care management as well as in community care planning. Groups previously marginalized can now expect to have a greater say in how things are organized. Paragraph 3.28 of the policy guidance (Department of Health 1991) acknowledges that most support of vulnerable people is provided by families, friends and neighbours. It then sets out what is to be done:

> The assessment will need to take account of the support that is available from such carers. They should feel that the overall provision of care is a shared responsibility between them and the statutory authorities and that the relationship between them is one of mutual support. The preferences of carers should be taken into account and their willingness to continue caring should not be assumed. Both service users and carers should therefore be consulted – separately, if either of them wishes – since their views may not coincide. The care plan should be the result of a constructive dialogue between service user, carer, social services staff and those of any other agency involved.
>
> (DoH 1991: 28)

One cannot help but be struck by the use of terms such as 'shared responsibility', 'mutual support', 'constructive dialogue', suggesting an orientation towards negotiation and partnership rather than professional dominance (Fisher 1994). This, however, is not easy to square with the Department of Health guidance (DoH/SSI 1991: 14) on the definition of need, which is 'a dynamic concept, the definition of which will vary over time in accordance with changes in national legislation, changes in local policy, the availability of resources, and the patterns of local demand. Need is thus a relative concept' (DoH/SSI 1991: 14).

What the definition seems to be saying is that the determination of need is very much in the hands of the enabling authorities rather than something shaped by what users and carers say they require. The scope for negotiation within the stated definition would appear to be wrested from users and carers. Twigg and Atkin (1994) suggest that case management is 'carer neutral' in that it can run on high or low budgets and can target carers or neglect them. Whether or not care management is directed primarily towards helping carers to continue caring or to enjoy an enhanced quality of life remains to be seen. An optimistic interpretation would be that there is everything to play for, and that there is nothing to stop carers taking the initiative and making their needs and circumstances clear. A more cynical interpretation would be that as resources come under pressure it is more likely that the carer perspective will drop from the equation and that carers will return to becoming invisible. Although the new Carers (Recognition and Service) Act 1995 should theoretically prevent this, the Act has many limitations, as we will describe later.

A study by Ellis (1993) considers the extent to which both users and carers are included in needs assessment and highlights many of the above tensions. She illustrates how professionals come to the assessment process with a set of preconceived and largely implicit beliefs about what constitute appropriate services, with such beliefs being heavily influenced by their own training and background. In terms of carers' needs, value judgements about 'deserving cases' strongly influence the decision to allocate services or not, a situation compounded by the tendency to view services in stereotypical terms and thereby fail to explore their potential, for example respite care. Such a stereotypical and limited view of the wider potential of services such as day hospitals and respite care has also been described in other studies (Nolan 1986; Nolan and Grant 1992a; Montgomery 1995). Ellis (1993) noted a persistent reliance by assessors on the physical functioning and dependency of the cared-for person as the main eligibility criterion for services, a practice which in her opinion resulted in other sources of carer stress being ignored.

The study by Twigg and Atkin (1994) of social workers, community nurses, GPs and home help organizers suggested that only social workers appeared to incorporate carers into assessment procedures in anything approaching an organized way, although this apparently did not lead to their receiving extensive support. Furthermore, the absence of any explicit policy for carers meant that professionals relied upon more tacit sources of knowledge such as professional values, the 'culture of the office' and the assumptive worlds of individual practitioners. Moreover, as noted above by Ellis (1993), the use of moral judgements about deserving cases also influenced decision-making processes. Also of considerable concern, given the gate-keeping role occupied by many doctors, is the belief held by most medical practitioners that they have no real role to play in assessing carers' needs (Twigg and Atkin 1994).

More recently, Manthorpe and Twigg (1995) studied needs-led assessment processes for carers in two local authorities. They found that the translation of the ideal of a separate assessment of carers' needs into the reality of practice was extremely problematic. They commented in particular on the absence of a 'tradition of practice' with carers, which meant that assessors generally lacked an adequate framework for the assessment. Compounding these difficulties, Manthorpe and Twigg believe that there is little incentive to be creative during the present climate of financial retrenchment, a finding consistent with that of Ellis (1993).

Whilst these studies provide a broad indication of the relative difficulties experienced in implementing community care policy, some of the finer points of detail can be more readily appreciated when viewed from a minority group perspective. Black and ethnic minority groups can be taken as an example. The government's 'Caring for People' White Paper (Secretaries of State for Health, Social Security, Wales and Scotland 1989) addressed 'people from ethnic minorities' in only 57 words, committing itself to taking account of the circumstances of minority communities and advocating that community care will be planned in consultation with them (Gunaratnam 1993). The subsequent policy guidance (DoH 1990a) talks about making 'information about assessment and services available in braille, on tape and in appropriate ethnic minority languages. Staff need to be recruited from a range of racial or ethnic minorities' (para. 3.21). Reference is made later (para. 3.23) to finding ways of overcoming language barriers. No references are given in the policy guidance to other reasons for underrepresentation of black and ethnic minority people as service users or carers. Neither does there appear to be a recognition that this might concern problems with the acceptability and relevance of services for these groups.

Guidance for practitioners on issues of race and ethnicity (Department of Health/Social Services Inspectorate 1991: 58) does little more to help with blandishments like: 'It is important that all assessment staff have a knowledge and understanding of racial and cultural diversity, and the impact of racism, as well as having access to specialist advice.' Given the apparent dearth of research one is forced to ask: What knowledge is being sought here? Where is it to come from? How can it be accessed? Unless it is available how can practitioners be trained?

Gunaratnam (1993) reflects on the community care legislation in the light of her research and draws two stark conclusions affecting carers from ethnic minority groups. First, lack of accessible information about services and inappropriate provision are still in evidence. Second, the kinds of resources valued by carers and service users in community organizations are threatened, she argues, by the contract culture. The push towards block contracts with large-scale providers is seen as disadvantaging small black groups with unusual or more varied patterns of need (Local Government Information Unit 1990). Whether this is the case remains to be seen.

Some indications of the tensions involved can be seen in the results of a recent report about assessment and care management practice amongst different ethnic communities (Begum 1995). Community groups and informal carers played significant roles in referring people to services, sometimes working with care managers in assessments; they were also important as interpreters and advocates. There were some indications that spot purchasing worked well in helping care managers to devise highly individualized care packages. However, locating interpreters was not always easy. Special problems were encountered amongst refugees, who were sometimes reluctant to come forward because of the perceived risks of deportation. Religious and cultural practices which had important meanings to individuals could easily be submerged in the needs assessment process. The complexity of the care package required often determined whether authorities were able to respond to the needs of a person from an ethnic minority community. At the time of writing little work had been done with the black and ethnic minority voluntary sector to enable them to take on service level agreements or contracting on an individual basis. Practice was further blighted by the policy confusion surrounding the issue of whether services should be 'mainstream' and generic or more specialized.

Askham et al. (1995) meanwhile have reported that only two-thirds of the Social Services Departments and District Health Authorities they studied provided some form of training or cultural-awareness teaching to staff working with elderly people from black and ethnic minority groups. From their scrutiny of the evidence about such training they concluded that it was often very limited in scope. They further reported in relation to individual needs assessment that assessment forms did not directly explore religious or cultural requirements.

Bewley and Glendinning (1994) include black and ethnic minority communities amongst those most likely to be excluded from consultation procedures in community care planning. Such exclusion, plus inappropriate needs assessment, the complexities of care management, the strictures of the welfare market, and the lack of a core body of good conceptually grounded research provides mounting evidence that many people from black and ethnic minority communities remain marginalized: it is difficult not to be drawn towards conclusions suggesting the persistence of discriminatory practices and institutional racism. If this problem is to be dealt with it will require a reordering of policy, research and practice priorities.

Despite the intention behind the NHS and Community Care Act (DoH 1990b) with respect to carers, concerns about provision for carers continued unabated, culminating in the Carers (Recognition and Services) Act 1995. Policy and practice guidance has recently been issued (DoH 1996; SSI 1996) and, with the exception of reference to the Welsh Language Act 1993 in connection with equal opportunities in the Welsh guidance, the guidance for England and Wales is identical.

The Carers Act is primarily concerned with informal carers who are providing or intending to provide *regular* and *substantial* care, a decision which appears to be shaped by the findings of Parker and Lawton's (1994) analysis. The reference to *regular* and *substantial* means that not all carers will be eligible for an assessment under the Act, and the policy guidance indicates that it will be for local authorities to determine locally how to interpret these terms and to make their interpretation known. This suggests that definitional criteria will subsequently vary throughout the country. The policy guidance reminds the agencies responsible that they should continue to use their general powers to support carers by means of carer support groups and information without requiring an assessment. The continued focus on 'regular and substantial' care as the eligibility criteria for service seems to be reinforced within the draft guidance, and this can be seen as a cause for concern, given the evidence that we will highlight later. Importantly the Act recognizes the contribution and special circumstances of young carers, and therefore seeks to integrate provision with that laid out within the terms of the Children Act 1989.

Local authorities are asked to carry out a carer's assessment when requested by a carer at the time of a user's assessment where the carer is (i) an adult (aged 18 or over) or a child or young person (under 18) who provides or intends to provide a substantial amount of care on a regular basis, or (ii) parents who provide or intend to provide a substantial amount of care on a regular basis for disabled children. The explicit linking of the carers' assessment to that of the user also raises questions about the ability of carers to seek an assessment not so linked.

Indeed, the Act links the results of the carer's assessment to the local authority's decision about services for the user. The aim is to 'encourage an approach which considers support already available from family, friends and neighbours, the type of assistance needed by the person being assessed and how and whether the current arrangements for care can sustain the user in the community' (DoH 1996, para. 9). Hence the orientation is one aimed primarily at facilitating continued caring. The policy guidance nevertheless stresses that the focus of the carer's assessment should be on the carer's ability to care and to continue caring, taking account of their circumstances, age, views and preferences, and support available to them. A willingness to continue care, or to continue providing the same level of support should not automatically be assumed.

A statement is incorporated about equal opportunities which recognizes that assessment is equally available to all members of the community, including: all potential users and carers; those who have communication difficulties arising from the disability, in which case special arrangements to include carers should be made; people from ethnic minority backgrounds; and those with stated language preferences.

The very existence of the Carers Act 1995 is a signal success for the ability of carers and carer organizations to lobby effectively. It will be for prospective study to assess whether the Act is capable of delivering what carers want. A recent report for the Carers National Association (Warner 1994) suggests that local authorities will have a great deal to accomplish if even the modest expectations of the Act are to be fulfilled. Based on a survey of 420 carers undertaken about one year after the community care changes of April 1993, the survey found that three-quarters who had been assessed said that the assessment had been difficult to obtain; only half thought that it had met their needs; and half were of the opinion that assessments were limited by available budgets. Nearly four out of five felt that the community care changes had made no difference to their lives.

Given the aforementioned difficulties in achieving an adequate assessment of carers' needs (Ellis 1993; Twigg and Atkin 1994; Manthorpe and Twigg 1995), there are few grounds for optimism that the introduction of a Carers Act will really do much to improve the situation. The lack of a practice tradition with carers and the use of tacit, implicit and professionally focused forms of knowledge do little to instil confidence. If the opportunities presented by the Carers Act are to be capitalized upon then there is a pressing need for a rethink about the taken-for-granted nature of the caring experience.

Framing questions about carers' needs and circumstances

Some final questions are worthy of consideration at this stage. First, it seems that the emphasis in much of the research and in policy is on the tangible, instrumental dimensions of care. These dimensions are more readily measurable. As we will illustrate in the next chapter, carers on the whole do not construe what they do in this manner and there is a real danger that the more invisible aspects of care will remain overshadowed. This is important as there is growing evidence that carers struggle to balance the overt and covert aspects of care, which means that assessors and care managers will have to pay close attention to those parameters which are meaningful to carers themselves.

Second, an increasing amount of research and accumulated practice experience suggests that it is vital to understand caring within a temporal perspective. The course of a disability or chronic illness can require major adjustments to kinship relationships and to the roles that the various parties perform. We are beginning to appreciate that a capacity and preparedness to care within the family circle can depend upon many antecedent factors, so that biography is an important part of understanding the status of a carer at any one point in time. Equally, ways of charting the onset, course and time phase of a person's disability (Rolland 1988, 1994) can provide vital clues about the likely future demands upon carers and families. The ability to predict the nature of such demands and the reasons for them is of considerable importance to carers and is likely to help them to develop more coherent approaches to planning and providing care. Of course the ability to do this will vary with the nature of a person's disability – some like multiple sclerosis are episodic and can involve long periods of remission, others like acute or long-term mental illnesses may also have symptom-free periods, yet many conditions follow a reasonably definite course. As we will show, many carers are given little information about these patterns and how they might anticipate and manage the more demanding periods. Patterns of coping and the preparedness for caregiving roles will also be explored in subsequent chapters.

Third, if plotting the course of a person's disability or chronic illness is feasible then it would make sense to do this in relation to a schema for charting family stages. The reason for this is that periods of family formation, child-rearing, children leaving home, middle and later years tend to be associated with discernible family challenges (Aldous 1994), and these can be as demanding, constraining or liberating as caring itself. The support network perspectives described earlier have a relevance in this context as they can provide a backcloth to understanding change and stability in family support. If a change in the condition of a disabled relative is anticipated to occur at about the same time as one of the family carers is about to marry or leave home, this may trigger some early decisions about the planning of care which can help all concerned. The importance of integrating differing forms of care 'work' with the trajectory of an illness and the biographies of both disabled people and their carers has been well described (Corbin and Strauss 1988, 1992). Therefore the integration of the relevant literature about chronic illness with what we know about caring is also important. Such a synthesis is attempted in Chapter 6.

Finally, it seems apparent that much of what we know about family care is from a majority white culture perspective. Markers of the plural society in which we live need to figure more prominently in carer research. Some of the evidence incorporated into what we have discussed so far suggests that factors such as race and ethnic identity, gender, marital or kinship relationship and age or life stage are implicated in how people come to assume caring roles and, to a degree, how they perform them.

2

Towards a More Holistic Conceptualization of Caring

What is this thing some call caregiving?
(Gubrium 1995: 268)

In the introduction to a special edition of *Qualitative Health Research*, focusing on the topic of 'The Caregiver Relationship', Jaber Gubrium (1995) 'takes stock' of the existing state of knowledge in the field of caregiving. Although succinct, the text is insightful and cogent, posing a number of fundamental questions, the most telling of which is quoted above. For whilst Gubrium acknowledges the extensive literature on caregiving he bemoans the fact that much of what has emerged from several years of study does not capture adequately the nuances of caring but instead 'second-guesses' the lived experience of carers by relying primarily on a causal modelling approach. The way towards a better understanding is, he argues, 'definitely not more of the same'. He signals the need for a critical assessment, not simply another literature review, which attempts a deconstruction of the taken-for-granted language of caregiving, including the term 'caregiving' itself. Others have also taken a similar view (Langer 1993; Opie 1994; Brody 1995), recognizing that whilst the terms 'caring' and 'caregiving' have been extensively used, they remain poorly defined (Abrams 1985; Bulmer 1987; Arber and Ginn 1990).

It is the intention of this chapter to outline an alternative perspective on caregiving and to present a reconceptualization of the differing types of care first described by Bowers (1987, 1988). This revised and extended typology is based on a reanalysis of several years of data collected by the authors from a variety of family carers providing care both to individuals with learning difficulties and to older people with varying forms of physical and/or cognitive frailty. The chapter begins with a brief overview of the ways in which both family and professional caring are currently construed, highlighting in particular the instrumental focus that dominates service ideologies. This is followed by a consideration of how responsibilities are negotiated within 'normal family' life as described by Finch and Mason (1993), providing a backcloth to Bowers's work and our revision of it. The chapter concludes by addressing the implications of an alternative conceptualization of caring for the planning and delivery of services.

Caring: often used, rarely defined

Although the above question posed by Gubrium appears deceptively simple, providing a comprehensive answer is much more complex. This challenge was identified several years ago by Bulmer (1987), who noted that whilst the meaning of care is intuitively fairly obvious, the types of help, support and protection it connotes are far from clear. Parker (1981), in attempting to disentangle care, draws a distinction between 'care' which can be construed as 'caring about' – as for example in generalized 'concern for' another person, in expressed emotion, or perhaps in financial donations and gift-giving – and 'care' as expressed in 'tending', as seen in more practical 'hands-on' terms. Survey studies typically concentrate on the latter. Green's (1988) national sample survey, for example, categorized the tasks of informal care into personal care, physical help, help with paperwork and finances, 'other practical help', keeping the person company, taking the person out, giving medicine and surveillance. These were used as the basis of the secondary analysis carried out by Parker and Lawton (1994) which, following a cluster analysis, resulted in six mutually exclusive categories of care: personal *and* physical care, personal *not* physical care, physical *not* personal care, other practical help, practical help only and other help. What emerges nevertheless is a largely instrumental model of caring.

Parker and Lawton alluded to other possibilities for developing a typology of caring activity based on the characteristics of the carers or of those being cared for, the nature of the caring activity or some combination of these. They also noted that 'tending' activity can be defined in terms of timing, frequency, urgency, complexity and how long tasks take. Context also provided another set of parameters such as the nature of impairment, the level of responsibility carried by the carer and so on. The primary purpose behind their reanalysis of Green's data, however, was to distance caring from its social or relational context.

Like Parker and Lawton, other writers have noted the lack of a comprehensive model for understanding family care and have attempted to extend how it may be visualized, though what emerges is not dissimilar to Parker's (1981) earlier description. Qureshi (1986) sees caring in two dimensions of practical tending and catering to social and emotional needs. Pearlin *et al.* (1990) suggest that caring is best taken as referring to the affective component whereas the term 'caregiving' more closely describes the behavioural aspects. Bulmer (1987) includes both affective and practical domains but suggests that caring also involves a more generalized concern for the welfare of others. The dual focus suggested by these commentators has perhaps been the most pervasive within British family care studies.

On a more philosophical level, Griffin (1983) contends that caring is a primary mode of being, a fundamental concept in our understanding of what constitutes human nature, a point captured by Benner and Wruebel (1989), who suggest that caring is 'the most basic way of being in the world'. This possibly helps to explain why people have been reported to continue providing care in the absence of affection (Qureshi 1986). Other studies have emphasized a categorization of care and carers based on a hierarchy of obligations, responsibilities and position in the life-cycle (Ungerson 1987; Qureshi and Walker 1989; Finch and Mason 1993), which may give rise to a set of informal rules by which individuals assume responsibility for the care of other family members.

Some writers have cast their ideas about care within the context of social support, viewing care as no more than an integral part or extension of ordinary interpersonal relationships. Based on how ordinary people construct ideas about the issue, Kahn and Antonucci (1980) for example have defined social support in terms of the three As: namely affect (caring and emotional intimacy), affirmation (provision of information about the rightness or wrongness of one's actions or thoughts) and aid (direct help through money, time and effort). Barrera and Ainlay (1983) discuss six categories of support drawn from a content analysis of reviewed research papers: material aid, behavioural assistance, intimate interaction, guidance, feedback and positive social interaction. Although taking definitional parameters beyond a concern with the instrumental, these studies are still primarily concerned with care as a set of tasks or activities.

Some have taken the analogy between care and a set of tasks or activities a stage further and used the metaphor of labour or work to categorize what carers do. Arber and Ginn (1995) for example cite James (1992), who describes caring in terms of three essential components:

- physical labour
- emotional labour
- organizational/managerial labour.

Arber and Ginn (1995) note that whilst physical labour is the most obvious and visible form of caring, the latter two are likely to be more important to the quality of life of an elderly cared-for person. Others have commented on the 'hard physical labour' component of caring (Bulmer 1987; Lewis and Meredith 1989; Twigg and Atkin 1994) but have also reasserted that caring is about more than just physical work. Lewis and Meredith (1989) consider that caring may also involve loving attention, and that for some carers it constitutes both an activity and a source of identity.

An appreciation of the role of emotional or affective components is clearly central to a more complete understanding of caregiving, although the emotions engendered are often mixed and may comprise such conflicting reactions as love, guilt, compassion and gratitude (Ungerson 1987), stirring both ambiguous and ambivalent feelings (Lewis and Meredith 1988a,b). Twigg and Atkin (1994) add another dimension to this already potent mixture, that relating to a perceived sense of responsibility whereby a carer becomes the 'arbiter of standards'. Indeed these authors go as far as to suggest that such a sense of responsibility may be the 'core feature that underpins all caregiving'. We will pursue this in more detail later, as the notion of carers maintaining and monitoring excellence in care is one that has considerable empirical support. Recognition of this is important, as the perceived ownership of expertise greatly influences the interactions between family and professional carers.

From a different but related perspective others have attempted to delineate various types of *caregiver* as opposed to the components of care itself. Lewis and Meredith (1989) for instance differentiate between carers who adopt a *balanced* mode in which they are able to combine caregiving with other important parts of their lives such as paid employment. They compared this type of carer with those who *integrated* caring into their lives, with caring providing a sense of purpose and of satisfaction. The third category Lewis and Meredith describe is caregivers who become *immersed*, who invest heavily in caregiving and find it extremely difficult to disentangle themselves. According to Lewis and Meredith, the consequences for carers vary depending upon which caregiving position they occupy. The most negative effect is experienced by the immersed carer.

There are considerable conceptual similarities between the categories defined above and those outlined by Twigg and Atkin (1994), namely: the *engulfed* carer who subordinates their life to that of the disabled person; the carer who is able to *balance/set boundaries* and the carer who is able to construct a *symbiotic* relationship from which they gain positive benefits. The affective domains of caregiving described earlier by Opie (1994) of commitment, dissociation, obligation and repudiation also have clear parallels with those of Lewis and Meredith (1989) and Twigg and Atkin (1994).

The obvious diversity and complexity of caring has led some observers to the conclusion that the search for a single 'dichotomous' definition that distinguishes a carer from a non-carer is 'over ambitious and probably futile' (Arber and Ginn 1990). Yet all too often such a definition is sought. Table 2.1 presents a number of definitions of a carer that have emerged over the last 15 years. Whilst there is variation in the relative emphasis within these definitions, they are all consistent in that their primary focus is on the instrumental aspects of caring. In terms of service provision it seems that Twigg and Atkin (1994) were correct in their belief that physical dependency is the defining feature of family caregiving. It is just such a view that we seek to counter. However, before proceeding to outline an alternative

Table 2.1 Definitions of a carer

Date	Source	Definition
1982	Equal Opportunities Commission	Anyone who looks after or cares for a handicapped person to any extent in their own home or elsewhere.
1984	Social Work Services Development Group	A person who takes prime responsibility in the home care of a person who, because of handicap or illness, needs almost continuous care.
1988	Green	A person looking after or providing some form of regular service for a sick, handicapped or elderly person living in their own or another household.
1990	Braithwaite	People who assume the major responsibility for providing caregiving services on a regular basis to someone who is incapable of providing for him/herself.
1991	Social Services Inspectorate	A person who is not employed to provide the care in question by anybody in the exercise of its function under any enactment. Normally, this will be a person who is looking after another adult in the home who is frail, ill and/or mentally or physically disabled, and where the dependency relationship 'exceeds that implicit in normally dependent relationships' between family members.
1995	British Medical Association	A carer is someone who gives unpaid care to a relative or friend who is dependent because of age, physical or other disability and who would, if not cared for, require support from the state or other means.

view of family caring, we want to look at what is meant by professional caring. Such a consideration is necessary if a better understanding of the interface between family and professional care is to emerge.

The nature of professional care

If there is uncertainty about a definition of the nature of family caring, the meaning and components of professional care are equally unclear. The nursing profession probably lays greatest claim to base itself on an ethos of care; a brief consideration of the extensive literature on this subject brings into sharp relief the areas of similarity and contrast between family and professional caring.

The concept of caring has been the subject of considerable scrutiny within the nursing literature and yet despite extensive usage, its meaning, as with family care, is uncertain (Radsma 1994; Fealy 1995; Kyle 1995; Scott 1995). Radsma (1994) notes the linguistically ambiguous position of caring, suggesting that it can be used as both a noun, as in home care, and a verb, as in caregiving. Mirroring Bulmer (1987), she comments on the intuitive appeal of the concept, reflected in feelings of warmth, respect, nurturance and regard. Interestingly, there is also considerable concern within the nursing literature about the emphasis on the tasks of caring and the relative neglect of the less tangible emotional components (Radsma 1994; Kyle 1995; Scott 1995). As with family caregiving, nursing care is seen as complex, comprising a number of elements. These are defined by Kyle (1995) as behavioural, moral, cognitive and emotional, with each element also being culturally and contextually bound (Fealy 1995; Kyle 1995). Fundamentally, however, the essence of nursing care is the belief that the person who is the recipient of care in some way 'matters' (Nikkonen 1994; Fealy 1995; Scott 1995). 'The widest basis on which one cares for another is that the other is a fellow human being, worthy of dignity and respect. This is crucial to all caring' (Fealy 1995: 136).

Scott (1995) describes good professional care as 'constructive' care, the achievement of which requires both competence in the physical (clinical and technical) aspects *and* humaneness, sensitivity and compassion. This contention provides a most interesting comparison because although there are obvious similarities between the definitions of family and professional care so far considered, the notion that a family carer has in some way to be 'competent' to deliver care is rarely formally addressed – this is an issue that we shall return to at a number of points later in the book.

In synthesizing the requirements for acceptable professional care, Kitson (1987) identifies three criteria: respect for the person; an ability and willingness to care; and the possession of the necessary knowledge, skills and attitudes. However, it seems that such criteria are not seen as essential for family care. Qureshi (1986) for example describes how affection is not a necessary condition for family care, although in its absence caring is more difficult. In drawing comparisons between caring for a parent and child care it seems very likely that if a parent was not considered to have affection for her child and was deemed to lack the skills of parenting then considerable concern would be voiced. However, with regard to the care of older people, whilst the absence of affection and/or skills might be noted, it hardly seems to raise the same level of professional concern. It is interesting to speculate as to whether this is a manifestation of ageist attitudes, a desire not to interfere in family life or simply ignoring the issue for fear of the potential consequences in terms of the availability of family care.

Returning to professional caring, Morse *et al.* (1990), in undertaking a synthesis of 35 definitions of caring from the literature, outlined five main perspectives, defining care as either: an affective response; a human trait; a moral imperative; a therapeutic intervention or an interpersonal interaction. The similarities between such dimensions and family caregiving are apparent as, with the exception of care as a 'therapeutic intervention', the other criteria span both professional and family care. Yet, much of what family caregivers do could be seen to constitute a therapeutic intervention. This 'therapeutic' element will become apparent when we describe the satisfactions of caring in Chapter 4. At this point it is sufficient to note that although family carers might not use the term 'therapeutic', this is often their intent. It therefore seems that the differences between professional and family caregiving are not as great as might be thought, apart from the fact that one group is formally trained and usually quite well paid, and the other is not. As Twigg and Atkin (1994) note, recent feminist perspectives on care have much emphasized the notion of payment for family care.

Bond (1992) argues that it is time to 'professionalize' family caring, not in the 'traditional' sense but to the extent that 'the skills used by caregivers are valued in themselves, to be encouraged and improved' (p. 18). The concept of carer 'expertise' (Nolan and Grant 1992a) will be developed in greater detail later in this chapter.

From this brief overview of both family and professional caring, it seems that analytically they are characterized more by what they have in common than by how they differ. Both are seen to consist of a number of like attributes, some visible and obvious, some subtle and invisible. Moreover, there is concern in both the family and professional caring literature that it is the visible, physical components of care that are most recognized, whilst the less tangible but more important aspects are given tacit acknowledgement at best.

Family care: widening horizons

A useful starting point in developing a broader conceptualization of family caring is to look at the way in which responsibilities are negotiated in 'ordinary families' who are not providing care. In unpacking the manner in which help and assistance is organized within such families, Finch and Mason (1993) assert 'with some certainty' that there is no clear consensus about the division of responsibility nor are there universal normative rules. Rather a delicate and dynamic process of negotiation occurs in which the family history and biography interact, resulting in the 'development of commitments' over time. They identify a number of key components to the negotiation process, foremost amongst which are reciprocity and balance. The intention of these activities is to maintain as far as possible family perceptions of independence. To achieve this, negotiations are often tacit and implicit, rather than being open and explicit. Indeed, Finch and Mason (1993: 71) contend that often the potential recipient of help is deliberately excluded from discussions to protect their sense of independence: 'There is an analytic distinction between exclusions which are intended to protect people . . . and those which are intended to disempower.'

It is therefore the context and meaning of such exclusions that are paramount rather than the act itself. In other words it is not the *task* that is important but the *purpose* or *intent* behind it. Similar subtle processes underlie the maintenance of reciprocity and the giving of and asking for help, which is seen to involve much more than 'simply doing the tasks' (p. 93). A delicate balance is achieved between the offer of help and having to ask for it. Most people consider it wrong to expect help as a right, but having to ask for help is also seen as something to be avoided if possible. In situations where the need for help is therefore apparent, offering to provide it before someone has to ask is the most psychologically satisfactory outcome for all parties. This complexity is heightened by the fact that many negotiations occur in advance of any help being required.

Therefore negotiations relate to both real and 'anticipated' situations, especially when older family members are the potential recipients of help. Finch and Mason believe that during such interactions, 'Peoples' identities are being constructed, confirmed and reconstructed' (p. 170).

In trying to identify those factors which influence negotiation it seems that gender, ethnicity, culture or income do not explain support in any straightforward way. Moreover, there are no rules of obligation in terms of rights or duty, but rather guidelines for action, based upon responsibilities that have been created over time. In conclusion Finch and Mason contend that there are no fixed beliefs in the giving and receiving of support, but a negotiated balance in which people strive not to become too dependent and work to maintain at least an element of interdependence.

Though we have presented only an outline of what are quite subtle processes of negotiation and adaptation between parties, we believe that there is much of value that might profitably be applied to family caregiving in the present context. For if family negotiations are based upon the perceived purpose rather than the tasks of care, and gender, ethnicity, culture and income play relatively little part, it is likely that similar factors will pertain to family caregiving.

Certainly the instrumental aspects of care so prominent in the definitions previously considered seem inadequate to capture the above subtleties. It was such a concern that led Bowers (1987) to explore further the meanings and purposes of care as defined by carers themselves. Working on the premise that effective interventions to assist family carers could not be designed until there was a more adequate understanding of the carers' experience, she sought to develop a new typology of intergenerational care.

Data were collected using semi-structured interviews with mainly female adult children caring for their elderly parents suffering from various degrees of dementia. Bowers argued that most previous conceptualizations had defined caring by the nature of the task involved: that is, what carers do. This emphasis did not, however, accord with the accounts given by the carers themselves. This led Bowers to conclude that the process of caregiving is much more complex than these commonly used definitions would indicate, and that much of the stress of caregiving is unrelated to the presence of tasks.

On the basis of her data, Bowers suggested that much of the work of caregiving is 'invisible', in that it does not include overt behaviour and is not apparent to the cared-for person. Bowers considered that caring should be differentiated by purpose rather than task. Developing these arguments further, she outlined five distinct but often overlapping types of care.

First, there is *anticipatory care*, based on anticipated future need, with the key notion being 'just in case'. Anticipatory care can begin many years before any actual help is required and, as such, it is deliberately kept from the individual who is the focus of its attention. However, it can have a profound effect on the carer's life as major life decisions can be influenced by such anticipated future needs.

The second type of care in Bowers's model is termed *preventive care*, the main component of which is monitoring at a distance. As with anticipatory care, this does not usually involve directly observable assistance and therefore the 'cared-for' person may remain largely unaware of its existence. Examples of this type of care are keeping a subtle check that medication regimes are followed, that diets are adequate, and so on.

When such a monitoring role requires more direct intervention, such as assistance with actually taking medication, then Bowers considers that the stage of *supervisory care* has been reached. At this point, the cared-for person is more likely to be aware of the interventions but the carer may still try to minimize such awareness.

None of the above categories of care are accounted for in the definitions previously considered. As the need for direct assistance increases and the carer has to 'do for', then the stage of *instrumental care* has been reached. This is the type of care on which most of the previous research and current interventions have focused. The cared-for person is now largely aware of his/her need for help but carers will often try to maintain an element of reciprocity in their relationship. Bowers argues that carers find this aspect of caring the least stressful.

Underpinning the whole model is the notion of *protective care*, the purpose of which is to maintain the self-esteem of those being cared for. This involves minimizing their awareness of their failing abilities and maximizing the extent to which they still perceive themselves as independent. According to Bowers, carers see protective care as the most difficult, the most important and the most stressful. Furthermore, it is often in conflict with other aspects of caring, especially the instrumental functions. It can, for example, be very difficult both to do something for someone while, at the same time, maintaining his/her perceptions of his/herself as independent. Consequently, carers would often prefer to ignore certain instrumental tasks in order to preserve protective caring.

In a later paper describing carers' perceptions of care in a nursing home, Bowers (1988) replaced the notion of protective care with *preservative care*, based on the need to preserve the cared-for person's sense of 'self'. Four broad types of preservative activity were described which were intended to help maintain family connections, and the dignity, hope and sense of control of the person in care. According to Bowers, family carers considered that staff should work collaboratively with carers in order to ensure that the essential elements of preservative care were maintained in the family's absence.

Given and Given (1991) identify the potential of Bowers's typology; they believe that it captures the more complex and sophisticated observations and judgements that define much of family care. However, they suggest that it requires further empirical confirmation. An appraisal of some of the current literature provides additional support for many of Bowers's arguments.

With respect to the notion of anticipating care, Finch and Mason (1993) suggest that anticipating the need for future help is a feature of ordinary family life and that negotiations can take place even if such help is never actually needed. Similarly, in a study explicitly to determine the extent to which daughters anticipate the future care needs of their mothers, Conway-Turner and Karasik (1993) discovered that of their sample of 103 daughters, 99 per cent actively anticipated caring for their mothers, and 68 per cent said they did this either frequently or daily. Such anticipation was not confined to middle-aged daughters with elderly mothers but with daughters still in their twenties, with many of the potential recipients of care being fit and active and in their early to mid-sixties. On the basis of their study Conway-Turner and Karasik suggest that the anticipation of caring responsibilities is a normal part of life, occurring several years before any care may be needed and irrespective of whether the need for care ever materializes.

In terms of preventive and supervisory care, Lewis and Meredith (1988b) outline a caring sequence which, if not identical, is distinctly similar to Bowers's (1987). They note that periods of what they term 'semi-care' and 'part-time full care' precede care proper. In semi-care there is usually little or no need for physical support but daughters 'monitor' the situation 'just in case', a phrase applied by Bowers to anticipatory care. Lewis and Meredith point out that semi-care can go on for several years. They claim that despite its apparently nebulous nature it is in fact very tying. However, it is not explicitly recognized by professionals who therefore do not see carers as requiring support during this period.

Instrumental care is recognized by all authors, but as Bowers (1987, 1988) points out, carers often work hard to maintain an element of reciprocity and interdependence in their relationships. This is consistent with the results of studies by Finch and Mason (1993) and Ellis (1993) who describe how carers and cared-for persons often negotiate a finely tuned set of responsibilities in order to preserve the perceived independence of the older person. Indeed Ellis suggests that the receipt of services is sometimes seen as synonymous with deterioration and therefore help is rejected even if it is required. Likewise Qureshi (1986) argues that some older people may prefer to abandon a goal, such as bathing, rather than see themselves as dependent upon others.

All of these studies provide further support for Bowers's (1987) concept of protective care, which is explicitly confirmed in the work of Finch and Mason (1993), who draw the analytic distinction between excluding people from negotiations in order to protect their self-esteem and exclusion which is intended to disempower. The former is entirely consistent with Bowers's category of protective care.

Upon first reading Bowers's (1987, 1988) work we were struck with how it accorded with much of our own data collected from a number of studies. However, there also appeared to be a number of limitations which suggested the need for further elaboration, because it was developed:

- with respect to intergenerational care only (as were many of the other studies cited above in support of it);
- specifically with dementia caregivers;
- without adequately accounting for reciprocity within the caregiving relationship, taking only a carer's perspective;
- without reference to a longitudinal perspective, limiting (for example) anticipatory care to the early stages of the caregiving process.

This prompted us to undertake a reconceptualization of Bowers's typology in order that it could be tested against a more diverse set of caregiving circumstances (Nolan *et al.* 1995a). It is hard to trace the exact evolution of this new typology because it is not the product of a single discrete study but has emerged from several studies conducted over a number of years. On the basis of these studies a subtle dialectic and iterative process occurred, during which Bowers's original work was tested out against both new and previously collected data. Data analysis during the course of one particular study (Keady and Nolan 1993a,b) acted as a stimulus, honing emergent ideas and concepts into a more coherent whole. A tentative refinement of Bowers's typology was the result; this occasioned a return to data from early studies to check the veracity and robustness of the proposed revisions. The limitations of this approach need to be acknowledged as it constitutes only a partial and somewhat inadequate process – most of the data were not collected for the purpose of either developing or testing the typology. Nevertheless, the revised categories proved robust, and the data provided empirical support for the new dimensions as they are currently conceptualized. These are:

- anticipatory care
- preventive care
- supervisory care
- instrumental care
- protective care
- preservative care
- (re)constructive care
- reciprocal care.

As will readily be apparent, Bowers's categories remain at the heart of the typology, but we have redefined anticipatory care whilst retaining both protective and preservative care, rather than replacing protective care with preservative care as Bowers (1988) suggests. Moreover, we have added two new categories: (re)constructive care and reciprocal care. These constitute the broad *types* of care used by family caregivers.

Preventive care, supervisory care and instrumental care remain unchanged and these will not be described in further detail. However, anticipatory care has been extended considerably and the relationship between protective and preservative care has changed; these will be considered in greater depth, as will the new categories of care we have suggested (Nolan *et al.* 1995a).

Redefining care: a new typology

Bowers (1987) saw the key concept underpinning anticipatory care as being 'just in case'. She describes anticipatory care as being invisible (i.e. it is not based on overt behaviour, nor is it recognized by the cared-for person) and as occurring mainly prior to other forms of care being needed. Furthermore, she suggests that anticipatory care is used mainly by children who are not sharing a household with their parents.

This broad conceptualization is consistent with the other work we have cited, for example semi-care (Lewis and Meredith 1988b) and the studies of Finch and Mason (1993) and Conway-Turner and Karasik (1993). We would suggest however, that anticipation is a more pervasive and prolonged activity and is of relevance not only *before* but *throughout* the period of caring.

Anticipating some possible future event is not of course restricted to caring, and is probably a universal human activity. Bowers (1987) argues, however, that anticipating the need to care for a relative, whether or not this need actually materializes, can have profound effects on people's lives. To take an extreme example, anticipating the need to care for an ageing parent might be a factor dissuading an only child from emigrating abroad. On the other hand, we would argue that this form of anticipation is not confined to children thinking about caring for their parents and is of relevance in other contexts. Wenger *et al.* (1996) for example suggest that spouses often move to a smaller house, with a smaller garden and nearer to shops or adult children, in anticipation of potentially increased dependency. There are some subtle but important distinctions between anticipatory care as envisaged by Bowers and that described here. Anticipation in Bowers's sense does not usually result in direct action (although clearly it may inhibit certain activity) and is more of a cognitive activity, whereas a move of house is an overt act. Also Bowers contends that anticipation by adult children is not shared with their parents for fear of causing offence. Anticipation in spousal relationships, on the other hand, is more likely to be shared and explicit rather than implicit.

Furthermore, we would suggest that anticipatory care extends throughout the caregiving history but that it changes in nature and form over time. Therefore anticipatory care, which occurs before other forms of care are needed, is most probably largely invisible but this should not be seen as axiomatic. For instance, it is becoming increasingly more common for parents to express their own wishes and preferences for care options should they anticipate future dependency needs. Rather than the notion of 'just in case', which Bowers sees as underpinning anticipatory care, we would see the question 'what would I do if . . . ?' as being more appropriate for this type of anticipatory care. When other more overt forms of care are actually required, we would contend that anticipatory care does not diminish but rather that it changes in character. Therefore, whilst it might still be appropriate to ask the question 'what would I do if . . . ?', an increasingly more relevant question, especially in progressive conditions, is 'what will I do when . . . ?'.

This form of anticipatory care shifts the focus away from anticipated *possible* events to anticipated *likely* events. This shift in perception recognizes that anticipatory care develops along a continuum. At one end lies possible future caregiving before any overt help is actually needed, whilst at the other end lies a discontinuation of caregiving either because of the death of the carer or cared-for person, or alternative care being required. For example, for the elderly parents of disabled children, care of this type tends to focus increasingly on what will happen when the parents die (Richardson and Ritchie 1986; Grant 1989, 1990). Such care is still largely invisible and unknown to the ultimate recipient. Moreover, it is something which older parents have been contemplating throughout the life-cycle from the point at which a diagnosis of disability first came to light. Parents are known to adopt varied and changing strategies to prepare the way for the inevitable: some seek early reassurances from statutory services about continued formal care, others negotiate the transfer of responsibility for care with other siblings, still others find it so traumatizing that all they can do is live on a day-to-day basis. Anticipating care in this context is known to be the cause of stress and high levels of anxiety amongst these elderly carers.

We would also contend that in addition to a change in emphasis, anticipatory care may also change in form. We have coined the terms 'specu-lative anticipation' and 'informed anticipation' to differentiate these (Nolan *et al.* 1995a).

Speculative anticipation occurs when the carer has little information or advice on which to make a decision or a judgement. In such circum-stances the carer is likely to overanticipate or underanticipate possible future demands. Inadequate information has been recognized for some time to be a major deficit in responding to carers needs (Nolan and Grant 1989), and despite numerous calls for more information to be made available, little seems to have improved (Twigg and Atkin 1994). Adequate information is particularly important at critical transition points, especially at the start of caring (Nolan and Grant 1992b) or at the end of the period of instrumental care (Nolan *et al.* 1996). Information allows for a balanced perspective to be gained and facilitates the development of more effective coping strategies. For example, Archbold *et al.* (1992, 1995) have demonstrated that the 'pre-paredness' of a caregiver at the start of caregiving is a major factor influenc-ing the future burdens of care; however, little thought and attention is given as to how carers acquire their role (Stewart *et al.* 1993). Even when this occurs at a time of health crisis and hospitalization, when one might expect support to be available, there is little in the way of systematic professional input to help prepare carers (Nolan and Grant 1992b; Stewart *et al.* 1993). In such circumstances carers can take on their role with no idea of the level of commitment that is required, either in terms of the intensity or duration of care (Nolan and Grant 1992b; Opie 1994).

In contrast, informed anticipation occurs when the carer has adequate advice, information, and support which allows for informed choice. This is important throughout the caregiving history, but especially at transition points. For example, in a series of recent studies looking at the admission of older people to some form of residential or nursing home care (Nolan *et al.* 1996), it emerged that carers are increasingly making decisions on behalf of frail older relatives but are doing so in the absence of adequate guidance and advice. Moreover, because the carer and cared-for persons do not usually discuss preferences prior to alternative care being required, carers have few criteria upon which to choose a home. This compounds an already stressful period and further heightens existing guilt and anxiety.

However, information alone is insufficient for fully informed anticipa-tion, which can only occur when decisions are shared and options discussed. This can be illustrated with a quote taken from an interview with a wife caring for her husband who had recently suffered a stroke: 'He just clams up and won't express himself and tell me how he feels and that makes caring all the more difficult. I don't know his worries and fears for the future which means I can't share mine with him.'

Recognizing and acknowledging the importance of anticipatory care has a number of implications for those working with carers. In particular there is a need to ensure that sufficient information is available and that carers are adequately prepared for their role. This should include not only the provision of information but also emotional support to assist in the formation of realistic perspectives and facilitate informed choice. However, as Stewart *et al.* (1993) argue, carers usually acquire their knowledge and skills on a trial-and-error basis. This is eloquently but tellingly recounted in the following excerpt from an interview with a mother whose child has learning difficulties:

> It was a little GP hospital and there was no doctor there and I was having difficulty, so by the time the doctor came to the hospital things were looking pretty bad and she was delivered by forceps and apparently, though we've never really been able to get this on record, she was damaged with the forceps and it tore a membrane in her brain and she had a brain haemorrhage and it's left her as handicapped as she is. Though we didn't actually find out the extent of the handicap until she was about 2, the first that I really knew about it was when the health visitor came to the house and she always kept her little hands very stiff and her arms; and being naive, not knowing much about babies, I didn't realize that there was anything wrong and I asked the health visitor when she came to the house to test her hearing why were her hands so stiff and she said 'My dear, spastic children are always like this' and that's how we were told that she was cerebral palsied, and that was the first idea that we had that she was having problems . . . We knew nothing about her handicap, I just had to learn as the days went by and for a long time I lost myself because I just didn't know what had happened, and I didn't know really how to handle it and the best way I can describe it is I lost the shiny bits in my life, all my sparkle, you know, all my identity and I just became this caring machine, feeding, caring, coping and wondering why and blaming myself and generally lost my identity for a long time. And every time you visited a doctor or a specialist you were told something worse than you were told the time before and it became very difficult and it wasn't until my younger daughter was born that we realized the full extent of her handicap because she started doing things at six weeks old that — couldn't do at 5 and then it really hit home so that was a really difficult time.

Over a period of five years, the parents in this case were not adequately informed either about their daughter's handicap, nor her potential for future growth and development. Similar deficits have recently been described with respect to dementia care, with carers often returning to their GPs over several years trying to obtain a diagnosis and subsequent information and advice (Williams *et al.* 1995). This problem is not confined only to dementia caring, as in this example of a wife caring for her husband who has had a stroke:

The GP told me to get all the help I could but he never told me where to get it from or what was available. For years it was like wandering around in the dark. It took me 11 years to get a wheelchair and yet it's the best thing that ever happened to me. If only I'd had it from the start.

The whole issue of preparation for caring and the acquisition of knowledge and skills is considered later when the longitudinal model of caring is described.

Protective, preservative and reconstructive care

These are presented together, because they are considered to have a temporal relationship. Bowers (1987) conceptualized protective care as being primarily concerned with keeping the cared-for person unaware of their failing abilities and increasing dependency. She later substituted the concept of preservative care (Bowers 1988), the purpose being to maintain as much of the person's sense of 'self' as possible. By implication such preservative care denotes 'former self'.

In terms of protective care, we would argue that it is a strategy of relatively limited duration and value. Whilst it may be functional in the short term or in certain circumstances, as with denial (Lazarus 1993), there comes a point when protective care is counterproductive and covering up dependency is neither possible or desirable. This form of care undoubtedly exists and is often motivated by high ideals, such as 'protecting' the cancer patient from their diagnosis. However, although well meaning, it is essentially paternalistic and often not in the best interests of either the carer or cared-for person. The following example of a daughter caring for her mother with Parkinson's disease provides an illustration:

Well, mum is starting to have a few accidents during the night now, you know, wetting the bed. Nothing much, only a few drops but it still leaves a little stain. I don't think she's aware of it though, she's certainly never mentioned it and there doesn't seem to be a problem in the day. So I've not told her I've noticed, she's so particular and would be really embarrassed and upset if she thought this was happening.

Whilst one can see the logic and positive virtues of this approach it still leaves a number of questions unanswered, particularly the identification of potentially treatable causes for the mild incontinence.

Other forms of supposed protection are not so clearly altruistic and, whilst couched in terms of benefit to the cared-for person, are intended to save carers and/or professionals from having to face difficult decisions. For example in the studies of admission to care homes (Nolan et al. 1996), instances were identified where an older person had been admitted to care in the belief that this was a temporary measure when in reality the carer and the professional involved saw it as a permanent move. Explanations from carers and professional were frequently offered, usually in terms of not wanting to upset the older person. It was reasoned that when they settled in they would be told of their relocation. Although it is easy to see how a carer might construe such a perception, the fact that a professional colluded with them is a cause for some concern.

When protective care is no longer possible or desirable, preservative care becomes the preferred or main strategy. Bowers (1988) describes preservative care primarily in terms of preserving the dignity, hope and sense of control of the cared-for person; she developed the concept following a study of admissions to a nursing home. We would argue, however, that it occurs throughout the various stages of the caregiving history and extends beyond preserving dignity and self-esteem to include the preservation of skills, abilities and interests, as in this example of a daughter caring for her mother with severe arthritis:

> She's always been very proud of her skills in the kitchen, especially her baking. So when she moved in with us we thought, 'we need to keep her involved', so she sort of took over that part of the house. But now of course she's getting much worse and not only can't she walk but she can't do much with her hands. So making pastry is out of the question. She's still bright as a button though, so she's become the resident expert on cooking, who we turn to for advice and the like.

The value of such care is quite apparent but we would contend that it is only functional to a certain point. One of the main adaptive tasks in chronic illness or disability is to develop new but equally valued roles to replace former ones (Charmaz 1983, 1987). Brandstädter (1995) contends that the maintenance of self-esteem amongst older people can be achieved by balancing assimilative and accommodative activities. Assimilative strategies are aimed at maintaining former abilities and interests for as long as possible, whereas accommodative strategies seek to build new abilities and interests when old ones can no longer be sustained. Brändstadter reviewed several years of research conducted by himself and his colleagues which provides convincing evidence that self-esteem and psychological health in older age are optimized by those individuals who balance accommodative and assimilative strategies and develop realistic perceptions of their capabilities. Within this context it is easy to appreciate how a rigid adherence to preservative care (which has clear conceptual similarities with assimilative activity) is not necessary in the long-term interests of either carer or cared-for person. It is here that (re)constructive care begins to figure more prominently.

The purpose of (re)constructive care is to build upon the past in order to develop new and valued roles. We have named it *(re)constructive* care in recognition of the differences that are apparent in certain caring relationships. Parents of children with learning difficulties, for example, are more likely to engage in *constructive* care in order to build an identity and a set of roles for their child. On the other hand, carers of either spouses or parents are more likely to engage in *reconstructive* care where the purpose is to rebuild an identity on the foundations of past histories and biographies. As noted before, parents of children with learning difficulties strive to construct a future for them, as in this instance of a mother caring for her 21-year-old daughter:

> Well I think it's up to me and her Dad in a way to make things right for her. We have to do our best to make sure that what happens to her in the future is the best that we can possibly do for her. I don't want to see her stuck along with 200 or 300 other people in a large building where they're trying to cope with all these different disabilities and perhaps she'll be there from 9 till 5 for the next 40 years. I don't want that for her . . . So we have to look at the options and see just what is the best for her and I want people to be positive. I don't want them to see the handicap first. I want them to look at her and think: Gosh, she's lovely, she's happy, let's try, let's face the challenge, let's be more positive. Just don't write her off because they might need to pick her up and put her on the toilet so many times a day or somebody might have to give up ten minutes to feed her during the lunch time. I don't want that.

The message here is quite clear: the need to 'construct' an acceptable future is pressing. Such considerations apply equally well in other caring relationships but the emphasis, if not the purpose, is different. This is illustrated in an interview undertaken with a woman caring for her partner who had recently had a major stroke which left him with a degree of dysphasia and considerable residual motor deficits. Her partner was a newly retired bank manager who had been an extremely active person in both a professional and personal capacity, including charity work, hill-walking and amateur dramatics/operatics. Shortly before the stroke they had moved to the country with an active retirement in mind. The stroke had wreaked havoc with their well-laid plans. The interviewee spoke tellingly and eloquently about their efforts to rebuild a future and to substitute interests. Because active participation in dramatics was perceived to be unlikely, she struggled to develop skills in appreciation and active listening. Whilst this was difficult, she was of the opinion that good progress was being made. She was extremely disappointed, however, that those professionals who were involved seemed unable to see beyond her partner's physical deficits. Indeed when one of the authors was interviewing the sister of the respite unit that her partner attended, he was described as 'a depressed little dysphasia'.

This sort of insensitivity, although not conveyed quite so forcibly to the carer herself, was nevertheless apparent to her and was a cause of considerable concern. As a consequence she was considering withdrawing from the respite service despite desperately needing the break. Although an extreme example, this illustrates the legacy of an overemphasis on physical functioning and dependency, both as an indicator of the need for support and as the perceived outcome of successful rehabilitation. A less dramatic, although still telling example, is recounted by Ellis (1993) when she describes how an assessment of need of an elderly woman focused on the functional aspects, totally ignoring her love of painting which provided a major source of pleasure. Ellis describes a number of other insights into the way that professional assessment of need seems to run counter to the perspectives of disabled people themselves. This often undermines rather than sustains their efforts at (re)constructing an identity.

The metaconcept uniting the various components of our typology is what we term 'reciprocal care'. The major limitation of Bowers's model is its failure to account for the reciprocal element of care. Given the context in which it was developed, this is understandable, as the opportunities for reciprocity in dementia, especially the later stages, are probably more limited than in any other condition. But ignoring the reciprocal element in a caregiving relationship is not uncommon. Kitson (1987) suggests that the recipient of care is the more passive partner who more or less complies with the decisions made by the carer.

This statement also seems to imply that the cared-for person has an extremely limited role to play in decision-making. This may be true in certain cases but, as a generalization, it is untenable. Kitson (1987) later qualifies this by stating that dependence lasts only until the recipient is able to resume responsibility for their own welfare. This may not always be possible in chronic or progressive conditions. Whilst direct exchange of the same type and level of care *is* extremely unlikely, the supposition that there is no form of reciprocity in caring is based *only* on the notion of the exchange of instrumental care. We would suggest that care can be reciprocal on a number of levels. Indeed, the growing evidence on the satisfactions of carers (Clifford 1990; Grant and Nolan 1993; Nolan and Keady 1993) clearly indicates that there are diffuse and subtle reciprocities in the majority of caregiving relationships. Even at high levels of dependency, forms of reciprocal helping at the financial, material and psychological levels has been reported in some studies (Grant 1986, 1990). There is nothing new of course in asserting that reciprocity is important in caring, as various studies attest (Abrams 1985; Qureshi 1986; Bulmer 1987; Lewis and Meredith 1988a,b; Qureshi and Walker 1989; Ellis 1993; Finch and Mason 1993). We believe, however, that the role of satisfaction in caring has been neglected, possibly due to the theoretical stance adopted by many studies. Although we will deal with the satisfactions of caring in some detail in Chapter 4, we state here our belief that reciprocity and satisfaction should be seen as the norm in most caregiving relationships and that these can be sustained even in the face of objectively adverse circumstances. Indeed, the absence of reciprocity and satisfaction should act as a warning sign indicating the need for additional support and possibly the search for alternative caring arrangements.

The types of care we have described above are not of course mutually exclusive, and in presenting them in the way we have we are conscious of creating an overly neat and orderly perception. Clearly many types of care can and do occur simultaneously, and the manner in which protective, preservative and reconstructive care slip into one another is subtle and often insidious. We repeat our intention that the typology and subsequent models to be outlined are not meant to be viewed as literal representations of reality but as alternatives to the currently dominant instrumental viewpoint. Certainly carers would not label their activities and purposes as protective or reconstructive care or indeed any of the other categories we have employed. However, we believe that they do *deliberately* use certain strategies to achieve the types of outcomes described above, albeit with considerable variation depending upon the nature of the caregiving relationship and the stage of the caregiving trajectory. Of course instrumental aspects of care are a central component and must not be overlooked. However, we believe that typologies that focus exclusively or primarily on such aspects not only fail to capture the subtleties and meanings of care but, given their link to service delivery, have the potential to do carers a considerable disservice. If applied in an uncritical and unthinking manner they can deny access to support to the potentially most stressed carers (Levesque *et al.* 1995).

Applying the typology: implications for service delivery

Despite the lack of a coherent strategy for the delivery of services to carers, a number of actual and potential interventions are nevertheless available. We believe that the extent to which such support is deemed acceptable and successful from a carers' perspective depends in no small measure on the degree to which it is sensitive both to the caregiving trajectory and the caring strategies that are employed. For example, Bowers (1987) points out that services which threaten carers' efforts at protective care are likely to be rejected. Other authors have made similar observations on the need for professionals to work actively with carers, taking due account of the carers' knowledge and expertise (Lewis and Meredith 1989; Braithwaite 1990; Nolan and Grant 1992a; Harper *et al.* 1993; Schultz *et al.* 1993; Greene and Coleman 1995; Montgomery 1995).

We suggest that interventions can be viewed along a continuum ranging from *facilitative* to *obstructive*, with the position on this continuum being mediated by the extent to which service providers actively engage carers as partners in the intervention process, taking particular account of the carers' expertise and caregiving strategies. This is different to Twigg and Atkins's (1994) notion of a carer as a co-worker, because unlike the co-worker the intention of a partnership is not primarily to maintain the carer in their role. Rather it is to facilitate the best outcome for both carer and cared-for person.

In the majority of cases this will mean a continuation of the caring relationship; but working with carers as partners also means recognizing that in certain circumstances a search for alternative forms of care is the most appropriate strategy.

Facilitative interventions denote an overt, planned and relatively systematic input, augmented by instant access to additional help in cases of urgent need. A prerequisite for effective facilitative support is that it complements the type of care provided by the caregiver. This requires a sensitivity and awareness of the caregiving dynamic and of the expertise of the carer. For carers new to their role there may be a need to provide information, advice and training so that they are adequately prepared and feel competent to provide good care (Archbold *et al.* 1992, 1995; Nolan and Grant 1992b; Stewart *et al.* 1993). It also means that in certain circumstances family members should not be expected to adopt a caregiving role in the first place. As Qureshi and Walker (1989) argue, family care can be amongst the best and the worst of human encounters – forcing someone into the caring role is likely to result in 'potentially disastrous close physical and emotional relationships'. Yet this is often what occurs when reluctant family members are pressured to take on the role of carer, particularly at the time of hospital discharge (Nolan and Grant 1992b). Nolan and Grant noted that hospital consultants based their decisions about future care almost exclusively on physical dependency, whereas potential carers placed far more emphasis on the nature and quality of their previous relationships.

The potential for conflicting perceptions between consultant and carer readily became apparent. Carers who *wished* to take a *very frail* relative home were often advised not to, whilst others (particularly children) were *expected* to take a *relatively able* parent home despite the fact that they might not wish to. For children who voiced doubts about their ability and willingness to care for a parent, there often appeared to be little choice in the matter. One carer described how she had been asked to come and see the consultant and then 'given a good telling off', after which she felt obligated. Despite the relatively good functional ability of the mother in this case and the fact that she did not live with her daughter, the situation soon became very fraught: 'I knew as soon as I started that things could only go from bad to worse. We'd never been very close anyway but I was surprised how, in just a couple of days, I could grow to almost hate my mother.' Given the above reaction it is certainly questionable if all people should be expected to care, and the availability of a relative must not be taken to mean that such an individual should automatically assume the role of carer. Within the present climate of ever more rapid hospital discharge, the time available for both carers and cared-for persons to make important decisions about future care options is diminishing. It seems increasingly likely that growing numbers of carers will adopt the role without adequate thought, advice and preparation.

On the other hand, experienced carers often have considerable expertise of their own; facilitative interventions are sensitive to this and recognize that such knowledge should actively be drawn upon. A failure to do so can result in frustration and annoyance, as with this mother caring for her daughter with learning difficulties:

> Sometimes it can be very annoying because if you've had three hours sleep at night and you get this young woman come in straight out of college or straight out of training and she says: 'Well I think you're doing this wrong and you're doing that wrong' and you just want to sit there and let everything fold in around you with a Valium sandwich. That can be very, very annoying.

However, another excerpt from the same interview illustrates how even experienced carers value an outside perspective, as it can often help to sort out the 'wood from the trees':

> They can distance themselves, they can look from the outside in. They can see things that perhaps I'm too close to and they can make suggestions and I think: Oh yes, we'll try that, perhaps this will work, whereas my role is so intense with — I have to think, I have to anticipate, I have to be one step ahead a lot of the time, I have to be physically able to do the lifting and the caring and the general physical activities that need to keep her occupied during the day, so I am very intensively involved. So sometimes you need to be able to step back and have someone from the outside look in and just give you a general overview of the situation and say: 'Well you've tried this. Now try it this way and see if this will work', and I find that can be positive sometimes.

It is important to note that facilitation is not a function of the *amount* of help or support given. The key determinant is that services are planned in conjunction with the carer and cared-for person to complement their needs. Such services are, unfortunately, not the norm.

Contributory interventions are based on a more *ad hoc*, unplanned and less systematic basis but nevertheless still more or less complement the primary caregiver's role. However, in contrast to facilitative interventions this complementarity has not been achieved by a process of genuine negotiation. Rather, it has arisen in a serendipitous manner, occurring more by chance and good fortune than reasoned judgement. Services, especially those provided by the statutory agencies, which actually complement the primary carer's role, more usually do so on this basis.

Efforts to support the primary caregiver which are neither facilitative nor contributory serve little or no useful purpose. Indeed, they are likely to do more harm than good. Unfortunately, all too often, formal services fall into this category by failing to take account of the caregiver's needs and dominant type of care.

We have termed such services either *inhibitory* or *obstructive* (Nolan *et al.* 1995a), both of which run the risk of being rejected by carers. Inhibitory services are usually not rejected out of hand as, on balance, the benefits are seen to outweigh the costs. However, such services are often accepted reluctantly and carers experience guilt at using them. Respite care provides a good example. It has been suggested that most elderly users of respite care 'tolerate' the admission at best (Nolan and Grant 1992a), finding the experience one of boredom and inactivity. In such circumstances, their self-esteem and morale may fall. However, as carers need the break, they still accept the respite care but feel guilty at doing so. Such a service, whilst maintaining the caring relationship, can inhibit carers' efforts to engage in preservative, reconstructive and reciprocal care.

This is illustrated by the following case history taken from a study of day care provision (Nolan and Cunliffe 1991). During one of the interviews a husband caring for his wife with dementia told of his experience of a respite service. The carer in question carried out all his wife's personal care whilst she was at home and took particular pains to ensure that his wife's hair was well washed and set in a certain way. The style he chose was his wife's favourite and the one that he felt she would have chosen for herself had she been able to. When his wife went in for respite care, he explained this to the staff involved. He was therefore disappointed and distressed to see that, when he visited his wife, her hair had been set in a different style. Whilst he appreciated the fact that the staff were attending to his wife's personal hygiene needs, their efforts were negated by their failure to heed the advice he had given them. Although he still used the service in question as no alternative was available, he was less than happy about doing so.

Obstructive interventions, rather than inhibiting the carer's efforts, are perceived as a direct effort to block them. This is again illustrated by a case study taken from a study of respite care (Nolan and Grant 1992a). One interviewee, an elderly woman caring for her husband with dementia, experienced difficulties with his wandering behaviour. However, she never sedated him but had developed an effective way of dealing with the problem. She attributed her husband's wandering to the fact that he had been a prisoner of war in the Second World War and had made repeated escape attempts. She rationalized that when he wandered he was going back to that period and his often quite desperate attempts to get out of the house were an effort to 'escape'. To forestall this, she would notice the signs of his increasing agitation and let him 'escape'. She normally found that once he had gone a few steps out of the house that he could easily be distracted and would return home quite happily.

She had accepted the initial offer of respite care only reluctantly. On the first admission she had tried to explain her way of dealing with her husband's agitation and wandering to the sister. She was told that, as 'experts', the unit had ways of dealing with wandering patients (it was not a specialist EMI unit). Not wanting to argue, she accepted this. She returned on her visit to find her husband heavily sedated with his mouth full of half-chewed food. She took him home immediately and vowed never to let him go for respite care again.

Twigg and Atkin (1994) suggest that one of the core features that underpin caregiving is the role as the 'arbiter of standards' – the continuum of interventions we have outlined above illustrates this process. Carers consider the appropriateness and relevance of services with regard to their own caregiving strategies and the degree to which professionals acknowledge the carer's expertise. At the extremes of the continuum, services are either welcomed or rejected, whereas for the two intervening positions a delicate balancing act occurs. The need for a break or help is measured against the guilt carers experience and the perceived benefit/disbenefits for the cared-for person. Motenko (1988) described a conceptually similar process in studying the reactions of husbands to their wives' use of respite care. He noted that husbands took pride in what they did as carers and considered themselves to have a store of knowledge and expertise. They required respite workers to exhibit the same qualities and attributes as themselves and only temporarily relinquished care of their wives to workers who met their standards. On the basis of his study Motenko argued that the perceived quality of a service is more important than the quantity.

In relation to social work practice, Fisher (1990: 244) too believes that carers should be seen as experts, 'experts in their own caring arrangements, in communicating with a dependent relative, in balancing competing demands, in interweaving practical and emotional care and in surviving'.

Taraborrelli (1993) argues that the expertise of family carers frequently surprises formal carers and must be better acknowledged. Taking a similar line of reasoning, a number of authors have called for the creation of closer partnerships between carers and professionals (Nolan and Grant 1992a; Ellis 1993; Hughes 1993; Harvath et al. 1994). This will require that professionals are prepared to learn from caregivers (Hasselkus 1988; Nolan et al. 1994), who often have a strong desire to 'teach' staff how to care. Recognition of the different but complementary skills and knowledge possessed by family and professional carers is therefore essential (Hasselkus 1988; Pitkeathley 1990; Nolan and Grant 1992a; Harvath et al. 1994). As Ellis (1993) notes, this will require a considerable reorientation of current professional practice and attitudes. Most fundamentally of all this must include a shift away from the preoccupation with the instrumental and physical aspects of care. Such components cannot and should not be ignored, but as Schultz et al. (1993: 5) argue, interventions based solely or primarily on the tasks of care have very little impact 'precisely because they fail to address the inner world of the carer and related major concerns such as loss and grief, guilt, anger and resentment'.

We opened this chapter with a question posed by Gubrium (1995), 'What is this thing some call caregiving?'. In attempting to provide a more complete (although still partial) answer we have outlined an extended typology of care based around carers' purposes and intentions rather than the tasks they perform. Implications for service delivery have also been addressed. In the next chapter we narrow the focus somewhat and consider how carers cope with the varying demands they face.

3

STRESS AND COPING: IMPLICATIONS FOR FAMILY CAREGIVING

> To care is to experience stress.
> (Opie 1994: 39)

Stress and burden have provided a dominant backcloth for many studies of family caregiving (Kahana and Young 1990; Twigg and Atkin 1994; Kane and Penrod 1995) and this is reflected in the extensive literature on these subjects. Twigg and Atkin (1994) are critical of the influence such studies have exerted, in particular the extent to which they have 'pathologized' caregiving. In many respects such criticisms are warranted, but the application of a stress-coping framework need not result in an exclusively negative view. That this has been the case is more a consequence of the manner in which stress-coping models have been interpreted rather than an inevitable consequence of their use. It is now increasingly recognized that *any* framework which is too deterministic (Burr *et al.* 1994) and focuses primarily on simplified causal models (Gubrium 1995) will not capture adequately the diverse and dynamic nature of family caregiving (Thompson *et al.* 1993; Burr *et al.* 1994; Opie 1994; Brody 1995; Gubrium 1995). However, stress-coping approaches do not *have* to be applied in a deterministic way, nor should they be seen as literal representations of reality (Pearlin *et al.* 1990). What they do provide, however, is a useful heuristic device to explore many dimensions of family care. This is the manner in which we will apply them here.

Working from an explicitly qualitative perspective, Opie (1994) asserts that caring is necessarily stressful, and whilst it is impossible to eliminate stress altogether, the manner in which it can be ameliorated is important. It has also been argued that although burden has made an important contribution to the caregiving literature, there is a need to identify a less pejorative term (Kane and Penrod 1995). Implicit in this suggestion is the notion that caregiving must be seen in other than exclusively negative terms. Others, like Opie (1994), have recognized that although stress is an inevitable part of caring and indeed life in general, it can also be a positive experience providing opportunities for growth and challenge (Boss 1988; Benner and Wruebel 1989). This more holistic perception of the nature of stress is one that we will employ.

The primary purpose of this chapter is to consider the way that carers cope with or manage the challenges they face. We will be drawing on data obtained from a survey using a new assessment index, the Carers Assessment of Managing Index (CAMI) (Nolan *et al.* 1995b) to underpin our arguments; we shall also discuss the implications for interventions designed to assist family carers. In order to provide a context for these discussions we begin with a brief overview of the main theoretical approaches to understanding stress and coping.

Stress: a brief overview of theoretical models

Whilst there is considerable evidence to support the view that family carers of people with long-term illnesses or disabilities suffer psychological and physical stresses, with some studies reporting findings which suggest the existence of psychiatric disturbance (Bradshaw and Lawton 1978; Burden 1980; Quine and Pahl 1986; Grant *et al.* 1990), the extent to which this is an inevitable consequence is in doubt. A recent review of the effects of caregiving raises questions about the longer-term impact on physical and mental well-being (Taylor *et al.* 1995) and highlights a number of methodological and theoretical limitations in many studies. Taylor and co-authors conclude that there must be a more careful targeting of those carers most at risk of negative health outcomes rather than a blanket approach that sees all carers as being in the risk category. This will require an individual assessment of carers which takes account not only of the challenges they face, but how they perceive such challenges and the coping measures and strategies they employ. In achieving such an assessment it is now generally recognized that the transactional model of stress provides the most adequate explanation of how people deal with potentially adverse life events. In order to appreciate this approach it is useful to compare it with other competing theoretical explanations.

The 'stimulus–response' model

There is in fact no explicit stimulus–response model of stress, but some writers describe the process as if this is what is implied. Stress is seen simply as the result of some kind of antecedent stimulus or event. The implicit assumption is that stress is objectively determined by the nature of the event itself. At least one carer stress scale has been published which appears to work in this way (Robinson 1983), with carers simply providing a yes/no response to 13 questions, with each yes response being given a score of one. Carers who score seven or more are deemed to be stressed. The additive nature of the scale makes a number of simplistic and unwarranted assumptions, considering all events to be either:

- stress-provoking all the time;
- equally stress-provoking; or
- stress-provoking for different carers or the same carer at different points in time.

This makes little sense. Individuals react to events in different ways. We may perceive things in the same way and still behave differently, or we may change our reactions from one day to the next. The model is accordingly oversimplified and would appear to have little explanatory power.

Stress and life events

'Life events' theorists see stress as stemming from interactions with the environment. Here, stress is seen as the result of the cumulative effects of major life events like divorce, moving house, serious illness or bereavement (Dohrenwend and Dohrenwend 1974). The assumption is that life events like these, if occurring in close temporal proximity, are more likely to result in physical or psychological stress than single events.

Time and appraisal are mediating factors in this model. Time is implicated because it is the great 'healer'. Where an individual is faced with multiple life events happening concurrently, their personal resources may become overtaxed and therefore it may take them longer to recover. Beliefs and values are also accorded an important role, hence the response to stress in the future may be quite different.

A 'life events' approach to understanding stress in relation to caring may be particularly relevant at times of significant life transition (a house move, change within a person's support network, a service transition, for example). It is probably less relevant to an understanding of how family carers manage on a day-to-day basis, although there will of course be occasions when significant life events and the 'daily grind' of care come together as key challenges to a person's adaptive capacity. Writers have shown that depression and self-esteem, for example, are better understood when both life events and life conditions are taken into account (Makosky 1982). Even here, however, it was shown that life events added little to the predictability of a variety of mental health measures beyond the contribution of life conditions.

The transactional model of stress (and coping)

In the context of developing a closer appreciation of how people deal with potentially stressful demands in their daily lives as carers, there now seems little doubt that the transactional model of stress (Lazarus and Folkman 1984; Folkman and Lazarus 1985) has become the most influential. Folkman and Lazarus (1985: 152) define stress as 'a relationship between the person and the environment that is appraised by the person as relevant to his or her well-being and in which the person's resources are taxed or exceeded'.

Within this model the existence of events or conditions in a person's life is not automatically assumed to be stress-provoking. Rather, the individual determines or appraises whether the event or occurrence is stressful in relation to his or her own resources. Stress is said to occur when there is a perceived mismatch between the nature of the demand and the person's ability to respond. Hence the appraisal process becomes the subject of interest. Basically the model runs as follows:

Stressor	$\rightarrow$	appraisal	$\rightarrow$	coping	$\rightarrow$	outcome
Antecedent	$\rightarrow$	mediating	$\rightarrow$	moderating	$\rightarrow$	criterion

From reviews there is growing support for the transactional model in understanding stress and/or coping (Edwards and Cooper 1988; Burr et al. 1994), and empirical tests in studies of carers seem to confirm this. Nolan et al. (1990) found that 47 per cent of psychological stress could be accounted for in this way even without including coping responses as a mediating variable. Quine and Pahl (1991) reported being able to explain 55 per cent of the variance in stress, with the inclusion of coping responses as a mediating variable, through application of the same underlying model.

Without longitudinal studies it is very difficult to be sure about the causal ordering in the above model, and writers express a degree of caution in interpreting results. In their discussion of mothers with children with severe learning disabilities, Quine and Pahl (1991) point out that 'difficult' behaviour can be stressful for mothers; but stress may also make mothers feel tired and irritable, less affectionate toward and less able to deal with a difficult child, who in turn becomes even more difficult to deal with. Hence their child's difficult behaviour may be both a cause and a consequence of stress.

In their comments on the basic transactional stress model, Edwards and Cooper (1988) suggest that other considerations also need to be borne in mind. It may be that coping occurs before appraisal. This would seem most likely when reflex responses are required to sudden emergencies, in other words when there is little or no time to think first. At the other extreme, for example where domestic routines have already been established, it may be less necessary to appraise what needs to be done before a coping behaviour is adopted. Edwards and Cooper also make the point that coping may itself be stressful, in which case the stressful condition to be dealt with *itself* provokes further stress in the coping response required. On the other hand, where successful coping is evident a positive reappraisal of the self may occur. Pearlin *et al.* (1990) have suggested that models like these should not be seen as end points in themselves but as problem-solving devices by which to explore the empirical world. They also imply that such models should not be viewed in a deterministic sense; the models need to accommodate the individuality and variability of responses to effectively similar events. These authors state that it is 'Virtually always observed in stress research that people exposed to seemingly similar stressors are affected by them in dissimilar ways' (p. 389).

Whilst a transactional approach has proved powerful in explaining variations of stress amongst large samples of caregivers, it is also a mechanism for exploring individual circumstances. It therefore provides a framework for the assessment of carers' needs on a one-to-one basis (Nolan *et al.* 1994).

Perhaps because transactional models place a greater emphasis on understanding how events and predisposing conditions are interpreted and appraised, they have usefully expanded our thinking about the social context of disability and chronic illness. Findings from studies in this mould would suggest that 'life conditions' or 'environmental' factors like interpersonal relationships with care recipients, social support, the carer's attitude to caring, household finances and other coping resources are all implicated in understanding stress (Nolan *et al.* 1990; Quine and Pahl 1991). However, it is how these are appraised that is the key. Importantly, the objective characteristics of these and other variables – the nature of the care recipient's disability, the amount of help required, for example – appear to be less relevant in people's stress reactions. A recent review of the extensive literature led to the 'overwhelming conclusion' that it is the subjective interpretation of events and not their objective characteristics that best determine stress (Kane and Penrod 1995). This would suggest that effort should be put into listening to carers in order to determine *how* and *why* they do what they do, rather than using beguiling but invalid objective criteria as proxy indicators of stress or need. More is said about this in the section on coping.

Similar to this transactional model of stress and coping is the rather impersonally titled Double ABCX model of stress and coping (McCubbin and Patterson 1983). In this model a family's use of resources (B) and their perception of the stressor event (C) are examined to determine their relation to the stressor (A) and the stress experience (X), the argument being that the ordering flows in the direction A–B–C–X. Orr *et al.* (1991) carried out an empirical test of the model in a study of families with learning disability. Their findings in fact suggested that the ordering runs in the direction of A–C–B–X. This is quite important as it suggests that the use of (coping) resources is contingent not so much upon the objective features of the stressor but more particularly on how that stressor is perceived and appraised. The lesson seems to be, 'Unless there is an indicated need for a resource on the part of the help seeker, there may not be a need regardless of what a professional perceives to be the case' (Dunst *et al.* 1988: 13). The immediate implications for professionals would be to listen, first of all, to carers and families and explore with them their perceptions of the care process and how these appear to affect the family.

Another important distinction to be made is the unit of analysis. Thompson *et al.* (1993) believe that there have been two major perspectives applied to an understanding of caregiver stress and burden. They call these the *stress* perspective and the *social context* perspective. The focus of the first perspective is on the *individual* caregiver, resulting in studies about *caregiver* burden. In the second a broader approach is taken to include, where relevant, the wider *family unit*. Consequently such studies focus on *caregiving* burden. A number of other writers have also argued that a more inclusive approach is required and that studies must move beyond the present dominant focus on the main or primary carer (Boss 1988; Patterson 1993; Burr *et al.* 1994; Brody 1995). This is an issue that we will discuss in more detail in subsequent chapters.

Who is most at risk of stress?

With the development of more dynamic models of the stress process, simple assumptions about the relationship between stress and the personal characteristics of carers or care recipients no longer hold. Despite this, some of the literature seeks to explain stress variation in this way in the hope, presumably, of identifying 'at risk' groups. The results are on the whole inconclusive, perhaps because underlying theory has not been fully developed.

For example, in economically developed countries there seems little doubt that most informal carers are women (Stone *et al.* 1987 (US); Green 1988 (Britain); Chappell *et al.* 1995 (Canada)). Congruent with ideas about women 'caring for' and 'caring about' (Dalley 1988) in rather different ways than men, it is often assumed that in taking on more of the onus for daily care, women would be more likely than men to experience greater stress. Intriguingly, in studies of carers of older people, there is both supportive evidence (Cantor 1983; George and Gwyther 1986) and non-supportive evidence (Zarit *et al.* 1980; Fitting *et al.* 1986; Carlson and Robertson 1993). Reviews of stress research in the mental health field draw similar conclusions in relation to gender (Biegel *et al.* 1994).

Whether one acts as a primary carer or as secondary to someone else is thought to be a consideration here (Chappell *et al.* 1995). Jutras and Veilleux (1991) report that primary carers experience more burden than secondary carers, yet Staight and Harvey (1990) found no differences in loneliness, depression, financial worries or life satisfaction among these two groups. George (1986) reported that normative conflict over equity issues arose most frequently for secondary carers who were adult children concerned about the sharing of responsibility for care with other siblings. But stress needs exploration and explanation in relation to a wide range of structural factors like age, gender, race, ethnicity, class and kinship relationship if the nature of differential vulnerability and risk amongst carers is to be exposed. Whilst the influence of such variables has an importance for policy considerations, ultimately – as Thompson *et al.* (1993) point out – interventions with individual carers and their families will only be successful when their unique circumstances and belief structures are explored more fully. In this context transactional models are more likely to hold the key to understanding stress. However, if effective interventions are to be designed, individual reactions to stress also need to be compared with the way in which people cope with potentially adverse events.

About coping

This section considers the nature of coping and its relationship to stress in caregiving. This is particularly important because supporting and enhancing carers' coping efforts is, or should be, a major intention underlying professional support (Milne *et al.* 1993; Nolan *et al.* 1994, 1995a). However, if such support is to be effective, a better understanding is required about the nature of coping and how it changes over time and across contexts (Lazarus 1993; Thompson *et al.* 1993; Ingebretsen and Solen 1995).

Before discussing these issues, it is necessary to allude briefly to the use of the term 'coping' itself. Although 'coping' is the term employed by the majority of authors when referring to the way individuals deal with difficult situations, some suggest that it is misleading. Patterson (1993) believes that the word 'adaptation' is to be preferred, whereas others opt for 'managing' (Boss 1988; Burr *et al.* 1994). Boss (1988) in particular presents a cogent argument when she states that the use of the term 'coping' both as a *resource* and as an *outcome* results in tautology. She suggests that 'coping' should be used when referring to the strategies used or activities performed and the term 'managing' applied to the outcome. This line of reasoning has considerable merit and requires further conceptual debate. Indeed we have used the term 'managing' in developing our new index, the Carers Assessment of Managing Index (CAMI) (Nolan *et al.* 1995b). However, in order not to misrepresent the views of the majority of authors we cite it is necessary to use the term 'coping' throughout the following discussion.

Coping and its relationship to stress

In reflecting upon the traditional paradigm of welfare, Titterton (1992) drew an important conclusion about vulnerability and risk which is relevant at this point:

> We still know little about those vulnerable individuals who are not involved with the welfare system. Indeed we also know very little about

the resilience of vulnerable individuals in the face of misfortune and adversity. We have much to learn about the 'invulnerables' – those individuals who have somehow overcome adversity and stress encountered in the life course.

(Titterton 1992: 3)

As Braithwaite (1990) suggests, we need to discover what enables some carers to tread their difficult path more successfully than others. But related questions also arise. What constitutes successful coping? What can be learned about the efficacy of different coping strategies? What are the 'mediating structures' that interpose between the individual and the wider society that allow some individuals to access and expand coping resources? And how can services intervene to reinforce successful coping?

Titterton (1992) argues that the welfare system currently conceives the issue of coping or adaptation in a rather static way. He suggests that more dynamic perspectives are required which take account of life-cycle or life-course models, in order to recognize the simple fact that at different life stages individuals and families face different life stresses and have different resources to fall back on.

But what is coping? An early definition was offered by Pearlin and Schooler (1978: 1): 'Behaviour that importantly mediates the impact that societies have on their members'. This is probably too general to be useful as a working definition even though Pearlin and Schooler's early work has proved very influential. Based on Lazarus's (1966) earlier seminal work, Lazarus and Folkman (1984) are generally credited with introducing the idea of cognitive appraisal into discussions about stress and coping. This is a mental process in which people assess whether demands pose a threat to well-being and appraise their resources for meeting the demands. Hence, in Lazarus and Folkman's terms, coping is defined mainly in terms of the problem-solving efforts that people employ when a perceived demand is seen to tax their adaptive resources.

Whilst broader than the definition of Pearlin and Schooler (1978), this is also too limited as it restricts coping to *problem-solving* efforts alone. Although problem-solving coping is often held to be the most effective (Braithwaite 1990; Lazarus 1993; McKee *et al.* 1994; Ingebretsen and Solen 1995), it is now recognized that a range of strategies are employed of which problem-solving is only one (Lazarus 1993; Thompson *et al.* 1993; Burr *et al.* 1994). The definition provided by Turnbull and Turnbull (1993: 11) better reflects the diversity of coping: 'The term coping refers to the things people do (acting or thinking) to increase a sense of well-being in their lives and to avoid being harmed by stressful events.'

The place coping occupies within the transactional model of stress is illustrated in Figure 3.1. It can be described in the following way. A demand or event occurs and a primary appraisal is made. Essentially this involves asking 'Is this something to which I need to respond? Does the event pose

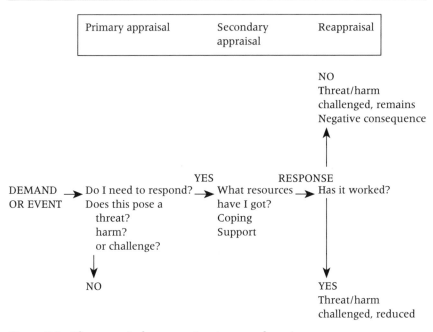

Figure 3.1   The appraisal process in stress and coping
Reproduced with permission from Nolan *et al.* 1994: 34.

a threat, harm or challenge?' If the answer is 'no' then no action is required. If the answer is 'yes' then a secondary appraisal occurs. This time the question is asked: 'What resources have I got to help deal with the event?' The individual then selects a response or resource (coping) to deal with the event. If the person feels that they cannot make an appropriate response at this stage, then a reappraisal of the situation may occur, leading to a fresh approach to coping, or else some manifestation of stress may be the result. Applications of this kind of model can be found elsewhere (Dill and Feld 1982; Birchwood and Smith 1987; Quine and Pahl 1991), and empirical testing has demonstrated its usefulness (Nolan *et al.* 1990, Quine and Pahl 1991).

This leads us to a consideration of the types of coping responses people can make.

Coping strategies and coping resources

Pearlin and Schooler (1978) considered that all coping behaviour involves efforts to either (a) change and alleviate a difficult situation, (b) alter or reduce the perceived threats, or (c) manage the symptoms of stress arising from the situation. The literature is littered with examples of coping responses of one

Coping aim

Type of coping effort	Preventive action	Direct action	Reframing	Deal with consequences
Behavioural	Assemble information about the problem	Call an individual plan meeting		Take sleeping pills
Cognitive	Plan to get help	Ruminate about what to do	View others as worse off	Daydream

Figure 3.2   A conceptual framework of coping strategies
Adapted from Brown (1993).

kind or another, but for convenience these can be split into two broad groups of *coping strategies* and *coping resources*. Coping strategies, sometimes referred to as coping styles, concern *how* people cope. Coping resources, on the other hand, usually refer to the *kinds of resources people might call upon* in managing situations.

Coping strategies

Coping strategies are extremely difficult to depict since they cover such a wide range of activities, making them hard to classify. There is a tendency to talk about behavioural and cognitive approaches to coping in the same breath, but as others have pointed out, these involve very different strategies which can be considered against different coping aims. These can be represented by taking an example (Figure 3.2).

To illustrate the distinctions we may consider the case of a middle-aged woman, a lone parent, supporting at home her severely disabled daughter whose temper tantrums have suddenly increased. *Preventive action* can be taken by assembling information about the problem or by planning to get help, examples respectively of behavioural and cognitive attempts to get to grips with the source of the problem with the aim of preventing or ameliorating it in the future. *Direct action* by the mother could be taken behaviourally by calling an individual plan meeting in order to assess how an agreed plan could be designed to reduce the incidence or the effects of her daughter's challenging behaviour. At the cognitive level the mother may choose alternatively to ruminate over her feelings, unsure of what to do, effectively delaying other courses of action. *Reframing* simply means creating alternative meanings about events or changing one's perceptions of these. A common cognitive approach would be for the mother to reappraise the importance of the challenging behaviour by convincing herself that there are others who are worse off. However, a recent survey of family carers in the Alzheimer's Disease Society and the Crossroads Care Network has indicated that the non-attribution of blame is the most used and the most useful strategy in this connection (Nolan *et al.* 1995b). This may in turn lead to a redirection of behavioural approaches to coping. Finally, there is the possibility that the problem cannot be prevented, dealt with directly or re-evaluated, so there is nothing left but to *deal with the consequences*. At the behavioural level the carer may consider taking sleeping pills in an attempt to catch up on night-time disturbances which can be quite common in these circumstances (Pahl and Quine 1987). At the cognitive level there may be nothing left to do but daydream in the rather vain hope that the problem will disappear.

Numerous studies have attempted to explore the coping efforts carers employ and devise typologies of coping strategies (Birchwood and Smith 1987; Braithwaite 1990; Rohde *et al.* 1990; Knusson *et al.* 1992; Orford *et al.* 1992; Jivanjee 1993; Milne *et al.* 1993; McKee *et al.* 1994). These have used both qualitative methods and a variety of quantitative instruments such as the 'Measure of Daily Coping' (Stone and Neale 1984) and the 'Ways of Coping questionnaire' (Folkman and Lazarus 1985). There is considerable overlap in the results of many of these studies, and also parallels with paradigms applied in other contexts such as occupational stress (see, for example, Carson *et al.* 1995).

Three general points are important here in regard to coping strategies. First, individuals usually access more than one coping strategy in their attempts to manage stressful encounters, and these can involve behavioural as well as cognitive approaches (Lazarus 1993; Thompson *et al.* 1993; Kiernan and Alborz 1995; Nolan *et al.* 1995b). Second, the processual nature of the adaptive response needs to be better understood. For example, in the early stages of stressful encounters attempts to manage the emotional consequences of stress, even if they involve escape and withdrawal, may be a necessary first step towards solving the problem (Lazarus 1983 quoted in Brown 1993). During the processes of appraising problems to be managed or overcome, a phase some have coined *strategic thinking*, strategies may be shaped or constrained by the individual's values, predispositions and inner resources (Dill and Feld 1982). The relevance of these factors to individuals, and how they impact upon personal coping strategies, are matters warranting much further investigation in a variety of contexts. Third, we appear to know very little about the economic and social costs and benefits to individuals of different coping strategies. Coping may be liberating but it may also prove to be a stressful experience in itself.

One of the difficulties of outlining a framework for understanding approaches to coping is the sheer range of strategies involved. It is unlikely that individuals simply dip randomly into a pool of alternatives in the hope that the selected strategy will work. What seems more likely is that individuals strive to achieve what Antonovsky (1987) refers to as a sense of 'coherence', this being defined as:

A global orientation that expresses the extent to which one has a pervasive, enduring, though dynamic, feeling of confidence that (1) stimuli
deriving from one's internal and external environments in the course of
living are structured, predictable, and explicable; (2) the resources are
available to one to meet the demands posed by these stimuli; and (3)
these demands are challenges, worthy of investment and engagement.
(Antonovsky 1987: 19)

Of the three elements described were Antonovsky views *meaningfulness*,
the third of these, as the key to understanding coping, representing as it
does a basic and relatively enduring disposition.

Although this approach has not been applied extensively to family
caregiving, there are indications that it is potentially very useful (Coe *et al.*
1992; Gallagher *et al.* 1994). Certainly the concept of 'meaningfulness' has
been applied a number of times in relation to coping (Brown 1993; Lazarus
1993; Turnbull and Turnbull 1993). The sort of global or meta-level orientation referred to by Antonovsky (1987) was suggested some time ago in the
field of learning disabilities (Bayley 1973) and has been elaborated by
Patterson (1993), who differentiates between context-specific beliefs and
global beliefs. The influence of beliefs, values and culturally determined
factors merits further exploration, as do variables such as age, gender and
socio-economic groupings. Quine and Pahl (1991), for example in a study
of mothers of children with severe learning disabilities, found that being
middle class with few financial worries helped significantly in buffering the
effects of stress. The implications of findings such as these for interventions
are significant.

Similarly the importance of an understanding of cultural diversity is
well illustrated by the following observation on Chinese carers: 'For example, emotional discharge is not a dominant coping strategy of Chinese individuals, whereas forbearance, seeking supernatural power, and praying to
ancestors are relatively common ways of coping, especially among older
Chinese individuals' (Cheng and Tang 1995: 12).

Other studies demonstrate cultural differences in carers' expectations
and coping strategies (for example Wood and Parham 1990; Cox 1995),
suggesting that it is a fertile ground for further research.

Coping resources

Coping resources, although in many ways more tangible than coping strategies, are not well understood. Coping resource typologies are even less in
evidence. More often than not coping resources are taken as given and
accepted uncritically within study designs. It is also likely that a reliance on
the use of coping strategy inventories leads to the assumption that coping
resources are subsumed within these.

Although there seems to be no particular route to depicting coping resources, it is helpful to distinguish between 'internal' and 'external' resources
(Lazarus and Folkman 1984). These authors consider that coping resources
are part of an individual's internal or external environment not under direct
control; they lie dormant until called upon in a stressful encounter.

Within a person's internal resources we may consider factors like personal skills, relevant life experiences, psychological disposition, and analytic
ability. These resources are likely to be more directly under the personal
control of the individual though their use will be subject to degrees of
negotiation with the care recipient. These factors appear to be amongst the
least studied.

External resources are rather more familiar and include, according to
Lazarus and Folkman (1984), things like utilitarian resources (income, housing, socio-economic status, formal services) and social resources (social networks, support available through such networks). These resources are more
likely to be shared and thus be subject to considerable degrees of negotiation
regarding their use.

Titterton (1992) expresses the view that coping resources have the
potential to tell us much about inequalities or relative disadvantage amongst
individuals. There is certainly strong empirical evidence for this (Pearlin and
Schooler 1978; Quine and Pahl 1991), suggesting that some families start
out with innate and inherited economic advantages in resource terms, giving them an enhanced repertoire of potential coping responses.

As an influence on stress and stress adaptation, social resources have
been widely studied. House *et al.* (1988) contend that three aspects of social
relationships – their existence and quality, their formal structure, and their
functional content – need to be conceptually and empirically distinguished.
Bulmer (1987) meanwhile suggests that the function or content of relationships within social networks is most important as it indicates something of
the goods and services exchanged, the closeness or intimacy between members, the intensity of their interactions and the exchange of information
involved. The structural properties of social networks, for example their size,
membership, density or linkages between members, are commonly used to
define the potential or *opportunity structure* for support. This is merely a
short-hand way of defining the human resources that may be available to
an individual. The opportunity structure in itself does not necessarily imply
supportiveness (Forrester-Jones and Grant 1995).

Social support, besides conferring benefits of one kind or another, can
also have iatrogenic effects upon givers and receivers, either because the
support provided is not relevant, too much or too little, or makes individuals
feel overconfident, or results in raised expectations about the continuity of
informal support (Rook 1992). This again serves as a reminder of the possible costs and consequences of certain kinds of coping responses. In relation
to the accessing of social resources in particular, this may place considerable
demands and expectations upon the help seeker in terms of negotiating

skills (getting people to agree to help), organizational and planning skills (scheduling the help when it is needed), reciprocity (deciding whether or not a *quid pro quo* lies at the basis of the support and how this is to work), and so on, all of which can be time-consuming as well as stressful. In the final analysis, the support expected may not necessarily be what is delivered.

On the whole, however, there is overwhelming evidence to suggest that social resources (both structural and functional) are heavily implicated in mediating stress and coping (Stoneman and Crapps 1988; Nolan *et al.* 1990; Quine and Pahl 1991; Boss 1993; Beresford 1994).

Coping effectiveness

McKee *et al.* (1994) suggest that coping can be considered effective depending upon the extent to which it reduces demand, increases capacity or both. By implication this places the primary emphasis on those coping efforts which are concerned with taking direct action to change or ameliorate a situation. There is a strong tendency, possibly linked to the dominant western cultural ethic, to see problem-solving coping strategies as being the most effective, and a number of studies seem to support this (Braithwaite 1990; McKee *et al.* 1994; Ingebretsen and Solen 1995; Kiernan and Alborz 1995). However, as Patterson (1993) points out, such strategies are only possible in certain circumstances; despite the fact that cognitive strategies have often been given a bad press (Turnbull and Turnbull 1993) there is now a wider appreciation that to focus on problem-solving alone represents an overly simplistic view.

Lazarus (1993), in a recent conspectus on the study of coping, raises a number of significant issues and challenges. In debating whether coping is a trait (a relatively permanent feature of an individual's personality) or a state (a context-specific response), he argues that both are needed and in fact represent opposite sides of the same coin. McKee *et al.* (1994) similarly suggest that individuals may have a dominant coping mode (a trait) but also a range of strategies that are context-specific (a state). Moreover, the diversity of coping needs to be explored and the primacy placed on problem-solving questioned (Lazarus 1993). Certainly problem-solving strategies are of little use, even harmful, in circumstances where events are not amenable to change (Boss 1988b; Lazarus 1993; Patterson 1993; Burr *et al.* 1994; McKee *et al.* 1994; Ingebretsen and Solen 1995). In such circumstances efforts either to construe a different meaning or to deal with the effects of stress are more useful.

Lazarus (1993) suggests that *all* strategies are *potentially* useful but must be matched with the nature of the stressor or threat faced. Effectiveness should therefore be considered with regard to the intended outcome and whether the stressor and coping effort are appropriately matched (Birchwood and Smith 1987; Burr *et al.* 1994). Stressors that are ambiguous (Boss *et al.* 1988, 1993) or unpredictable (Archbold *et al.* 1992, 1995) pose the most problems as it is difficult to select the type of response needed. Individuals therefore need to be able to select from a range of coping strategies, suggesting that coping as a *state* is the most desirable characteristic. Certainly it seems that individuals who can draw on a variety of coping responses are likely to be less stressed (Birchwood and Smith 1987; Brown 1993; Burr *et al.* 1993; Lazarus 1993; Thompson *et al.* 1993; Nolan *et al.* 1995b). On the other hand, consistency also appears to be important. Individuals seem to have a dominant coping mode; this is functional provided that it does not become rigid and inhibit flexible responses (Birchwood and Smith 1987; Lazarus 1993; McKee *et al.* 1994).

Perhaps most important of all, however, and consistent with the work of Antonovsky (1987), is the role that meanings and perceptions play in coping. Indeed following his overview of the literature, Lazarus (1993) concluded by arguing that it is the ability to sustain serviceable meanings that is the key to understanding how people cope with the difficulties they face.

For instance it seems that if individuals are able to see events as a challenge, rather than a threat or harm, then they experience less stress (Lazarus and Folkman 1984; Stoller and Pugliesi 1989; Brown 1993; Turnbull and Turnbull 1993; Burr *et al.* 1994). This raises the very interesting issue of the role that *positive illusions* may play in mediating the effectiveness of coping strategies (Brown 1993). Brown reports evidence suggesting that people with high self-esteem, strong beliefs in personal efficacy, and an optimistic attitude are more likely to initiate active coping targeted towards the source of stress. He terms this a 'high can do' attitude. It would appear that such individuals are more able to sustain coping efforts in the face of initial obstacles and ultimately cope more effectively. He suggests that when people feel confident of success they are capable of conjuring a clear image of themselves achieving a goal. Visualization in this way makes goal attainment more likely. On the other hand, there would seem to be a fine line between *illusions* and *delusions*. People may become unrealistically optimistic about what they can accomplish and consequently ignore risks associated with their actions.

Carers, for example, can place themselves and care recipients at risk by continuing care beyond reasonable endurance in the belief that no one else can provide the same quality of support. Hence in considering outcomes it is necessary to pay attention to the implications for the well-being of care recipients and significant others as well as the carer.

Beliefs and meanings are also important in drawing a distinction between an individual's ability to master a particular coping strategy (self-efficacy) and the perceived effectiveness of that strategy (outcome beliefs). Drawing from work by Bandura (1982) and Schultz *et al.* (1990), we can ask on behalf of the carer: 'Can I do it?' and 'Will it work?'. From this a matrix can be constructed which outlines four coping typifications (Figure 3.3).

In situations where a carer both feels confident about accomplishing a strategy and where it is perceived that the strategy will be effective, *assured*

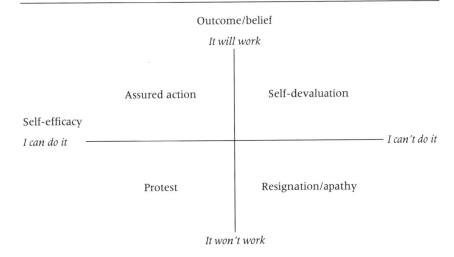

Figure 3.3 Self-efficacy and outcome beliefs
Reproduced with permission from Nolan *et al.* 1994: 39.

action is the likely result. Where the carer has little confidence in the ability to take action when the action is deemed effective, then the likely result is *self-devaluation*. Where mastery over a strategy is believed but the strategy is seen to be of dubious value, a situation of *protest* can be envisaged. Finally, where personal mastery and outcome beliefs are both questioned, *resignation or apathy* is likely to be the result. The matrix has a practical usefulness in aiding thinking about the circumstances in which outcome beliefs perhaps need redirecting or where assistance with coping skills is required. The implications of non-intervention are just as much thrown into relief. However, other questions can be posed at this juncture. Coping mastery and a belief in whether a particular coping strategy works make no assumptions about whether the strategy is a satisfying one to the carer (or the care recipient) or whether it implies some element of personal cost to either party. These are likely to be further factors entering into people's frameworks for appraising their coping strategies.

We can summarize the factors influential in coping in the following way. It seems that coping resources and coping strategies are potentially an integral part of an individual's coping framework, to the extent a framework exists in people's minds. However, coping strategies adopted are constantly reviewed in the light of an appraisal process which takes account of how individuals feel they are performing, including the rewards and stresses experienced, and the sense of mastery they gain, reinforced by feedback from other family members. Finally, it is assumed that coping strategies in the end are shaped by what is achieved for either the care recipient or the carer (coping effectiveness). For the most part the connections implied by such a model still remain to be empirically tested.

We agree with Milne *et al.* (1993) that working with carers to augment their coping efforts is one of the most potent of interventions. However, this requires that a comprehensive assessment of each carer's unique circumstances is undertaken which includes a consideration of the type of stressors they face, the coping strategies they employ and their perceived effectiveness (Lazarus 1993; Thompson *et al.* 1993; Burr *et al.* 1994). Generic coping checklists tell us little about helping carers with specific problems (Hinriden and Niedireche 1994), but indices based on a transactional model of stress which are caregiving-specific have considerable potential. We go on now to consider the use of two such indices: the Carers Assessment of Difficulties Index (CADI) (Nolan and Grant 1992a) and the Carers Assessment of Managing Index (CAMI) (Nolan *et al.* 1995b) and their implications for work with family carers.

Helping carers cope: the role of assessment

We have argued above that if carers are to be assisted to cope more effectively with the difficulties they face, then a range of factors need to be taken into account. First, and most important, is the recognition that stress and coping are essentially subjective experiences. As has been suggested, 'stress is in the eye of the beholder' (Nolan *et al.* 1990). Second, the nature of coping needs to be addressed and a better understanding of coping effectiveness achieved. We have as yet no clear evidence about which coping strategies are the most effective, but a number of general principles can be applied to points of growing consensus in the literature. These may be summarized as follows:

- Coping efforts can take a number of forms: action taken to deal with or prevent the stressor itself; a reappraisal or creating a differing perception of the stressor; efforts to deal with the resultant stress. Coping may involve direct action (behavioural) or cognitive strategies, or both.
- Although problem-solving has been regarded as the most effective method, this is now being questioned. It is more widely recognized that the coping strategy should be matched to the nature of the stressor. Therefore it is of little use trying to solve an insoluble problem, but on the other hand, relying on a reappraisal of a preventable stressor is similarly ineffective.
- Individuals who have a range of coping strategies are likely to cope more effectively. Although individuals may have a dominant coping style (a trait), flexibility is also required so that differing approaches can be utilized as appropriate (state).
- Meanings are particularly important to coping: being able to see things as a challenge rather than a threat or harm, having a sense of competence and mastery, and perceiving efforts as meaningful are all important mediating factors.

It seems self-evident that if interventions are to be successful then it is essential to gain a carer's perspective of their situation. Yet this is often not the case, with professionals imposing their own views of what is or is not stressful. Whilst professional perspectives are influenced by a number of factors such as training and background, work culture or the assumptive worlds of practitioners (Twigg and Atkin 1994), the main criteria determining perceived stress are the instrumental aspects of caring. However, it is now widely recognized that these are the least stressful aspects for the majority of carers and that other factors such as the nature and quality of relationships, a range of behaviours from the cared-for person (e.g. manipulation, overdependency) and the adequacy of financial resources are far more important.

In an assessment of the stresses of care, the first task must therefore be to establish the nature of the problems that carers face and to identify which of these are seen to be the most stressful. This is the purpose of the Carers Assessment of Difficulties Index (Nolan and Grant 1992a), which has proved useful in determining the most stressful aspects of caring both in epidemiological-type surveys (Nolan *et al.* 1990; Nolan and Grant 1992a) and in one-to-one situations (Nolan and Grant 1992a; Keady and Nolan 1993a,b). However, establishing the nature of the carer's difficulties and their perceived stressfulness is only the first step. It is also necessary to determine the coping efforts they employ and to consider if these match the difficulties they encounter. This is the purpose of the Carers Assessment of Managing Index (CAMI) (Nolan *et al.* 1995b), the properties and usefulness of which we will now consider.

CAMI: assessing and supporting carer's coping efforts

CAMI was developed following a series of interviews with family caregivers and a review of the available literature (Nolan *et al.* 1995b). It comprises 38 coping statements. For each statement, carers indicate whether: they don't use this approach; use it but don't find it helpful; use it and find it quite helpful; or use it and find it very helpful. In this way not only is the frequency of use determined but also the perceived effectiveness of individual strategies.

Following development and pilot work, CAMI was recently used in a postal survey of members of the Alzheimer's Disease Society in Wales and Scotland, and the Crossroads Care Network in Wales (Nolan *et al.* 1995b). Two hundred and sixty completed indices were returned from carers who were supporting a variety of individuals. The characteristics of the sample can be found in Appendix 1. The majority of carers were providing support to older people; most carers were themselves elderly. Seven out of ten were women (72 per cent) and three out of ten men (29 per cent). In most cases care was being provided either to a spouse (50 per cent) or to a parent (38 per cent). Within the spousal caregiving group the gender ratio was roughly equal (46 per cent men/54 per cent women) whereas most children caring for parents were either daughters or daughters-in-law (89 per cent women/ 11 per cent men). The sample provides interesting insights into the coping strategies of what might be termed 'heavily involved' carers, and the results are discussed below. Before proceeding, however, it is important to recognize the limitations of the sampling method adopted. First, as the sample was non-random it is not possible to generalize the results to other caring populations. Second, because the exact number of questionnaires distributed is unknown it is not possible to calculate a meaningful response rate. Both these factors need to be borne in mind when interpreting the results.

The results focus mainly on the nature of the coping strategies and their perceived usefulness. In order to aid interpretation these have been presented in three tables which contain strategies aimed at managing events/ problem-solving (Table 3.1); managing meanings/perceptions (Table 3.2); and managing stress (Table 3.3). The broad similarities in these tables will be discussed prior to addressing potential differences in coping by gender and relationship (spousal or child/parent).

Managing events/problem solving

These strategies are generally considered to be the most useful in circumstances where events or stresses are amenable to change. A quick perusal of Table 3.1 provides an indication of the diversity of strategies that carers employ and also how frequently they are both used and seen as helpful. Of the 14 strategies listed, seven are used and seen as either very or quite useful ('useful' from now on unless specified otherwise) by over 75 per cent of the sample, and of the remaining strategies, six are seen as useful by over 50 per cent of the sample. Even the least-used strategy – being firm with the cared-for person and pointing out what is expected – is considered helpful by four out of ten carers. Clearly then for this sample, problem-solving strategies are both heavily employed and seen as effective.

The single most useful strategy (85 per cent of the sample) is to find out as much information as possible. The value of information to carers has been apparent for some time, with Abrams (1985) seeing it as essential. Yet it appears that carers still receive too little information, or that which they do get is inappropriate (Ellis 1993; Twigg and Atkin 1994). This is well illustrated in a number of recent studies of admissions of older people to residential or nursing care (Nolan *et al.* 1996). Although the reports of the local social services inspection units have been in the public domain for a number of years, not one carer in three separate studies was aware of their existence despite the fact that all of the carers interviewed had been in contact with formal service agencies. There seems to be very little point in making such information publicly available if no one knows of its existence.

Table 3.1 Managing events/problem-solving (n = 260)

	Very helpful %	Quite helpful %	Not really helpful %	I don't use this %
Finding out as much information as you can about the problem	61	24	8	7
Getting as much help as you can from professionals and other service providers	51	32	10	7
Talking over your problems with someone you trust	51	31	7	12
Relying on your own experience and the expertise you have built up	50	32	8	10
Keeping one step ahead of things by planning in advance	52	27	5	16
Establishing a regular routine and sticking to it	49	29	8	14
Establishing priorities and concentrating on them	50	26	12	12
Thinking about the problem and finding a way to overcome it	41	34	17	9
Altering your home environment to make things as easy as possible	45	23	10	23
Keeping the person you care for as active as possible	43	26	18	13
Trying out a number of solutions until you find one that works	38	37	9	16
Preventing problems before they happen	35	34	12	18
Getting as much practical help as you can from your family	29	28	9	35
Being firm and pointing out to the person you care for what you expect of them	18	21	33	28

The value of obtaining professional support is highlighted as the second most useful problem-solving strategy adopted, and yet this too is often inhibited by a lack of awareness of how to obtain formal services. Abrams (1985) suggested that most carers exist in a 'deep fog of ignorance' about where to get help, and he considered that this was 'well nigh criminal'. Little seems to have changed, with the more articulate, vocal or strident carer still getting the lion's share of support from formal agencies (Nolan and Grant 1992a; Ellis 1993). Evers (1995) believes that access to services will get increasingly difficult as systems become more fragmented; he argues that a major strategy should be to increase the social competence of carers so that they are better able to access available support. The new Carers Act is hardly likely to help in this regard by tying the carer's right to assessment to circumstances where the user is also being assessed.

The other strategies in Table 3.1 have a number of important implications for assisting carers, highlighting the need to talk over problems with a trusted confidante. A combination of other items also signals that carers can be very proactive and adopt a range of problem-solving approaches built around their experience and expertise. The importance of recognizing carer expertise has already been alluded to and is discussed in greater detail in subsequent chapters. The role and influence of routines is also something that merits attention, as services which do not fit in with carers' priorities are usually rejected (Lewis and Meredith 1988a,b, 1989; Braithwaite 1990).

Managing meanings/perceptions

There is growing recognition of the importance of cognitive coping strategies aimed at changing perceptions of an event or the circumstances surrounding it. Certainly in situations where problems cannot be resolved, such cognitive methods are generally the most useful. The value that carers accord them is quite apparent in Table 3.2.

The single most used and useful strategy in the entire index is the non-attribution of blame – realizing that the cared-for person is in no way culpable. Over nine out of ten carers (92 per cent) saw this as helpful. Achieving this perception is, however, often intimately linked to an understanding of the disease process so that, for example, difficult behaviour is not viewed as deliberate. This is especially important in certain mental illnesses such as dementia or schizophrenia (Twigg and Atkin 1994). The role of adequate information in the non-attribution of blame illustrates the reciprocal and interactive nature of coping, providing further support that a range of strategies are likely to prove more effective than relying on a single dominant approach. The use of positive comparisons (seeing someone else as worse off – 81 per cent) is also recognized in the literature (Brown 1993), and this is linked to seeing the positive side of things (74 per cent). These sort of tactics have been termed 'positive illusions' (Brown 1993) and are generally seen to be functional and helpful providing they do not become

Table 3.2   Managing meanings/perceptions (n = 260)

	Very helpful %	Quite helpful %	Not really helpful %	I don't use this %
Realizing that the person you care for is not to blame for the way they are	70	22	5	3
Taking life one day at a time	65	23	6	7
Realizing there's always someone worse off than yourself	54	27	14	5
Realizing that no one is to blame for things	54	26	15	6
Seeing the funny side of the situation	47	29	12	12
Gritting your teeth and just getting on with it	46	30	15	9
Remembering all the good times you used to have with the person you care for	46	26	17	12
Looking for the positive things in each situation	40	34	13	14
Accepting the situation as it is	38	35	20	8
Believing in yourself and your ability to handle the situation	44	32	18	6
Drawing on strong personal or religious beliefs	33	24	11	32
Keeping your emotions and feelings tightly under control	24	29	31	17
Realizing that things are better now than they used to be	17	17	31	35
Forgetting about your problems for a short while by daydreaming or the like	14	21	20	45
Ignoring the problem and hoping it will go away	2	2	20	76

too unrealistic or detached from reality. The whole point of such positive illusions is that they are not entirely consistent with objective events. Therefore it does not matter if the person the carer perceives to be worse off is in an objectively better position – it is the perception that is most influential.

Counterbalancing such positive illusions, stoicism also represents an important cognitive coping strategy (gritting your teeth – 76 per cent – and accepting the situation as it is – 73 per cent). These bring an element of realism to the situation but there is a fine line to be drawn here between stoic acceptance and possible nihilism. This returns us to the self-efficacy/ outcomes belief relationships depicted in Figure 3.3, in which for an action to be taken there has to be both a belief that it will be effective and that it is within the individual's capacity to perform. Therefore accepting things as they are may be valuable when things cannot be changed, but such a perception is not helpful when positive action can be taken. It is interesting to note that the more passive forms of cognitive coping (daydreaming – 35 per cent – and ignoring the problem – 4 per cent) are not seen as being particularly effective. Humour, on the other hand, is perceived as helpful by over 75 per cent of carers.

As with the problem-solving tactics, cognitive strategies aimed at managing perceptions and meanings are characterized by diversity and pervasiveness. Of the 15 strategies to which carers could respond, six were seen as helpful by over 75 per cent of the sample and another five by over 50 per cent. Combining these figures with those from the problem-solving strategies paints a very different picture than that of the passive or helpless carer. Indeed carers here can be seen as resourceful and inventive in bringing to bear a broad range of coping strategies. There is a repertoire of problem-solving devices based around information-gathering, forward thinking and a belief in the expertise that carers hold. This is tempered by the need to talk and the value of having a trusted confidant.

In circumstances which are not amenable to change, carers are also able to select from a number of cognitive approaches. Generally, passivity and running away from issues do not appear to figure highly, consistent with the problem-solving efforts that are employed. Non-attribution of blame, positive illusions (including humour) and a belief in one's own ability seem central to this group of strategies. The importance of caring as a long-term relationship is suggested in the role played by remembering previous good times with the cared-for person.

Managing stress

There are certain situations in which events can neither be prevented nor a different perception created. In such circumstances the most helpful response is to deal with the stress that results. Table 3.3 lists responses to these strategies in CAMI that can be seen as efforts to manage stress. It will be seen that when compared to other coping strategies, responses to stress are

Table 3.3   Managing stress (n = 260)

	Very helpful %	Quite helpful %	Not really helpful %	I don't use this %
Keeping a little free time for yourself	55	24	4	18
Taking your mind off things in some way, by reading, watching TV or the like	49	32	13	7
Maintaining interests outside caring	41	29	5	26
Getting rid of excess energy and feelings by walking, swimming or other exercise	30	22	9	40
Trying to cheer yourself up by eating, having a drink, smoking or the like	20	22	14	45
Attending a self-help group	20	17	6	57
By having a good cry	18	17	22	44
Letting off steam in some way e.g. shouting, yelling or the like	10	20	24	46
Using relaxation techniques, meditation or the like	10	14	5	72

neither as frequently used nor are these generally seen to be as helpful. However, three statements are particularly valued by carers and these are:

- keeping a little free time to yourself (79%);
- taking your mind off things for a while (81%);
- maintaining interests outside caring (70%).

Taken together these items give a strong indication of the need for carers to be able to maintain a life outside of caring. This is particularly important in a number of regards. Braithwaite (1990) argues that if carers perceive their social interactions to be threatened then they are far more likely to experience stress; others have suggested that the ability to engage friends and kin in meaningful activities outside caring is a powerful form of stress relief (Thompson *et al.* 1993). Indeed Thompson and co-authors believe that engaging significant others outside of caring is far more effective than instrumental support, material aid or physical assistance as a means of reducing carer stress. This relates to what has been termed the 'restrictedness' of caring (Twigg and Atkin 1994) and provides a powerful indication, if any were needed, of the value of some form of respite care (Nolan and Grant 1992a; Levin *et al.* 1994; Montgomery 1995).

Unfortunately respite care frequently fails to live up to its potential, as its purpose is often conceived in a narrow and restrictive way (Nolan and Grant 1992a; Montgomery 1995). As Montgomery argues, it is the quality and convenience of respite that are the most influential factors, but services often fail to deliver these as they both rely on dependency as an eligibility criterion and are kept in reserve until a crisis point is reached. It will be seen from Table 3.3 that both keeping a little free time and maintaining interests outside caring are perceived as helpful by nearly everyone who uses them – 95 per cent effective for keeping a little free time and 93 per cent effective for maintaining interests outside of caring. This provides the strongest possible signal that more effort should be invested in assisting carers to achieve these goals.

A similar logic can be applied to other strategies which, although not used all that often, are nevertheless seen to be effective. For example, attending a self-help group is only used by 43 per cent of the sample but is considered to be helpful by 86 per cent of those attending one. Similarly, relaxation techniques are utilized by only 28 per cent of the sample but are considered helpful by 82 per cent of carers who use this strategy. This perhaps suggests a lack of opportunity, rather than a lack of effectiveness, and again provides pointers for the development of services which afford carers greater choice as to how to manage stress. On the other hand, some ways of dealing with stress are neither used all that often, nor are they seen to be particularly helpful (having a good cry, letting off steam), and this illustrates the need to keep an open mind as to what is effective and in which circumstances.

Coping with caring: variations by gender and relationship

A key message which emerges from the foregoing is the sheer diversity of coping strategies in evidence. Of the 38 items in CAMI, 15 are used and seen as helpful by over 75 per cent of the sample, and a further 11 are seen as helpful by 50 per cent of the sample or over. This diversity is further demonstrated in the way that coping varies by gender. Although the literature on this point is underdeveloped and equivocal, it is the received wisdom that men are generally seen to cope more effectively than women and that they are also more likely to employ the purposeful, problem-solving approaches. Our results suggest that such 'truisms' do not stand up to close empirical scrutiny.

Table 3.4 summarizes the differences in coping by gender and is divided into three categories. Category 1 includes items in which there is a difference in the frequency of use but not in the perceived helpfulness (or otherwise) of a strategy. The second category includes items where there is

Table 3.4   Differences in coping strategies by gender

1 Variations in frequency of use but not perceived helpfulness	Percentage who use it
Getting as much practical help as you can from the family	49% men/71% women (χ^2 11.20 p<.01)
Being firm, etc.	59% men/77% women (χ^2 8.86 p<.05)
Having a good cry	24% men/66% women (χ^2 43.94 p<.0000)
Using relaxation techniques	18% men/32% women (χ^2 7.64 p<.05)
Daydreaming	66% men/51% women (χ^2 9.42 p<.02)
2 Variations by perceived helpfulness but not frequency of use	Percentage who used it and found it helpful (or very helpful)
Finding out information	82% men (56% very helpful) 93% women (69% very helpful) (χ^2 10.68 p<.005)
Attending a self-help group	80% men (23% very helpful) 89% women (55% very helpful) (χ^2 8.80 p<.01)
Maintaining outside interests	87% men (49% very helpful) 97% women (62% very helpful) (χ^2 9.79 p<.01)
3 Variations in both usage and perceived helpfulness	Percentage who used it and found it helpful
Talking over problems with someone you trust	Used by 76% men/93% women (χ^2 33.87 p<.0000) Found helpful by those using it: 81% men/96% women (χ^2 21.07 p<.0000)
Keeping a little free time to yourself	Used by 76% men/84% women (χ^2 8.44 p<.05) Found helpful by those using it: 53% men/73% women (χ^2 7.40 p<.02)

no difference in the frequency of use but there are differences in perceived helpfulness. The third category is concerned with situations in which there is variation both in the frequency of use and perceived helpfulness. These figures indicate that women employ both a more diverse set of coping strategies and that they perceive these to be more effective.

The implications of these findings are particularly important in those circumstances where the strategy in question is seen to be helpful – that is, section 1 of the table. For example, obtaining family help is seen as very useful (88 per cent/86 per cent) by both women and men but is utilized by 71 per cent of women and only 49 per cent of men. The data of course provide no explanation for this (it is not mediated via relationships, as daughters and wives are equally likely to use this strategy), but it may be that men are reluctant to seek help, not wishing to appear to be failing to cope. It might be expected that women would have a cry as a coping strategy more than men, as is indeed the case (66 per cent/24 per cent). However, there is no significant difference between men and women as to how useful they find this (61 per cent/55 per cent). It may well be that men are reluctant to admit to crying and therefore do not indicate this in their responses; or it could be that cultural and gender stereotypes are denying men access to a potentially useful form of emotional release. Similar considerations apply to the use of relaxation techniques. Again, perhaps contrary to expectations, women in this sample are more likely to be firm with the cared-for person and point out what they want (77 per cent of women/ 59 per cent of men) but this is not seen to be helpful by everyone. Nevertheless about 50 per cent of those using this strategy find it helpful.

The second set of circumstances in which there is variation in coping occurs when strategies are used with a similar frequency but when they are perceived to be differentially effective. Such variations are illustrated in section 2 of Table 3.4. It will be seen that significant differences are apparent in three coping strategies. Although there is no difference in the frequency with which men or women seek information (93 per cent in both cases), attend a self-help group (41 per cent/44 per cent) or maintain interests outside caring (74 per cent/73 per cent), women find all of these approaches more helpful than do men.

Notwithstanding these differences, it is interesting to note that 93 per cent of both men and women adopt an information-seeking approach, serving to underline its importance. With regard to attending a self-help group 89 per cent of women find this either useful or very useful compared to 80 per cent of men, but 55 per cent of women find it very useful compared to only 23 per cent of men (p<0.01). A similar trend is apparent with maintaining interests outside caring, with 97 per cent of women who use the strategy finding it helpful, 62 per cent very helpful and 87 per cent of men finding it helpful, 49 per cent very helpful.

It is not possible to determine why these differences exist but we might speculate that, with men normally perceived to utilize direct problem-solving more than women, these more passive methods might be seen as less helpful. Whatever the reason it is clear that for the present sample, women have both a wider range of strategies than men and find these strategies more helpful. This is confirmed in the third type of difference in Table 3.4, where there are differences both in the frequency with which coping efforts are employed and in how helpful they are perceived to be.

Once again it is the female carers who are most in evidence here. They use two strategies more frequently: talking over a problem with someone they trust – 93 per cent/76 per cent (p<.0000); and keeping a little free time yourself – 84 per cent/76 per cent (p<.05). They also find these approaches more helpful: 96 per cent of women find talking over problems either helpful or very helpful (68 per cent very helpful) compared to 81 per cent (47 per cent very helpful) of men (p<.0000); 73 per cent of women find keeping a little free time very helpful compared to 53 per cent of men (p<.02).

Table 3.4 clearly indicates that women in the present sample employ a more diverse range of coping strategies than men. They are also significantly more likely to find the strategies they employ helpful. A number of these strategies are of the more passive type (relaxation, having a good cry, talking over problems, attending a self-help group) that the previous literature suggests are employed more by women. However, whilst the literature indicates that men use direct problem-solving methods more than women, this is not apparent in our sample. Women are equally likely to use purposeful problem-solving as men but in addition have a better array of tactics aimed at managing stress symptoms. Given the importance noted earlier of having some time and interests away from caring, and the benefit of being able to draw upon a range of coping efforts, women in this sample, irrespective of relationship (i.e. wife or daughter), appear to cope more effectively than do men. We would reiterate here that caution is needed in generalizing from these results given the nature of the sample. However, the findings do suggest the need to question a number of the hitherto taken-for-granted assumptions about the nature of coping employed by male and female carers. Harris (1993) argues that in addition to recognizing the difficulties that female carers face, greater attention also needs to be given to some of the different problems male carers face. Our results provide support for this contention.

Such differences were not so apparent by relationship, with significant variation emerging on only one variable: spouses are significantly more likely to find remembering all the good times they had shared with the cared-for person helpful than are children (χ^2 9.79, 3df p<.02). Therefore although this tactic is used by over 90 per cent of both groups (93 per cent spouses, 91 per cent children) 60 per cent of spouses find this very helpful compared to 38 per cent of children. This reinforces the importance of past relationships and biography in understanding both stress and coping in family caregiving.

Despite the differences in coping discussed above, what emerges most clearly from these results is the diversity and pervasiveness of coping strategies that carers utilize. Far from being a passive and largely reactive group, carers are characterized by being proactive and purposeful in bringing a broad range of methods to bear on the difficulties they face. Moreover, a number of coping efforts that are not used all that frequently – for example relaxation techniques or attending a self-help group – are still seen as help-ful, suggesting that their low uptake is possibly more a lack of opportunity or skill rather than desire. The only strategy that was universally seen as unhelpful (ignoring the problem and hoping it will go away) is in any case generally recognized as inappropriate.

Helping carers cope: the focus of professional support

The importance of coping to an understanding of how people deal with adverse or potentially adverse life events is beyond question (Lazarus 1993); recently there has been an emerging consensus that adaptability and flexibility is the key to successful coping, especially the ability to match the coping response with the nature of the stressor (Brown 1993; Lazarus 1993; Thompson *et al.* 1993; Burr *et al.* 1994; McKee *et al.* 1994). In terms of inter-ventions to assist carers, a number of authors are of the opinion that coping offers a potentially fertile and productive avenue (Milne *et al.* 1993; Nolan *et al.* 1994; Triantafillou and Mestheneos 1994). However, if such interven-tions are to be successful it is essential that coping is viewed from a carer's perspective (Boss 1988a, 1993; Sharp 1992; Ingebretsen and Solen 1995).

We have already suggested a number of specific ways in which carers can be assisted to cope, and these are underpinned by a number of general principles. Elsewhere (Nolan *et al.* 1994) we have identified four such gen-eral principles, namely that professionals should:

• identify and reinforce carers' appropriate coping responses;
• identify and seek to reduce inappropriate coping responses;
• help carers to develop new coping resources/responses;
• augment existing coping resources by building larger support networks.

To these we would add:

• services should substitute for carers only when the above interventions prove unsuccessful;
• services should not support carers beyond the point at which their own health suffers;
• services must adopt a more enabling and facilitative role working with carers as partners (not co-workers) in a way which is sensitive to carers' existing expertise and the stage of the caring history.

Discussing the future support for carers from a European perspective, Evers (1995) argues that services must primarily seek to supplement and complement carers' efforts rather than substitute for them. This is not to argue that there are no circumstances in which services should be substitutive. However, at the moment this is the dominant, indeed almost the exclusive, *modus operandi* for formal services. Greene and Coleman (1995) contend that services function primarily by breaking down caring into discrete tasks, failing to capture the dynamics of caring. There is a need to move beyond this perspective before progress can be made. As Schultz *et al.* (1993) note, this will mean basing interventions around a model of caring, the purpose of which is to improve a carer's ability and positive adaptation by means of empowerment, problem-solving and skill development approaches. This requires a multidimensional model of assessment (Levesque *et al.* 1995) which captures the specificity of caring situations (Brodatey *et al.* 1994) and allows for an individually tailored programme of support to emerge (Jerrom *et al.* 1993). We believe that CADI (Nolan and Grant 1992a) and CAMI (Nolan *et al.* 1995b) are one means by which such an approach could be developed. However, for a more holistic assessment of this kind to be undertaken two further criteria must be met. First, it must include attention to the potential satisfactions of caring, and second, the entire process should be informed by a temporal and longitudinal perspective on caregiving (Given and Given 1991; Brodatey *et al.* 1994; Greene and Coleman 1995). These issues form the substance of the following two chapters.

4

SATISFACTIONS OF CARING: THE NEGLECTED DIMENSION

The identification of positive aspects of a situation – the silver
lining effect – may be one of the most powerful cognitive coping
strategies of all.

(Summers *et al.* 1989: 37)

According to Ungerson (1987: 8), Bayley's description of caring as being 'onerous, emotionally demanding, hardly reciprocal and only rarely rewarding'
provides the most adequate account of the caregiving experience, and this
is an impression that most of the literature would sustain. However, over
the last few years there has been a growing realization that such a perception is far from accurate. A number of authors have become critical of the
predominant focus on the stresses and burdens of care, and have suggested
that a true picture will not emerge until the potentially satisfying aspects of
caregiving are explored in greater detail (Motenko 1988, 1989; Summers
et al. 1989; Walker 1990, 1992; Farran *et al.* 1991; Nolan and Grant 1992a;
Grant and Nolan 1993; Langer 1993; Cohen *et al.* 1994; Levesque *et al.* 1995).

It has been recognized for some time that support for the belief that
caring has invariably negative consequences is marginal at best (Gilhooly
1984), and recently there has been growing empirical evidence of potential
satisfactions or rewards. These studies, as with virtually all caregiving research, are based on non-random samples (Kane and Penrod 1995) and
make generalization difficult. Nevertheless, the sheer weight of evidence is
impressive and highlights the need for the satisfactions of caring to figure far
more prominently on a number of agendas. Studies typically report the
percentage of carers identifying satisfying aspects of their role as ranging
from 55 per cent (Cohen *et al.* 1994) to well over 90 per cent (Clifford
1990), with this figure being greater than 80 per cent in the majority of
studies (Crookston 1989; Summers *et al.* 1989; Braithwaite 1990; Clifford
1990; Farran *et al.* 1991; Kane and Penrod 1995).

This has led to a greater appreciation of the diverse and often subtle sources of satisfaction that carers experience, permitting both a more complex and a more complete understanding of the caregiving dynamic to emerge. However, knowledge in this area is still relatively sparse and there have been few systematic efforts to study the sources and types of satisfactions that carers may experience. There appear to be several reasons for this. First, despite the growing sophistication of stress and coping models of informal care, there has been a tendency to view caring in largely pathological terms (Titterton 1992; Nolan *et al.* 1994). Hence, carers may be seen as victims, trapped in their roles or obligated to support dependent relatives, often with minimal material, psychological or financial support. The primary role of services here becomes one of stress reduction, something which remains high on the policy agenda. Second, carers may be regarded as well-meaning individuals whose interests and motivations may lead them to patronize or overprotect relatives who need their support or care. Here, services are more likely to be directed towards helping the care recipient to live a more 'ordinary' life independent of carers. Third, there has been a historical tendency to view carers, like many 'clients', as passive recipients of welfare services (Titterton 1992). This has reinforced models of care which may have little relevance to the everyday realities which carers face. Viewed as passive agents, carers are not expected to express their feelings about what they do. This merely serves to perpetuate invalid assumptions about caring because concepts are not rooted in the everyday experiences of carers themselves.

In this chapter we consider the satisfactions and rewards of care in some detail. Following a review of the existing literature we draw upon what we believe to be the most extensive empirical data on the satisfactions of caring yet collected in Britain, and use this to highlight the pervasive and diverse nature of rewards that carers may experience.

Reciprocity, relationships and meanings: key concepts in the satisfactions of caring

Compared to the literature on the stresses and burdens of care, that on the rewards and gratifications is still relatively embryonic. Nevertheless, the possibility that caring may provide positive outcomes is not a new concept and was identified early in the genesis of caregiving research (Davies 1980). Since that time a number of studies have generally provided descriptive accounts illustrating the frequency of certain sources or types of satisfaction, whilst others have attempted to go further by seeking to build a more adequate theoretical account using concepts such as *mutuality* (Hirschfield 1981, 1983) and *enrichment* (Archbold *et al.* 1992, 1995; Cartwright *et al.* 1994). From a synthesis of this literature it is possible to identify a number of emerging themes that summarize our present state of knowledge. Prominent

amongst these is the notion of reciprocity, the purpose of which is to maintain a sense of balance and interdependence in relationships. Finch and
Mason (1993) suggest that reciprocity is the driving force behind much of
'normal' family life. It is asserted that this concept provides the best analytic
key to understanding the giving and receiving of help and support. As they
point out, reciprocity in this context does not necessarily or usually refer to
the equal exchange of comparable help or support. Rather it is the product
of a complex set of often implicit negotiations shaped largely by the history
and biography of relationships. Similar considerations apply to the satisfactions
and rewards of caring. In most instances caring grows out of established
relationships; as Wenger et al. (1996) suggest, it can best be understood in
this context.

The early literature on the potential satisfactions of care clearly signalled the importance of relationships to achieving or construing rewards
(Fengler and Goodrich 1979; Davies 1980). Davies (1980) for example argued that satisfactions are only possible when the recipient of care is seen
as a valued person rather than as a problem. Similarly, when studying
carers of people with dementia, Hirschfield (1981, 1983) contended that the
development of mutuality (the ability to find gratification and meaning in
caregiving) was dependent largely on the extent to which the cared-for
person was perceived to reciprocate 'by virtue of their existence'. This returns to the arguments developed in Chapter 2 about professional (nursing)
care where 'constructive' care (Scott 1995) can only be achieved when the
cared-for person in some way matters (Kitson 1987; Fealy 1995; Scott 1995).
Although it is recognized that family care can be delivered in the absence
of affection (Qureshi 1986), we will argue later that the absence of satisfactions
can and should be taken as an indicator of a fragile and potentially abusive
relationship, a conclusion consistent with other studies (Walker et al. 1990;
Archbold et al. 1992; Cartwright et al. 1994). The importance of relationships
to an understanding of the satisfactions of care has been signalled by a
number of other studies (Motenko 1989; Archbold et al. 1992; Nolan and
Grant 1992a; Grant and Nolan 1993).

A closely related concept is that of the meaning ascribed to caring. The
argument here is that if caring is to be construed as positive there has to be
at least some element of meaning or worth attached (Farran et al. 1991;
Given and Given 1991; Archbold et al. 1992; Jivanjee 1993; Langer 1993).
The most detailed arguments appear to be those suggested by Farran et al.
(1991), who adopt an existential paradigm. They contend that caring can be
seen as meaningful in terms of provisional and ultimate meanings. Provisional meanings are constructed within the day-to-day elements of care
whereas ultimate meanings are more intimately tied to the philosophical or
spiritual beliefs that an individual holds. Caring, Farran et al. (1991) suggest,
provides a number of avenues to finding meaning, including creative routes
(as a means of developing new skills for example); experiential routes (via
relationships and feelings); and attitudinal routes (via the exploration of

personal beliefs and values). The creation of meaning in this context is primarily seen as an individual process rather than being circumscribed by race, gender and other 'givens' (Farran *et al.* 1991). This is an interesting conceptualization, but our understanding of the influence of factors such as race and gender is as yet too rudimentary to discount the role these variables may play.

Although not operating from such an explicitly existential perspective, the concept of *caregiving enrichment* (Cartwright *et al.* 1994) is also dependent upon the meanings ascribed to care. These authors define enrichment as 'the process of endowing caregiving with meaning or pleasure for both caregiver and care-recipient'. The linking of meaning and pleasure with a satisfying relationship highlights the integral nature of these concepts, consistent with the conclusions of a number of authors (Davies 1980; Hirschfield 1981, 1983).

Reinforcing the importance of subjective and constructed meanings, the typology of care we outlined in Chapter 2 is underpinned explicitly by the meanings or purposes of carers rather than the tasks undertaken. These concepts appear central to a better understanding of caring in general and caring satisfactions in particular.

Conceptualizing the rewards and gratifications of caring

Given the importance of reciprocity, one way of exploring the satisfactions of caring is therefore in terms of the main perceived beneficiary of an exchange. In some circumstances this is clearly the cared-for person; in others there is a more obvious form of mutual benefit; and at the opposite end of the continuum the primary gain appears to be for the carer (Nolan and Grant 1992a).

An alternative conceptualization is to consider the source or derivation of satisfactions, with three main types having been identified: satisfactions deriving mainly from the interpersonal dynamic between carer and cared-for person; satisfactions deriving primarily from the intrapersonal or intrapsychic orientation of the carer; and satisfactions deriving mainly from a desire to promote a positive or avoid a negative outcome for the cared-for person (Grant and Nolan 1993).

We will use these two analytic devices to impose an element of conceptual order on the current literature on caregiving satisfactions. The categories created are not intended to be conceptually discrete. There is considerable fluidity between the categories and some represent experiences that are more prominent than others. At one level it could be argued that all the satisfactions of caring are a product, at least in part, of the dynamics of the caring relationship. Moreover, as satisfactions are largely a subjective perception, similarly all must in some measure result from the cognitive or intrapsychic orientation of the carer. What we seek to identify is the *relative emphasis* within differing satisfactions of caring. Therefore in applying our two analytic schemes, *major perceived beneficiary* (cared-for person ←→ both ←→ carer) and *derivation of satisfactions* (the interpersonal dynamic; the intrapersonal/ intrapsychic dynamic; the outcome dynamic), we can better identify and understand differing types of satisfaction. For example, in some instances the major perceived beneficiary will be the cared-for person and the source of satisfactions will derive from the interpersonal dynamic between carer and cared-for person. In another instance both carer and cared-for person will benefit but the derivation may be from the intrapsychic orientation of the carer. These two dimensions can be used to create a matrix comprising nine cells as indicated in Figure 4.1.

There is a danger that these arguments appear tautologous. It might be assumed that if satisfactions are in evidence the carer must *always* benefit in some way. Moreover, it will be argued later that a carer who experiences satisfactions is likely to provide better care, so in satisfying caring relationships the cared-for person must similarly *always* gain. This merely highlights the inherently reciprocal nature of good caring relationships and can be seen as reinforcing rather than countering our arguments. We accept therefore that in this broader sense all the satisfactions of caring provide some reciprocity for both parties (and often others such as the family as well). However, it is still useful, theoretically and practically, to explore the relative emphasis within differing types of reward. Although at this point much of what we discuss will relate to dyadic interactions it is apparent that satisfactions relating to wider family relationships also pertain.

The importance of the relational aspects of caring suggests that any attempt to synthesize the literature on the satisfaction of care should begin with an analysis of the interpersonal dynamic between carer and cared-for person.

The satisfactions of caring: deriving satisfactions from the interpersonal dynamic

We will begin our consideration with those satisfactions that can be construed as arising largely from the interpersonal dynamic between the carer and cared-for person and where the main perceived beneficiary is the cared-for person. That is the top left-hand cell of the matrix in Figure 4.1.

Based on a series of in-depth interviews and a large-scale postal survey of members of the Association of Carers (now Carers National Association), it was found that the largest single source of satisfaction identified by carers was the act of giving to the cared-for person (Nolan and Grant 1992a; Grant and Nolan 1993). Frequently this involved the maintenance of simple pleasures, as the following quotations illustrate:

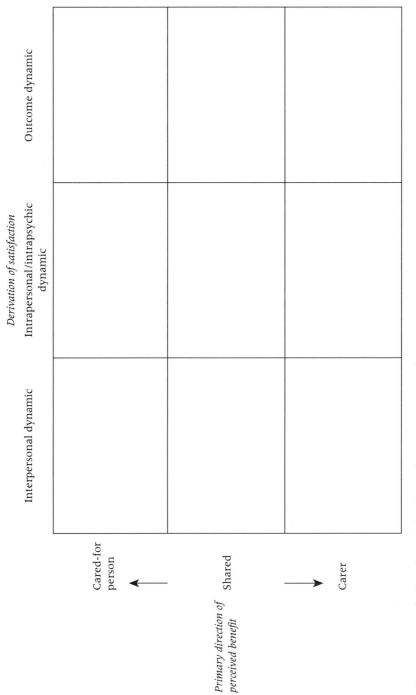

Figure 4.1 Exploring the satisfactions of care: a conceptual matrix

When my mother gets pleasure from something I've planned and when I manage to turn her unhappiness to happiness.

When my husband can remember something about where he has been or what we have done. This means he has enjoyed himself and that makes all the hard work worthwhile.

Seeing her smile, her pleasure when things go well, my pleasure when she is contented. It's a joy to help her, to always be near her, bringing her a cup of tea in the mornings.

Jivanjee (1993: 9), in a study of dementia caregivers, noted similar rewards and was surprised to discover 'the creativity of people in finding rewards in seemingly insignificant events or activities, and the capacity for people to find their own resilience in oppressive situations'.

These findings are consistent with other studies which suggest that simply seeing the cared-for person happy and contented is a source of considerable satisfaction for carers (Lawton *et al.* 1989; Clifford 1990; Cartwright *et al.* 1994; Kane and Penrod 1995). The maintenance of such simple but important interactions is seen by Cartwright *et al.* (1994) to provide one of the main mechanisms serving to enrich relationships. They argue that enrichment should constitute a major therapeutic intervention whereby carers and cared-for persons are encouraged and assisted to maintain customary pleasurable routines, whilst also developing innovative ways in which everyday life events can attain new symbolic meaning.

At a much more abstract level it has been suggested that maintaining the dignity and self-esteem of the cared-for person is also a major source of satisfaction (Nolan and Grant 1992a; Grant and Nolan 1993). In order to achieve this, carers often draw on their intimate knowledge of the cared-for person, particularly in terms of sustaining or rebuilding meaningful roles. This is one of the main purposes of protective, preservative and (re)constructive care described in Chapter 2.

That carers see such activities as satisfying (Nolan and Grant 1992a; Grant and Nolan 1993) suggests that they also gain some benefit, and yet the intended beneficiary is clearly the cared-for person. We believe that this provides strong empirical support for the concept of altruism as reciprocity described by Abrams (1985).

Remaining within the caregiving dynamic there is also evidence that the interpersonal relationships between carer and cared-for person provides for satisfactions which are more obviously of mutual benefit to both parties. For example Clifford's (1990) study indicated that 62 per cent of carers of older people and 50 per cent of carers of people with learning difficulties felt closer to the cared-for person than they were at the beginning of the caring experience. Other authors have reached similar conclusions (Motenko 1989; Walker *et al.* 1990; Nolan and Grant 1992a; Grant and Nolan 1993; Coleman *et al.* 1994). Such improved relationships are not confined solely to the caregiving dyad, with studies also reporting that caring has resulted in an improved relationship within families (Stoller and Pugliesi 1989; Farran *et al*. 1991; Nolan and Grant 1992a; Grant and Nolan 1993; Patterson 1993; Burr *et al*. 1994; Kane and Penrod 1995). Patterson (1993) for instance describes the emergence of what she termed *collectivity*, whereby family members experience greater affirmation of each other and *shared control*, where a better understanding of the relative contribution of each family member emerges. Farran *et al*. (1991) identified the development of better family and social relationships as the single most frequent source of satisfaction and meaning in care, cited by 63 per cent of the 94 carers in their study.

In circumstances where the primary source of satisfaction is the interpersonal aspects of care but the main perceived beneficiary is the carer, expressions of appreciation have been identified as a major source of reward (Lewis and Meredith 1988a,b; Clifford 1990; Nolan and Grant 1992a; Grant and Nolan 1993; Beresford 1994). Such appreciation is particularly valued when it comes from the cared-for person (Lewis and Meredith 1988a,b; Nolan and Grant 1992a; Grant and Nolan 1993) but can be considerably reinforced by appreciation received from relatives, friends and professional carers (Grant and Nolan 1993; Beresford 1994). The quotations below, cited by Grant and Nolan (1993), provide an indication of the importance carers attached to feeling valued, whether by the cared-for person or others:

The fact that he has a lovely disposition and is appreciative of the help I give him more than compensates for any extra care he might need.

When my mother puts her arms around me and says she knows what I am doing (although this clarity doesn't last long) and when my aunt says thank you for everything (she always means it).

The impression that she still appreciates my caring even after ten years of Alzheimer's disease.

To see an appreciative smile on the face of my severely mentally and physically handicapped son.

When one of her sons or daughters say thank you for looking after their mam, then I feel appreciated and that's all I want.

Compliments from friends and relatives – I never get any from the patient.

Someone saying well done (very rare!).

Other sources of reward for the carer rooted primarily in the interpersonal dynamic include receiving the love and affection of the cared-for person (Clifford 1990; Kane and Penrod 1995) and the opportunity to reinforce marriage vows, out of love rather than duty (Motenko 1988; Grant and Nolan 1993).

Deriving satisfactions from intrapsychic sources

The majority of those rewards and satisfactions derived primarily from factors relating to the intrapersonal or intrapsychic orientation of the carer will axiomatically be located within the bottom middle cell of the matrix depicted in Figure 4.1. The literature indicates a diverse set of potential rewards for carers, ranging from some of the most lofty to some of the most basic of psychic needs.

The potential for caring to meet existential needs, providing life with meaning and purpose, has long been identified (Davies 1980) and reaffirmed a number of times subsequently (Pearlin *et al.* 1990; Farran *et al.* 1991; Nolan and Grant 1992a; Grant and Nolan 1993; Harris 1993). It seems that women more often cite existential satisfactions than men (Davies 1980; Ungerson 1987; Lewis and Meredith 1988a,b) although these studies focused primarily or exclusively on women, so that it is uncertain whether this conclusion represents a genuine gender difference or is an artefact of the samples studied. Other studies suggest that men also invest significant meaning in caring (Motenko 1988; Harris 1993), which is not motivated primarily out of duty, but rather out of pride and love (Motenko 1988). At a similar level of what has been termed 'ultimate' meaning (Farran *et al.* 1991), caring provides many people with a vehicle for expressing strongly held religious or personal beliefs (Clifford 1990; Farran *et al.* 1991; Nolan and Grant 1992a; Grant and Nolan 1993; Coleman *et al.* 1994). For example 91 per cent of Coleman *et al.*'s (1994) sample considered that caring had brought them closer to God. It is interesting to speculate whether this is a cohort effect and if such perceived rewards can be sustained in an increasingly secular society.

No less important, but perhaps somewhat lower down the 'psychic hierarchy', caring has been described as providing opportunities to meet a wide range of caregiver needs such as developing competence and mastery (Motenko 1988; Summers *et al.* 1989; Kahana and Young 1990; Pearlin *et al.* 1990; Jivanjee 1993; Langer 1993); maintaining a sense of achievement (Stoller and Pugliesi 1989; Beresford 1994; Kane and Penrod 1995); providing opportunities to overcome challenges (Nolan and Grant 1992a; Grant and Nolan 1993); developing personal qualities such as greater tolerance and patience (Crookston 1989; Clifford 1990). Not surprisingly therefore caring is often seen to be a source of self-esteem for carers (Motenko 1988; Given and Given 1991; Cartwright *et al.* 1994), which illuminates the inherently meaningful nature of care for some caregivers (Archbold *et al.* 1992).

Other sources of psychic reward for carers include opportunities to fulfil a sense of duty (Coleman *et al.* 1994; Kane and Penrod 1995) – although this is not as significant as might be anticipated – and a reduction in feelings of actual or potential guilt. Certainly guilt is a pervasive emotion even when carers are providing all that might reasonably be expected in the way of help and support. There is likely to be a reciprocal relationship between the genesis of guilt and the ability of carers to set reasonable expectations and limits. Pratt *et al.* (1987) suggest that as there is little discussion on the moral dimensions of family caring, carers can find it difficult to establish meaningful parameters. Consequently they may set unattainable standards which they cannot meet, making guilt an integral part of care (Nolan and Grant 1992a). The implications of this for the design of interventions with family carers will be considered later.

Some of the above aspects of personal benefit and development for carers have also been noted to relate to families. Whilst still a source of reward that is primarily concerned with the psyche, the psyche in question here is that of the family as a unit rather than the individual carer. This most logically fits within the centre box of the matrix. For example, Patterson (1993) has described three sets of benefits accruing to families which might be conceived of in this way, these being the development of shared purpose (greater value placed on the small, less materialistic things in life); framability (a generally more optimistic outlook on life); and relativism (the development of a more tolerant and less judgemental set of values).

Also within the reciprocal cell of the matrix we would place satisfactions deriving from the repayment of past kindness (Nolan and Grant 1992a; Grant and Nolan 1993) and what has been termed 'hypothetical' exchange (Grant and Nolan 1993), which is the belief that if the situation were reversed then the cared-for person would provide care for the carer. We see these satisfactions as being reciprocal because they provide strong motivations for care and its continuance, ensuring that the cared-for person receives the help they need; they are also satisfying for the carer because they permit freedom from a perception of indebtedness. Maintaining such a perception has been described as one of the prime motivations behind the giving and receiving of help in ordinary family life (Finch and Mason 1993).

It has been recognized for some time that providing the physical aspects of care may meet the needs of some carers, particularly female carers, to tend and nurture (Lewis and Meredith 1988a; Motenko 1989; Kahana and Young 1990; Nolan and Grant 1992a; Grant and Nolan 1993). We would place these in the top-centre box of the matrix, as the prime beneficiary is the cared-for person but the carer also gains by having an important psychic need met.

Deriving satisfactions from promoting positive or avoiding negative consequences

The last broad category of satisfactions in our conceptualization concerns those which derive from the desire to promote positive or reduce negative consequences, usually for the cared-for person. We have termed this the outcome dynamic. Once again this represents a diverse and potent source of satisfactions. In terms of promoting positive consequences, many carers have a strongly held belief that they are able to provide the best care possible for the cared-for person, primarily because of their intimate knowledge of the individual's needs and circumstances (Crookston 1989; Pearlin *et al.* 1990; Farran *et al.* 1991; Nolan and Grant 1992a; Grant and Nolan 1993). It is here that carers most clearly exercise their role as the 'arbiter of standards' (Twigg and Atkin 1994). The flipside of this coin is the belief that as no one else can provide an acceptable standard of care then the carer perceives that they must continue at all costs. Whilst providing a source of satisfaction, this can also serve to bind the carer to their role, making it very difficult to relinquish, even when institutional care is under consideration (Davies 1980; Hirschfield 1981, 1983; Nolan and Grant 1992a; Grant and Nolan 1993). These sentiments are captured in the quotations below (Grant and Nolan 1993: 153, original emphasis)

A few of my mother's contemporaries are in nursing homes that we visit. I'm determined that she is *not* to go into a nursing home or hospital as *I know* the neglect that occurs when staff are overstretched.
(anonymous)

Great satisfaction because I know that care in hospital would be much worse than care at home and this would apply to the nursing homes I've investigated.
(retired consultant)

Returning to positive consequences, one of the chief sources of satisfaction, especially for parents caring for children with learning difficulties, is to see their child develop, grow and reach their full potential (Clifford 1990; Grant and Nolan 1993; Beresford 1994). The following are illustrative of this:

I find caring very rewarding. I daily see the results of love and loving care. I have a delightful, well-balanced, undemanding and grateful 21-year-old daughter who is admired and loved by all she comes into contact with. My hard work has been very worthwhile.

Seeing a child who was a limp rag doll finally becoming a human being and knowing that I was a major part of it.

Bringing my severely handicapped daughter up to be a well-educated, witty, amusing and intelligent human being has been the most satisfying achievement of my life.

Such caring roles have been termed 'symbiotic' by Twigg and Atkin (1994). These authors argue that such carers are reluctant to give up their role and only accept help if it is consistent with their own frame of reference. By implication the arguments propounded by Twigg and Atkin (1994) suggest that carers do not wish caring to end because their *own* needs would no longer be satisfied. Whilst this may happen in exceptional circumstances, in our experience carers are reluctant to give up care not for primarily sel-fish motives but simply because alternatives are perceived to be unacceptable.

An allied, but distinct, form of satisfaction occurs when the cared-for person has experienced some form of sudden physical or mental catastro-phe. Here carers derive satisfaction from assisting in the recovery process, especially when this is contrary to expectations. This is illustrated below:

I was told six times that my husband wouldn't last the night. Two years later he is driving a car.

When my mother left mental hospital I was told to accept what she had become. She just sat staring at the wall. I have worked hard to reha-bilitate her and though this has cost me a great deal both mentally and physically, I have a great deal of satisfaction seeing that my efforts have been worthwhile and have proved the medical profession wrong.

The biggest satisfaction is knowing that I have kept him going five years after the medical profession gave him up.

Dimensions of the outcome dynamic that might be perceived as result-ing in shared benefit are the development of a new set of joint interests or activities (Cartwright et al. 1994). Similarly, the development of new skills and expertise in carers themselves (Pearlin et al. 1990; Nolan and Grant 1992a; Grant and Nolan 1993) and a widening of interests and contacts for carers (Nolan and Grant 1992a; Grant and Nolan 1993) are best located in the bottom right-hand corner of the matrix where the main benefit is to the carer. In this way all the cells of the matrix can meaningfully be filled.

It will be apparent from the foregoing that the potential sources of satisfaction from caring are diverse, complex and often subtle. Figure 4.2 provides a completed matrix with the relevant sources of satisfaction in-serted into the appropriate cells. We would stress at this point that our thinking on this matter is still emergent and we present our ideas here as evolving rather than fully formed. Others may interpret things differently and take issue with the manner in which certain satisfactions have been located. We would welcome such a debate and would be happy if a differ-ing, more adequate conceptualization were to emerge. Our heuristic device would then have served its purpose. Nevertheless at this point we consider the matrix to be a realistic attempt to capture the nuances of caring satis-factions. The empirical data we present below adds support to this contention.

Exploring the satisfactions of caregiving

With a few exceptions, for example Motenko (1989), the studies we have cited have included satisfactions as a small component of a larger investiga-tion rather than focusing primarily on this aspect. For instance, Lawton

Derivation of satisfaction

Primary direction of perceived benefit	Interpersonal dynamic	Intrapersonal/intrapsychic dynamic	Outcome dynamic
Cared-for person	Maintaining/providing small pleasures Seeing cared-for person happy Maintaining dignity/self-esteem of cared-for person	Nurturance and tending	Providing best care available Avoiding institutionalization Helping cared-for person reach full potential, development and growth Aiding recovery
Shared	Closer caring relationships Improved family relationships	Developing family values and meanings Repayment of past kindness Hypothetical exchange Altruistic behaviour	Developing new shared interests
Carer	Expressions of appreciation from: • cared-for person • family/friends • professionals Love and affection from cared-for person	Existential satisfactions Expression of religious/other beliefs Developing competence/mastery Sense of achievement Personal quality e.g. tolerance or patience Fulfil sense of duty Reduce guilt	Developing new skills and abilities

Figure 4.2 Exploring the satisfactions of care: a completed matrix

et al. (1989, 1991) included a small number of items on the satisfactions of caring as one part of their study but the source of the items is unclear. However, the growing recognition that an absence of satisfactions can act as a risk factor in identifying poor caring relationships (Clifford 1990; Walker *et al.* 1990; Archbold 1992, 1995), coupled with the belief that identifying satisfactions can serve as a therapeutic intervention (Langer 1993; Nolan and Keady 1993; Cartwright *et al.* 1994) suggests that 'particular attention' should be given to exploring the range and diversity of caregiver reward (Levesque *et al.* 1995). The Carers Assessment of Satisfactions Index (CASI) (Nolan and Grant 1992a) was devised for just this purpose.

This index consists of 30 items which were derived from an extensive postal survey of carers and a number of in-depth semi-structured interviews. Items were therefore empirically based, being generated from sources of satisfaction identified by carers themselves. In completing the scale carers are asked to indicate if each item doesn't apply to them; applies but does not provide a source of satisfaction; applies and provides quite a lot of satisfaction; and applies providing a great deal of satisfaction. The index can be either interviewer-administered or form part of a postal survey. The results we report and discuss below are based on two main sources of data. The first data were generated from in-depth interviews with 38 carers of people with dementia (Keady and Nolan 1993a,b), whilst the remaining data were collected using a postal questionnaire survey. The questionnaire, which comprised CASI and a range of other variables such as age, gender, caregiving relationship, self-perceived emotional and physical well-being, levels of physical and mental frailty and so on was distributed by the Alzheimer's Disease Society Newsletter in Wales and Scotland and the Crossroads Care Network in Wales. This approach has the same two methodological limitations which relate to the survey described in the last chapter using CAMI. However, the majority of caregiving research has been based on non-random, usually 'clinical' samples (Kane and Penrod 1995), so that the difficulty in generalizing results is widely acknowledged.

Nevertheless, 206 completed questionnaires were returned, providing an extensive pool of empirical data focusing specifically on the satisfactions carers experience. The characteristics of the sample can be found in Appendix 1. Most carers were either spouses caring for a partner or children (usually daughters) caring for a parent. In order to make meaningful comparisons we will restrict further reporting to these two groups, giving a total sample of 200.

Sources of satisfaction are discussed using the matrix applied to the literature review. Utilizing the source of satisfaction as the main descriptor, the full results for the entire sample can be found in Appendix 2. However, for the sake of brevity these have been summarized in matrix form in Figure 4.3. Each source of satisfaction has been located in the relevant cell; the percentage of carers who found this item provided a great deal or quite a lot of satisfaction is in parentheses.

Derivation of satisfaction

Main beneficiary		Interpersonal dynamic	Intrapersonal/intrapsychic dynamic	Outcome dynamic
Cared-for person	←	Maintain dignity of cared-for person (96) See cared-for person happy (88) Give pleasure to cared-for person (87)	Like to see cared-for person well turned out (91) Cared-for person's needs tended to (79)	Keep cared-for person out of an institution (80) Give best care possible (78) Help cared-for person overcome difficulties (78) See small improvements in cared-for person (48) See cared-for person reach full potential (45)
Shared		Expression of love (89) Closer to cared-for person (49) Closer family ties (39)	Know I've done my best (90) Hypothetical exchange (79) Sort of person who enjoys helping others (78) Repay past kindnesses (66) One way of showing my faith (55)	
Carer	→	Cared-for person doesn't complain (46) Appreciation from others (56) Appreciation from cared-for person (59)	Provides a purpose in life (25) Stops feeling guilty (31) Grown as a person (43) Test out abilities (45) Provides a challenge (48) Feel wanted and needed (53) Fulfil sense of duty (67)	Widened interests (30) Developed new skills and abilities (42)

Figure 4.3 Frequency and source of satisfactions experienced by carers

Initially it is worth highlighting some broad trends which illustrate both the diverse and pervasive nature of satisfactions. Of the 30 items on the index, 12 were seen as providing quite a lot or a great deal of satisfaction by 75 per cent or over of the sample (we term these *major* sources of satisfaction), six provided similar levels of satisfaction for over 50 per cent of the sample (termed here *important* sources of satisfaction), and no single item applied to less than 25 per cent of the sample. On this basis Ungerson's (1987) contention that caring is 'hardly reciprocal and only rarely rewarding' does not stand up to empirical scrutiny. This diversity is also reflected in the sources of satisfaction, with nine items derived from the nature of the interpersonal dynamic, 14 derived from the intrapersonal/intrapsychic domain, and seven from the outcomes dynamic. This serves to highlight further the importance that relationships and ascribed meaning have to an understanding of the caring dynamic. If attention is focused on the main beneficiary, then ten items relate to the cared-for person as beneficiary, eight are more explicitly shared and 12 relate primarily to the carer. A more detailed look at these broad figures however reveals some interesting variations.

Satisfactions: cared-for person as main beneficiary

It is immediately apparent that those aspects of caring which provide carers with the greatest satisfaction relate to circumstances in which the main perceived beneficiary is the cared-for person. Of the ten items falling into this category, eight are seen as major sources of satisfaction by carers. Moving left to right across the top of the matrix these are as follows: maintaining the dignity of the cared-for person (96 per cent); seeing them happy (88 per cent); giving pleasure to them (87 per cent); seeing them well turned out (91 per cent); tending to their needs (79 per cent); keeping them out of an institution (80 per cent); giving the best possible care (78 per cent) and helping them overcome difficulties (78 per cent). Two of the remaining major sources of satisfaction are also clearly linked to providing benefit for the cared-for person: know I'll have done my best (for cared-for person) (90 per cent) and expression of love for cared-for person (89 per cent). We suggest that these results provide convincing empirical support for the concept of altruism as reciprocity first described by Abrams (1985). Such a notion has been criticized as forming an insufficient basis on which to consider a relationship as reciprocal, because the nature of the return is too vague (Wright 1986; Bulmer 1987).

On the basis of our results, however, we feel that Abrams was correct and that carers do indeed derive a good deal of satisfaction from acts, the prime motivation for which is to improve or maintain the quality of life for the cared-for person. As Jivanjee (1993) argues, it is often the seemingly insignificant events that provide the greatest pleasure, particularly in the context of caring, where once-trivial happenings assume greater import. It is here that the notion of caregiving enrichment as a therapeutic intervention (Cartwright *et al.* 1994) figures prominently. These authors believe that enriching activities provide pleasure for both the carer and cared-for person and that those professionals working with carers should actively encourage enriching activities by identifying customary routines that are seen as important and helping to maintain these wherever possible. This should be complemented by efforts to identify new routines or daily events that can be perceived as important. Cartwright and co-authors suggest that enrichment is based on an active process of interweaving two biographies in order to determine which 'mundane' activities are most likely to be endowed with symbolic meaning. These enriching activities provide a vehicle to maintain or strengthen dyadic relationships as well as to enhance the self-esteem and sense of identity of both the carer and cared-for person. Such interventions are not costly in terms of time or money but do require that service providers move their attention beyond instrumental care.

The importance of nurturance in providing carers with satisfaction is apparent from the high percentage who see this as providing a major source of reward. What is interesting here is that there are no differences by gender on the two items concerned with nurturing or tending activities, with both men and women seeing these as equally valuable. This perhaps suggests that there is a need for a critical reappraisal of some of the assumptions made about the generalized nature of caring. As we will illustrate shortly, gender differences appear in our sample but the type of kinship relationship also influences satisfaction.

In eight out of ten cases, keeping the cared-for person out of an institution and providing the best possible care also constitute a major source of satisfaction. At one level this represents nothing dramatic, indeed it is what might be expected, but combined with a perception of giving the best possible care there are major implications for the design and delivery of services to carers. These variables place carers in the role of 'arbiter of standards' (Twigg and Atkin 1994), and as already noted, in circumstances where services do not meet carers' standards, then they are likely to be rejected (Motenko 1988; Lewis and Meredith 1989; Braithwaite 1990; Nolan and Grant 1992a). A clear indication of the standards that carers are likely to apply can be discerned from the data here. Therefore carers wish to see that the cared-for person's needs are tended to, that their dignity is maintained and that pleasurable activities are provided in order to ensure their happiness. Unfortunately services often fail to meet these criteria and are seen to inhibit or obstruct carers' efforts with the consequence that they are either accepted reluctantly (and with considerable guilt) or are rejected.

The issue of creating acceptable alternatives is best illustrated by the case of institutional care. A strong motivation for and satisfaction of caring is to keep the cared-for person out of an institution, and community care policies have explicitly reinforced this. Carers see this as important primarily because institutional alternatives are perceived to be unacceptable, not necessarily in principle, but because of the standards of care with which they are associated. Sometimes such an alternative is unavoidable, and the carer can no longer continue to support the cared-for person. In such circumstances greater recognition of the difficulties surrounding entry to care from a carer's perspective is required. If carers have been receiving support at all, this is usually withdrawn following admission of the cared-for person to care. However, it is at just such a time that additional help, particularly of an emotional nature, may be needed. This is developed further in the next chapter. Whilst providing the best care is identified as a source of satisfaction, the role of arbiter of standards can also act as an Achilles' heel in maintaining carers in their role past the point where it is desirable.

Satisfactions of caring: other considerations

An appraisal of the three cells along the bottom of the matrix helps to identify situations where the carer can be perceived as the main beneficiary.

The value of being appreciated either by the cared-for person, significant others, or both has been alluded to a number of times (Lewis and Meredith 1988a,b; Clifford 1990; Nolan and Grant 1992a; Grant and Nolan 1993; Beresford 1994). Indeed Lewis and Meredith (1988a,b) argued that this may be the only source of reward for carers. Although our results belie this, the value of appreciation is still quite apparent. This again has implications for the delivery of services, not simply in terms of their acceptability, but as the basis of intervention in its own right. For instance Twigg and Atkin (1994: 124) have commented: 'What carers wanted was recognition, advice, validation of their worth and a chance to talk, rather than major service inputs.'

Recognition and validation of worth are potentially powerful means of enhancing a carer's sense of competence and of control, which as we demonstrated in the previous chapter are important components of successful coping. The reciprocal nature of satisfactions and stressors is illustrated by the fact that when the cared-for person is both appreciative and does not grumble or moan this can be an important source of satisfaction, yet someone who is unappreciative and does complain is viewed as being particularly difficult to care for (Lewis and Meredith 1988a,b; Nolan and Grant 1992a).

The role and importance of intrapsychic rewards are brought into sharp relief in the centre bottom cell of the matrix. Although these are not cited as frequently as many of the other items, they are wide-ranging and cover a broad spectrum of needs. These vary from fulfilling a sense of duty, through the provision of a challenge, to giving life a purpose and meaning. This latter is the least frequently identified source of satisfaction (25 per cent of the sample) but can hardly be considered as insignificant, either in terms of the number of carers identifying it or with respect to its possible impact. This is perhaps a particularly important consideration at the end of caring; for if caring has provided a purpose in life there is a potentially large void that will need to be filled.

The fact that reciprocity is perceived to exist in intangible forms of exchange is apparent in the mid-centre cell of the matrix, where eight out of ten carers identify hypothetical exchange (the perception that if situations were reversed the cared-for person would care for them) as a major source of satisfaction. Such a perception is most likely in circumstances where there is a well-established relationship between carer and cared-for person, as evidenced in the importance attached to the repaying of past kindnesses. Some years ago when discussing the nature of reciprocity in caring, Bulmer (1987) noted that the idea of a lifetime balance sheet of social care was not an inappropriate one.

Adopting a broadly similar metaphor, Antonucci and Jackson (1989) argue that reciprocity can best be understood within a life-course perspective in which the achievement of reciprocal relationships is central to successful ageing. Building upon Bulmer's (1987) notion of a 'balance sheet', they posit the idea of a 'social support bank' in which individuals monitor their social interactions in a relatively informal, often unconscious manner but keep a balance between what is deposited and what is withdrawn. They state that people who feel they have had reciprocal interpersonal relationships across the life course will cope more adequately with the challenges posed by advancing age. They further add that if individuals feel they have made a contribution to the world in which they live then an enhanced sense of personal competence is likely to emerge.

We suggest that the same probably holds true of caring, and that in circumstances in which a sense of reciprocity is maintained then both carer and cared-for person are likely to achieve a better quality of life. Both will meet and have met important needs at a variety of levels. In this sense, good caring relationships will be characterized by reciprocity and by some evidence of satisfaction for the carer. Conversely, in the absence of reciprocity and satisfactions, caring relationships are more prone to exploitation by one or other party and poor interactions would appear more likely. The significant point about satisfactions in caring is that they are diverse and often diffuse and may comprise contingent possibilities rather than actual, tangible exchanges. This is again consistent with the position of Antonucci and Jackson (1989), who suggest that it is in those relationships which are both long-standing and emotionally close that one finds reciprocity of the 'most general and non-specific manner'. Many, if not most of the sources of satisfaction we have identified fit into such a general and non-specific category. However, although satisfactions are both diverse and prevalent they are not necessarily uniform. Accordingly, we now examine differences in sources and types of satisfaction by gender and relationship.

Variations in caregiving satisfaction

In the previous chapter some of the assumed differences in coping strategies, especially those between men and women, were found not to hold true in our sample. With regard to satisfactions the literature is currently limited, so that there is less in the way of 'received wisdom' to counter. Certainly one can hypothesize about where potential differences by, for example, gender or relationship may lie but there is little current empirical evidence available to draw comparisons. Moreover, it may be as instructive to identify areas in which differences are *not* apparent as it is to seek variation. Therefore as already indicated, it would be reasonable to assume on the basis of the available literature that the 'nurturing' aspects of caring are more likely to be satisfying to women. Yet no such differences were found to exist. Here attention is turned briefly to the variation in sources of satisfaction in our sample. For the sake of brevity only the direction of the difference and its significance will be reported here.

In one of the few studies to comment, Levesque *et al.* (1995) indicate that men report more positive and less negative effects of caregiving than do women. This trend is also discernible in our data, as in all six items for which there were statistically significant differences, men reported more satisfaction than women. For example 73 per cent of men as opposed to 52 per cent of women found appreciation from the cared-for person a source of satisfaction (χ^2 9.01 3df p<.03) and 58 per cent of men as opposed to 41 per cent of women identified the fact that the cared-for person doesn't grumble or moan to be a source of satisfaction (χ^2 10.66 3df p<.01). Interpreting these results in a cross-sectional sample is of course problematic. It may well be that the psyche of men is such that appreciation constitutes a particular source of satisfaction, or it may be that women as cared-for persons are more likely to be appreciative than men. We can readily see how certain interest groups might interpret this finding in differing ways. A similar conundrum is posed when it is observed that men are significantly more likely to see caring as fulfilling a sense of duty (men 76 per cent/women 63 per cent – χ^2 8.93 3df p<.03) but also see caring more as an expression of their love than do women (men 93 per cent/women 86 per cent – χ^2 10.43 3df p<.01). Does this reflect Motenko's (1988) contention that men see fulfilling their marriage vows as a very tangible manifestation of their love or is an alternative explanation more likely? Others have produced findings consistent with those of Motenko, that male carers see the fulfilment of vows not as a duty but as an indication of an enduring and still highly significant relationship:

> What little I am able to do is for the love and the vows I took with my wife, with no sense of duty.

> For better or worse I fully believe in this. We have a very happy and satisfying marriage and I don't think we could live without each other.
>
> (Grant and Nolan 1993: 153)

Male carers in our sample are also more likely to see caring as having strengthened close family ties, and to hold the belief that if the situations were reversed their wives would do the same for them (men 90 per cent/ women 73 per cent – χ^2 13.11 3df p<.005).

Variations in satisfactions depending on whether a spouse is caring for a partner or a child is caring for a parent were more likely to be highly statistically significant than gender differences. In the eight sources of satisfaction where such differences were noted it was spouses in every case who perceived the greater reward. Therefore spouses in our sample were significantly more likely to see caring as satisfying because it:

	p<
enables them to give pleasure to the cared-for person	(.01)
helps them fulfil a sense of duty	(.005)
helps them grow as a person	(.005)
provides appreciation by friends and relatives	(.005)
strengthens close family ties	(.01)
provides a way of testing themselves out	(.0005)
provides a way of showing their faith	(.001)
makes them feel wanted and needed	(.0005)

Whilst differences are apparent by relationship and gender, the key message to emerge from the data is the strong support provided for the existence of caring satisfactions. These findings are consistent with other studies which suggest that at least 80 per cent of carers experience satisfactions (Crookston 1989; Summers *et al.* 1989; Braithwaite 1990; Clifford 1990; Farran *et al.* 1991; Kane and Penrod 1995). What we have been able to add, however, is a clearer indication of the sources and types of satisfaction within an emerging conceptual framework. Given this, what are the implications of the results, particularly for services and interventions for family carers?

The satisfactions of caring: so what?

The foregoing raises a number of interesting theoretical questions, particularly about the role and nature of reciprocity within family caregiving. Clearly, as in 'ordinary' family life, reciprocity does not operate on the simple and tangible exchange of goods and services (Finch and Mason 1993). The process is far more subtle, discrete and implicit, emerging from and being influenced by the nature of past and present relationships. We contend that our data provide further support for the concept of altruism as reciprocity (Abrams 1985) and also to some extent to the notion of a 'social support bank' (Antonucci and Jackson 1989). We would also agree with Antonucci and Jackson that this is a cognitive and subjective process that may not be apparent to others, even those closely involved with the carer. These provide potentially fruitful avenues for further exploration. What emerges most powerfully for us is the importance of the 'little things' in life, those apparently trivial and mundane events that can assume great significance, especially as horizons and opportunities appear to contract. We also have concerns that the sources of satisfactions for carers may be their Achilles' heel, serving to bind them in situations which perhaps should not be sustained. On the whole, however, these concerns are outweighed by the potential for the satisfactions of caring to be used in a number of positive ways to assist carers and cared-for persons achieve a better quality of life.

We have made reference throughout this chapter to some of the implications of caregiver satisfaction for the design and delivery of services. Here we would like to pursue these in more detail, under three main headings:

- satisfactions as a coping resource/therapeutic intervention;
- satisfactions as a quality control measure;
- satisfactions as a 'risk' indicator.

The quotation by Summers *et al.* (1989) which began this chapter suggested that the 'silver lining effect' – the identification of the positive aspects of a situation – may be one of the most powerful cognitive coping strategies of all. If this is the case then there is significant potential for satisfactions to act as a mechanism for improving the caregiving situation. We noted in the previous chapter that in circumstances where a stimulus is perceived as a challenge, rather than as a threat or harm, then it is less likely to be stressful. The same logic can be applied to caregiving, which represents a potentially very stressful encounter. However, there is evidence from our findings that caring allows for the realization of important aspects of self-esteem such as mastery, personal growth, overcoming challenges and feeling a valued and competent person. Where these are manifest, caring may become not a source of stress but rather a source of gratification. In terms of the stresses and burdens of care there is now overwhelming evidence to indicate that it is subjective appraisals and not objective characteristics that are important (Kane and Penrod 1995). Moreover, stress results primarily from problems in interpersonal relationships and certain types of behaviour which threaten them (for example, manipulative, demanding or unappreciative behaviour). Satisfactions represent the other side of the coin and reflect the desire to maintain and gain pleasure from cherished relationships. Such relationships are those that people choose to remain in as opposed to those that they are forced to sustain: 'As an unremarkable but nevertheless important principle, the more caregivers are able to define their role as positive, the less caregivers perceive themselves to be victims caught up by inexorable social forces that deny their autonomy' (Opie 1994: 40).

In all of the above examples, satisfactions may serve as coping resources, as a mechanism to buffer the inevitable difficulties of caring, and as well-springs of hope when all appears despair. However, in any long-term relationship there is a tendency to lose sight of the important but everyday interactions that help shape and define family life. In short, we can take things for granted, and the reason why someone is important to us becomes buried under a mountain of seemingly more pressing events. How much more likely this is to happen in caregiving situations. If satisfactions of caring are protective and functional then there may be a need to help carers and cared-for persons focus on these more effectively.

Following Cartwright *et al.*'s (1994) suggestion that caregiving enrichment should be used as a purposeful attempt to work with carers and cared-for persons to identify meaningful events and seek to maintain them or replace them with valued alternatives, it is our belief that CASI can be used for a similar purpose. During interviews the instrument helped many carers to reappraise their situation and begin to see caring in a different, more positive light. We are aware of at least one context in which it is being used as part of a counselling intervention with carers and is proving useful in this regard (Gilleard, J. personal communication). Therefore in addition to being used as an assessment tool in the traditional sense, CASI appears to have potential for more creative use. We think it may have a specific application at the end of caring in the community when the cared-for person is admitted to care. This is known to cause carers considerable guilt. Hence using CASI to review their period of care may well be therapeutic, helping them to develop a more positive impression of their efforts. Langer (1993) suggests that 'retelling' the caring experience, particularly the reasons why individuals became carers can be a powerful coping strategy. She believes that it helps carers to validate what they do and to renew a sense of purpose and competence.

Satisfactions may also be used as an important aspect of quality control when designing and delivering services to carers and cared-for persons. We have already suggested that services can be viewed along a continuum ranging from facilitative to obstructive, dependent upon the degree to which they are consistent with the mode of care being provided by the carer. Those sources of satisfaction of benefit to the cared-for person provide an indication of the importance carers attach to seeing that their needs are well tended to, that their dignity is maintained and that they have a good quality of life. Although services would putatively fulfil similar aims, it seems that the means to achieving these outcomes are perceived differently by family and professional carers. For a start, carers often find it difficult to ask for help even when they may need it (Lewis and Meredith 1989). What is provided is often inappropriate or unsympathetic (Lewis and Meredith 1989). As Taraborrelli (1993) notes, carers find it difficult to accept help unless they believe that those providing services know as much about the cared-for person as do the family carers, a point made some five years earlier (Motenko 1988).

There is also the danger that carers may take too much of an individualistic perspective, leading them to believe that no one else could ever provide the quality of care they do (Lea 1994). In these circumstances professional carers need to bring a wide range of knowledge and perspectives to bear in assisting carers to accept help (Hughes 1993). One of the main barriers to closer working between professionals and carers is the pathological perspective utilized by professionals whose interventions are usually intended to 'fix' the problem (Summers *et al.* 1989; Clarke 1995). Montgomery (1995) has argued, with respect to respite care, that two basic criteria must be met before carers will utilize a service: they must feel that they need help; and the service available must be the one they want. We would add a third and possibly more important criterion: the service available must be perceived to be of acceptable quality. Carers often seek to check on professional knowledge and understanding of the cared-for person's needs, such as seeing whether they know about their favourite foods or pastimes (Bowers 1988; Nolan and Grant 1992a). Working with carers and cared-for persons to identify these sorts of criteria would add another more relevant and sensitive dimension to quality assurance.

Another area in which attention to satisfactions is potentially useful relates to the assessment of risk. We believe this can occur in two broad areas: risk of poor emotional health of the carer, and risk of fragile and potentially abusive caregiving situations. It has been suggested for some time that carers who find positive aspects to their role are likely to experience better morale and well-being (Gilhooly 1984; Motenko 1989); Given and Given (1991) argue that the presence of caregiving satisfactions provides a significant predictor of less stressful situations. In this regard we think that the balance between 'uplifts and hassles' provides a better assessment of the caregiving situation than do either alone (Kinney and Stephens 1989). Therefore in situations of high mutuality, carers appear to cope well, even in the presence of objectively adverse circumstances (Hirschfield 1981, 1983; Archbold *et al.* 1992, 1995). Conversely the absence of mutuality signals poor caregiving circumstances, even if objectively the situation appears to be unproblematic. Lewis and Meredith (1989) believe that the potentially most fraught caring circumstances are those in which there is no positive feedback, and it seems that those carers who can identify no positive aspects to their role are likely to be near breaking point (Clifford 1990). On this basis it has been suggested that there is a need to target carers who get no satisfaction (Walker *et al.* 1990; Archbold *et al.* 1992), and either provide additional support or seek alternative caregiving arrangements – low mutuality should be 'taken very seriously' (Archbold *et al.* 1992). Mutuality might be assessed at various points in caregiving but is particularly important when entry to the caring role is made at a time of crisis, when efforts should be made to gauge the quality of past and present relationships. In circumstances where poor relationships exist, caution must be exercised before assuming that a caregiving relationship should be initiated. In an established caregiving relationship, the total absence of satisfactions suggests that close attention is paid to the advisability of sustaining care. We noted in the last chapter that the non-attribution of blame is seen by carers as the most useful coping strategy of all. We would suggest here that a blaming culture allied with the absence of satisfaction may well be a potent indicator of 'at risk' caregiving relationships.

In this chapter we have explored the satisfactions of caring and found them to be diverse, pervasive and subtle. It has also been suggested that satisfaction provides a fruitful avenue for further conceptual and theoretical development. However, just as importantly we believe that satisfactions provide a number of important therapeutic interventions. We recognize the difficult and often stressful nature of caring and that for some individuals it provides an intolerable burden. There are others, however, for whom caring is also a source of considerable pride, joy and satisfaction, indeed life's purpose. For the majority of family carers we would suggest that caring falls some-where between these two extremes and is at times difficult and stressful, and at others provides satisfaction and a sense of achievement. Learning how we can help carers minimize the former whilst maximizing the latter is likely to provide the key to more successful interventions.

5

FAMILY CAREGIVING:
A TEMPORAL PERSPECTIVE

[C]aregiving is clearly a dynamic process characterised by changing
caregiver and care recipient needs. In any event, much is yet to be
learned about the caregiving process, and such research may lead
to improved interventions.

(Greene and Coleman 1995: 59)

One of the major deficits in the caregiving literature has been a failure fully
to explore the temporal and longitudinal aspects. Such a failure is attributable to both methodological and theoretical limitations. Methodologically
the complexity and expense of conducting longitudinal studies have resulted
in a focus on cross-sectional samples. This has been exacerbated by a pre-
dominance of statistically orientated approaches generating the large samples needed to apply multivariate techniques. Such techniques are necessary
to test the deterministic assumptions underlying the theoretical orientation
of many researchers.

Virtually all we know about family caregiving has emerged in the last
15 years (Brody 1995), and despite the considerable research effort during
this period, Kahana and Young (1990) note that conceptual limitations are
increasingly apparent. The lack of a temporal and longitudinal model is one
such limitation that has been alluded to by a number of authors (Stoller and
Pugliesi 1989; Given and Given 1991; Miller and McFall 1992; Taraborrelli
1993; Thompson *et al.* 1993; McLaughlin and Ritchie 1994; Opie 1994),
signalling the need to develop a better understanding of how caregiving
changes over time. The purpose of this chapter is to outline a longitudinal
model of caregiving based on a study of dementia caregivers (Keady and
Nolan 1993a,b, 1995a) and to consider its potential application to individuals caring for people with differing needs and circumstances. Particular
attention is paid to the implications of the model for the design and delivery
of interventions intended to support family carers. It is argued that services
should be 'stage specific', tailored to need at varying times in the caring

trajectory (Given and Given 1991), for although each caregiving situation is unique, we consider that there are broad stages which help predict the occurrence of certain types of demand. In describing these broad stages we will indicate sources of potential variation dependent upon, for example, the type of illness or disability that occasioned the need for care. The chapter begins with a brief overview of some of the existing temporal models of the caregiving process.

Models of family care: longitudinal considerations

A number of the studies we have already referred to in some detail (Bowers 1987, 1988; Lewis and Meredith 1988a,b, 1989) have adopted what might broadly be termed a temporal or longitudinal perspective. However, it is within the field of dementia caregiving that the most sophisticated and elegant models have emerged. Although all of these studies have used a largely cross-sectional design they nevertheless provide useful insights into the processes that help shape and determine care in dementia.

The study by Wilson (1989a,b) represents a major influence and merits some detailed consideration. Wilson uses a grounded theory approach to study 20 carers' experience of people with dementia, and describes an eight-stage model (Wilson 1989a). These stages are summarized in Table 5.1.

At the end of her study, Wilson (1989a) acknowledged that she had provided only a 'beginning knowledge' about the temporal experience of family caregiving. Later (Wilson 1989b) she elaborated more fully on the three stages of 'taking it on'; 'going through it' and 'turning it over', which she characterized by the term 'surviving on the brink'. A range of coping strategies were described which differed according to the stage of the caregiving trajectory. The main premise underpinning Wilson's conceptualization is the belief that all choices in dementia caregiving are essentially negative, and strategies are devised to minimize negative impacts. Although this is clearly at variance with other contemporary studies of dementia which focused on the positive aspects (Motenko 1989), Wilson's work is useful as it draws attention not only to the varying stages of caring in dementia but also illustrates the stage-specific coping approaches that are evoked. She argues that it will not be possible to design appropriate interventions until there is a better understanding of the carer's rationale for the coping strategies they adopt.

Willoughby and Keating (1991), in a slightly later study, start from a similar premise, arguing that little previous work has considered the stages or processes of care. They identify in particular a dearth of knowledge about how carers progress through and manage the various transitions that are required. In their conceptualization the process of *taking on* and *relinquishing control* are the key elements. They suggest a five-stage model, the first of which is *emerging recognition*. Consistent with Wilson's (1989a,b) work,

Table 5.1   Stages in dementia caregiving (after Wilson 1989a)

Noticing	Gradual awareness of unusual or aberrant behaviour on the part of the person with early dementia. The stage is only recognized in retrospect.
Discounting/normalizing	Rational explanations for the behavioural changes are sought, e.g. acute illness or old age. This stage lasts until discounting is no longer possible.
Suspecting	Realization that something more serious is involved.
Search for explanations	This eventually leads to the reluctant search for an 'official' diagnosis.
Recounting	Once a diagnosis has been made there is a retrospective reappraisal of behaviour and events to date.
Taking it on	Decisions about future care options are now required, but are often made without sufficient information or awareness of the likely implications of assuming a caring role.
Going through it	The stage of caring for an increasingly frail and dependent person. The skills required are often learned on a trial-and-error basis.
Turning it over	A gradual realization that the carer's own physical and mental health is suffering and that other care options are needed. Even after admission to care, carers usually continue to play an active, albeit, different role.

Willoughby and Keating (1991) describe the gradual way that unusual or odd behaviour is noticed by the family member. The significance of this behaviour is denied initially until there is a gradual acknowledgement that something is wrong. During the second stage, carers seek to gain control by finding out as much information as possible. They often use proactive responses to maintain the dignity of the person they are caring for, for example by limiting interactions to activities in which they are competent. The similarities between this and Bowers's (1987) protective caring are obvious, as is the potentially paternalistic effect. As the disease progresses, carers rely increasingly on support from more formal sources and begin to consider admission to care. Once this decision has been made, carers need time to adjust to the admission and help to relinquish control of care to others (stage 4). Finally there is a process of *letting go* of caring, moving on and reclaiming a new life. Perhaps because Willoughby and Keating (1991) were primarily concerned with the admission process and its importance, their model provides a less comprehensive coverage of the middle phases of caring than Wilson's (1989a,b). Nevertheless it is complementary in reasserting the need for differing interventions which take account of stages of the disease process. On the basis of their study the authors suggest that more attention should be given to 'closure' (the term they adopt for admission to care), and that professional interventions at this time are particularly important. As we will highlight later, there is evidence that carers often do not get the level of support they would like during this period (Nolan *et al.* 1996).

Both of the above models pay little attention to the potentially rewarding aspects of caring, a trend not so apparent in the work of Wuest *et al.* (1994). They describe the process of 'becoming strangers', which they assert is characteristic of interactions between carers and people with dementia. They conceptualize this as comprising three major dimensions: dawning; holding on; letting go. These dimensions are mediated by the level of commitment between the carer and the person with dementia, the insidious nature of loss in dementia and the type and level of support received. In contrast to the models previously described, Wuest and co-authors accord the person with dementia a much more active role, particularly in the 'dawning' phase. It is here that both individuals begin to appreciate that something is amiss, and in so doing, three types of interaction occur:

- explaining – trying to find meaning for unusual behaviour;
- covering – both parties conspire to try and keep things normal;
- confirming – behavioural changes become more prominent and can no longer be explained or covered up.

Once both parties can no longer sustain a perception that things are normal, then the stage of holding on is entered. The primary purpose here is to maintain relationships and mutual quality of life for as long as possible. As with Willoughby and Keating's model (1991) the first strategy is to try and gain control; this may involve a number of tactics such as establishing routines, planning, gaining knowledge and 'self-talk', which allow for a more rapid and proactive response. This, however, cannot be sustained indefinitely; as caring continues there is a 'draining of resources' experienced by the carer. This gradual process of attrition results in the emergence of the third stage, that of 'letting go'. Here the carer reaches the painful decision that a place in an institution will probably be needed. This results in an often slow process of separation, although the final decision to seek alternative care is usually triggered by a specific event. Wuest *et al.* (1994) see the above process as a continuum which moves the carer and person with dementia from intimacy to strangers.

In marked contrast to the above models, the one proposed by Kobayashi *et al.* (1993), whilst also adopting a temporal perspective, pays far greater attention to the maintenance of closeness and warmth throughout the process of caregiving for a family member with dementia. They argue that many carers find fulfilment in their role which allows them to develop understanding, consideration and affection. This model comprises a seven-stage transition during which a range of emotions are experienced. During the early stages, carers often see odd behaviour as deliberate, leading to a confrontational situation. However, once dementia is recognized then the behaviour is understood in that context and confrontation subsides, but carers still retain the hope that things may return to normal. Eventually, however, they become resigned to the disease and adopt a 'hands off' approach. However, as the disease progresses and communication has to rely increasingly on non-verbal means, then Kobayashi and co-authors suggest that carers develop expertise in communicating with the person with dementia. As a consequence they feel empathy and recognize personal qualities in the cared-for person that transcend dementia. This is termed 'awakening'. The authors argue that intervention in the early stages may assist carers to reach the 'awakening' phase more rapidly. This model is also interesting as it was developed in a Japanese context and reflects certain cultural traditions. Nevertheless, there are clear conceptual similarities to many of the studies cited throughout this book, for example in carers finding satisfaction and gaining expertise.

Rather than focusing on the sequential nature of caregiving in dementia, other studies have attempted to describe more fully the coping strategies deployed by carers (Bowers 1987, 1988; Harvath 1994; Clarke 1995). Having considered Bowers's work in some detail already, attention is given here to other studies. Using a grounded theory method with a sample of ten female caregivers aged 51–80, Harvath (1994) explores the perceptions and interpretations of dementia-related problem behaviours and the strategies used by caregivers to manage such situations. Carers tend to use a trial-and-error approach to managing problem behaviours. Perceived stress is mediated by whether events are viewed as a threat or not, with carers reporting the use of cognitive strategies to decrease their level of anxiety. Clarke (1995) also utilizes grounded theory, but in addition to interviewing family carers she also collected data from professionals. She suggests that carers continually strive to redefine their domestic situation as normal in order to allow life to continue 'in a relatively problem free manner' (p. 144). This, Clarke contends, is achieved by seeking to normalize events by employing three strategies: pacing; confiding; rationalizing. These are described briefly below:

Pacing – the aim of this strategy is to allow the carer to 'hang on' for as long as possible. Pacing involves the utilization of services such as day or respite care, which are acceptable providing they do not threaten the perception of normality that is being created. Pacing also includes the management of emotional involvement with the person with dementia.
Confiding – a confidante is utilized to allow carers to put their difficulties into perspective and see these as being potentially surmountable. The confidante is rarely a professional carer but usually a close family member or friend.

Rationalizing – this strategy is employed by family carers to make sense of the situation in various ways, such as relating their present relationship to past experiences with the cared-for person.

Although there is considerable variation in the terminologies used in the above models, they are characterized more by what they have in common than by how they differ. They all highlight the gradual way in which dementia develops and how family members seek to normalize and discount behaviours. This can lead to tension in relationships in the early stages. There then follows a search for explanations or understanding via official diagnoses and confirmation that something is wrong. Once they have 'taken on' caring, efforts are focused on trying to hold on and maintain control for as long as possible. The process of 'turning it over' or 'letting it go' is seen as particularly difficult, and there is a perceived need for additional support at this time. The models differ in the extent to which carers may gain satisfaction from their role, but each is consistent in the assertion that if services are to be effective then far greater attention must be paid to both the carer's perspective and the stage of the caregiving process.

Conspicuous by its absence in the above studies is any concerted attempt to gain the perspective of the person with dementia. This is understandable up to a point due to the insidious nature of dementia and the fact that by the time many studies have commenced the disease is too far progressed to gain a true insight. However, a temporal account of the progress of dementia from the perspective of the sufferer has been outlined (Keady and Nolan 1994a, 1995b,c) and is seen to consist of nine distinct, but often overlapping phases: slipping; suspecting; covering up; revealing; confirming; maximizing; disorganization; decline; death. A recent study which involved interviews with 11 people with early dementia (Keady and Nolan 1995a,b) indicated that such individuals adopt a far more proactive response than has previously been described and have a range of coping strategies aimed at maintaining normality. One of their main strategies is to keep their failing abilities a secret for as long as possible. This often leads to conflict with their carer, who suspects something is wrong and seeks explanations. In some situations, however, a process of tacit collusion is sometimes initiated where both parties pretend to ignore the increasingly obvious 'slips' that are occurring.

The data generated from this study revealed a number of dynamic, subtle and often latent interactions that occurred during the early phases of dementia. In retrospect many of the interviewees and their carers wished that they had been open with each other at an earlier stage as this would have allowed them to make better use of the time available when meaningful interactions could occur. Although small scale, the study highlights the importance of considering the dyadic nature of caring relationships within a temporal perspective.

Transitions in care: developing stage-specific interventions

The argument we are advancing here is that interventions with family carers will not be effective until they are tailored to the stage of caregiving history. It is our belief that key transition points can be identified and that these serve as markers for the type of help and support that will be most useful at a given point in time. We base this contention on a six-stage model of the caring process developed following in-depth interviews with 58 carers of people with dementia (Keady and Nolan 1993a,b, 1994b, 1995a,b,c). Although the sample used was cross-sectional, interviewees were purposively sampled to include carers new to their role, experienced carers who had been providing care for a number of years, and those who had either recently placed a cared-for person in some form of alternative care or where the cared-for person had died.

The six stages of the model have been termed (Keady and Nolan 1994b):

- building on the past
- recognizing the need
- taking it on
- working through it
- reaching the end
- a new beginning

We elaborate each of these stages using illustrations from previously unpublished data to identify a number of key characteristics. Whilst developed from a sample of dementia carers, it is our belief that the model can be applied to other caring situations, albeit with variations depending upon the context. We will, at appropriate points in the text, illustrate some of the potential variations that might be anticipated in different caregiving circumstances.

Essentially two broad sets of processes are relevant throughout each of the stages, and these reflect the transactional nature of caring and the development of caregiver expertise over time. We term these 'common processes'. Those characteristics that are unique to each stage we term 'stage-specific processes'.

In order to highlight the transactional nature of caring, we have developed the A to E of caring. This captures the common elements occurring in each of the six above stages:

Acknowledging the challenge – here the carer recognizes that a situation has arisen that requires a response and determines whether this poses a threat, harm or challenge. This equates with the primary appraisal within stress theory. This is followed by:

Balancing the books – where the carer considers the range of resources that they have at their disposal, which allows them to:
Clarify the alternatives – when a range of possible courses of action are identified so that carers can:
Decide what to do.
Together these processes would constitute the secondary appraisal in the transactional model of stress and coping. After taking action the carer then:
Evaluates the consequences – or reappraises the effectiveness of what they have done.

As individuals progress through their caring history it is also our belief that they gain varying degrees of expertise, much along the lines described by Benner (1984) and Eraut (1994) as relating to professional carers. Eraut (1995), in tracing theories of professional expertise, considers that a revolution has occurred in the last 30 years. This has seen a shift away from the belief that professionals rely largely on propositional (theoretical) knowledge to inform their practice towards a realization that much of what they do emerges from their experience. In relation to work with carers, others have argued that due to a lack of a 'tradition of practice', i.e. experience in this area, professionals rely on the culture of the office and their own assumptive worlds (Twigg and Atkin 1994). We think that this denotes a lack of sufficient 'expertise' in this area of work.

One of the most comprehensive theories of how professionals may develop expertise from experience is that advanced by Hubert and Stuart Dreyfus (1986). They describe a five-stage process which forms a continuum ranging from novice (high reliance on rules and plans with little ability to make discretionary judgements) through advanced beginner (where individuals can appreciate discrete 'aspects' of a situation although they cannot prioritize which 'aspect' is the most pressing) to competent (the ability to see longer-term goals and make conscious plans), proficient (the ability to see situations holistically and to identify the most important aspect readily), eventually to expertise (where there is an intuitive grasp of a situation based on a tacit understanding of important aspects). The expert only uses conscious decision-making in new or novel situations. In commenting on this model Eraut (1994) highlights how the acquisition of expertise is dependent, not upon theoretical knowledge, but upon experience. He describes the latter stages of the process in the following:

> The pathway to competence is characterised mainly by the ability to recognise features of practical situations and to discriminate between them, to carry out routine procedures under pressure and to plan ahead . . . whereas proficiency marks the onset of quite a different approach to the job: normal behaviour is not just routine but semi-automatic; situations are apprehended more deeply and the abnormal is quickly spotted and given attention . . . Progression from proficiency to expertise finally happens when the decision-making as well as situational understanding

becomes instinctive rather than analytic; and this requires significantly more experience.

(Eraut 1994: 125–6)

Our data strongly suggest that carers go through an almost identical process, albeit starting from a different vantage point. Therefore professional 'expertise' usually begins with a period of formal training in which the rules (theoretical constructs) and basic competencies (practical skills) are introduced. However, it is not until these are practised and refined in the 'real world' that genuine expertise can begin to develop. To take an everyday example, you don't learn to drive until after you have passed your driving test. New carers, on the other hand, usually don't have the luxury of any 'formal' training and are lucky to get even basic information or advice (Nolan and Grant 1992b). Consequently they develop their skills largely by a process of trial and error (Stewart *et al.* 1993; Harvath 1994), potentially prolonging the novice and advanced beginner stages. Yet as the data we have already cited in Chapters 3 and 4 testify, experienced carers most definitely perceive themselves as experts. Earlier we used a quotation from a mother caring for her daughter with learning difficulties to illustrate how for several years she was in the dark about the extent of her daughter's difficulties. During this period she and her husband struggled to know what to do and how best to provide the care their daughter needed. Later in the same interview she described how her own expertise had developed over time. Here she illustrates how her intimate knowledge of her daughter allows her to select the most appropriate way of dealing with difficult and disruptive behaviour, termed 'eppies' (for episodes) within the family. She outlines a number of strategies dependent upon the context:

> It all depends. She hates being ignored, she hates to be left on her own, she hates to be isolated. So if I think one day that might work then that's what I do. I take her into her bedroom and say: 'Right, if you want to carry on you carry on on your own, I'm going and I'm going to do something else', which she hates, she absolutely loathes that. And another time, if I see that she's in distress, perhaps she's got a pain in her back or something, because she's had an operation to cure scoliosis and sometimes her back really aches, so if I think it's because of a physical problem, then I sit with her and I try and talk through it or whatever. We put a video on or we'll put the music on and we'll sing and she plays with her maracas, you know. But I can judge her pretty well. I can usually tell if it's physical or if it's just temper and bloody-mindedness, you know, and then you tailor the situation and you try and cut it and make sure that you've chosen the right option.

Similarly, in recounting how she had developed the physical skills of caring she describes how she manages to lift her daughter, who is now 21 and quite heavy:

Yes, it's something that I've developed over the years. I've always done it so I've done it in the way that suits me best. I've been able to . . . I mean I can pick her up even now and I flip her over on to the bed and get her toileted and whatever in two minutes and I can do all those different movements because I'm so used to the actual way that I lift her. Perhaps if a person of a more professional standing came and said: 'You're doing this the wrong way' and they showed me to do it another way, I wouldn't be able to do it at all. So I have to do it my way and I have to do it, otherwise I wouldn't be able to cope.

In an earlier interview the same mother illustrated how she was able to 'anticipate' needs in advance of them occurring, thereby avoiding increased work and disruption:

And I mean I know, I can sense it coming, and I know before, half an hour before she says anything what she wants. She's got the kind of handicap that you've got to be able to anticipate everything. I mean it's no good me going there ten minutes after it's happened. You know I can tell. If she's not asking anybody to go . . . if she wants to go to the toilet I can tell straight away what she wants just by the tiniest little movement. So it's easier for me. So I've always done it. My mother goes mad but I've always done it. I say 'Mam, by the time I get somebody else to do it I've done it.' People say, you should have a Family Aide in the mornings. But if they were here and they see the kind of aggro you can get – and she would be worse if she knew I was here and somebody else was doing it, I would have to go in eventually anyway – so I think, no, it's easier for me to do it myself, and it's less hassle, it's done twice as quick.

In our view these quotations well illustrate all the hallmarks of expertise as defined by Dreyfus and Dreyfus (1986) and Benner (1984). This mother's expertise is built upon long experience, it is intuitive, based on tacit understanding and it allows a more holistic view of caring possibilities.

Having outlined the core concepts of transactional processes and expertise that underpin our temporal model of caring, we now attempt to relate these to specific stages and consider their implications for the design and delivery of services for carers.

Building on the past

Strictly speaking it could be argued that this is not a stage of caregiving at all. Its name alone marks it as an antecedent event. However, we feel that it can legitimately be identified as an integral component of the caregiving process and, moreover, that it is of importance before, during and after caring. Twigg and Atkin (1994) suggest that caring occurs in the context of a relationship and, as most of the demographic data indicate (Green 1988,

Evandrou 1993), the relationship is usually close and familial. Therefore to understand caring requires a consideration of the nature and quality of past interactions. This is relevant in all caregiving situations, although the emphasis will vary. For example, the birth of a handicapped child might suggest that there is no past upon which to build. However, the nature of previous relationships between the parents and other siblings may be important considerations. In circumstances where caring relationships are formed between spouses or child and parent, it has been recognized for some time that the quality of past interactions are influential factors shaping present support (Quereshi 1986; Motenko 1989; Nolan and Grant 1992a). It is therefore axiomatic that caring 'builds on the past'; as we will illustrate shortly, this is crucial to the carer's perception of their role.

However, as well as being central to an understanding of the antecedents of care, building on the past also plays a critical role throughout the natural history of caring relationships. In some situations the past increases in significance and the future consists of diminishing horizons. For example, at the start of a caring relationship a mother and daughter may have a 50-year 'biography'; but after five years of caring the biography has extended to 55 years, the five most recent of which are in a carer–cared-for situation. These five years will undoubtedly have influenced the perception of the previous 50 years and may have overshadowed them altogether. For in some circumstances, caring can reaffirm and strengthen relationships whilst in others a previously good relationship may have become spoiled in some way. The latter is more likely to be associated with higher levels of carer burden and stress (Motenko 1989; Nolan and Grant 1992a). The balance is different, however, when parents are caring for handicapped or disabled children because the focus is much more future-orientated, but the past will still exert a significant influence. In a very real sense therefore 'building on the past' is both an antecedent to care and an integral part of it, and the longer the caring relationship is sustained the more integral it becomes. The role this plays is more fully elucidated in the following stages of care.

Recognizing the need

Recognizing the need refers to the process by which carers become aware of their changing relationship with the cared-for person. The description of this process that follows relates primarily to spousal or child–parent caring relationships because data collected from these groups informed the development of our model. This stage is just as relevant, however, in parent–child relationships. For instance in circumstances where an amniocentesis has indicated a Down's foetus but the parents decide to continue with the pregnancy, recognizing the need begins before the birth of the child. Similarly the manner in which parents are informed of the birth of a handicapped or disabled child and the support (or lack of it) that they receive at this time can have a profound effect on their future lives. In the example we cited earlier the parents were left for several years without adequate information and support so that recognizing the need was a constantly shifting process. Alternatively parents may be told of the extent of handicap or disability but inadequately supported subsequently. This too has deleterious consequences (see Cunningham and Jupp 1991 for a review). For our purposes, however, we elaborate upon the stage of 'recognizing the need' in spousal or child–parent relationships.

In terms of the typology of caring that we outlined earlier, it was noted that anticipatory care may take place several years before instrumental care is ever needed (Conway-Turner and Karasik 1993). Carers may begin to perceive a changing relationship at this time. However, recognizing the need is more likely to begin when preventive care is required and will become increasingly evident as supervisory care intervenes. However, as anticipatory care, preventive care and supervisory care occur in most relationships, recognizing the need is usually a gradual and cumulative process. It is at the interface between supervisory care and instrumental care that this recognition becomes prominent. In some instances recognizing the need will occur very rapidly whereas in others it will be far more gradual.

We can draw parallels here with the work of Lewis and Meredith (1988a,b, 1989) who describe a period of semi-care and part-time full care as preceding care proper. They conclude that most of the daughters in their study drifted into the caring role, rather than being thrust into it. This is often the case, especially in situations where increased dependency is an insidious process. Work in dementia illustrates this point well.

Keady and Nolan (1994a), building on the work previously cited and following a number of detailed interviews with carers of people with dementia, describe a series of intricate and subtle processes that accompany recognizing the need.

This begins with the process of *noticing*, when some behaviour of the cared-for person catches the carer's attention. This is usually a day-to-day, taken-for-granted act which for some reason is no longer performed adequately, for example, driving. Initially carers would seek to *normalize* this by searching for logical explanations, for example a temporary illness or having left glasses at home. This is necessary to create an image that everything is OK – a perception that things are still normal. Depending upon how aberrent or frequent such behaviour is, this stage may go on for some time. Eventually, however, a perception of normality can no longer be sustained and carers begin to *suspect* that something more serious is amiss – a cognitive shift occurs from 'things are OK' to 'this might be serious'. This is then accompanied by a more active search for explanations. This differs from the rather passive 'normalizing' in that now deliberate and conscious efforts are made to obtain evidence that allows a return to the perception that 'things are OK'. This might involve checking suspicions with other family members or occasionally addressing the issue directly with the cared-for person. Unfortunately this later tactic sometimes meets with a hostile reception from the cared-for person who is trying to cover things up. When this occurs, fears and anxieties are often submerged for a further period, as with this daughter caring for her mother with Alzheimer's disease:

> I tried to tell my mother about what she was doing and ask her if she recognized it, but she didn't want to know. I thought I had done all the right things, you know, planned what I was going to say and I waited until there was no one else in the house. She seemed happy enough at first but I couldn't get through to her. She just stopped me stone dead and said there was nothing wrong with her . . . (pause) but I knew there was.

In the face of this sort of defensive reaction both parties are reluctant to discuss the issue again; in these circumstances carers frequently keep an ever vigilant watch on the cared-for person until they are convinced that something is probably very wrong: 'I knew it was serious when he stopped going out. He always went out on a Friday night for a drink with his friends. Had done since we were married over 40 years ago.'

At this point some carers seek *confirmation* of their increasing suspicions, usually from the GP. Unfortunately in many cases the response they receive is off-hand, even dismissive; this often means that the carer returns to their situation until further more serious deterioration occurred.

> I went to the doctor because my wife was doing things that I just did not understand. I knew she was ill but nobody would believe me – she couldn't go with me, you see, and they had to go on what I said. All the doctor said to me was 'Come back again in six months if things have not improved'. Some help that was.
>
> (Male spouse carer, aged 54)

> When mum started to leave the gas on that was it. I went to see my doctor and he promised to look into it. He never did. I had to take her to casualty in the end to get someone to see her. Mind you that was three years later.
>
> (Adult child carer, male, aged 49)

This is by no means an uncommon event and has been likened to 'banging my head against a brick wall' (Keady and Nolan 1995a). Understandably this initial reaction inhibits further contact with formal services, often for a substantial period of time. During the interviews both carers and people with dementia voiced their anger at this, as it was considered to have 'robbed' them of valuable time when cognitive abilities were still relatively intact. Such a 'diagnostic quest' has been identified as one of the crucial periods both for people with chronic illness and their carers (Corbin and Strauss 1988, 1992). The more prolonged the 'diagnostic limbo' between suspicion and confirmation of the disease, the greater the stress. It is not until a diagnosis has been provided that 'recognizing the need' ends and the next stage of caring 'taking it on' begins, for as Taraborrelli (1993) suggests, the official diagnosis is often a turning point in caregiving relationships. In certain situations the diagnostic limbo can be extremely lengthy, even indefinite, heightening both the ambiguity and unpredictability of caring, making it even more stressful.

In other sets of circumstances, however, the process of 'recognizing the need' occurs instantly, overnight. Such is the case with a stroke. The sudden catastrophic nature of a stroke allows no time for preparation and very little time for anticipation. In contrast to a prolonged period of recognizing the need in dementia or certain diseases of childhood, the carer in this later situation has to 'take it on' with little or no advanced warning.

Taking it on

We consider that recognizing the need ends when there is a realization by the carer (and the cared-for person in many cases) of a fundamental change in their relationship. It is here that there is a cognitive shift towards the more formally recognized role of carer. The stage of 'taking it on' is a period, often brief, of decision-making – the carer is confronted by a series of questions and decisions such as: Is this for me? Can I do it? What will it mean? Should I 'take it on'? Three broad sets of responses are possible to this important latter question: Yes I'll take it on; Yes I ought to take it on, or No, I won't/can't take it on.

Many carers do not of course even think in such terms, as caring represents the continuance of a valued relationship and there is no decision to make. Others, if they do contemplate such questions, do so covertly with little advice or support. Only in the minority of cases does full and frank discussion occur.

Little previous attention has been given to the way in which carers adopt or 'take on' their role (Given and Given 1991; Nolan and Grant 1992b; Stewart *et al.* 1993), yet this is often a critical period. For example, those carers who feel that they have been able to exercise a genuine choice of whether to become a carer or not report less subsequent burden (Nolan and Grant 1992a). Opie (1994) strongly advocates that all carers, no matter how willing they are to adopt the role, should be encouraged to explore fully the implications of their decision. This is especially true for children who should consider their reasons for caring, if future ethical dilemmas are to be minimized (Selig *et al.* 1991). Yet frequently true choice is all but absent because assumptions are made about the willingness and ability of family members to take responsibility for care. The quality of previous relationships (building on the past) are critical at this stage, and caution is needed where there has always been a poor relationship, or previously good relationships have been spoiled (Phillips and Rempusheski 1986; Nolan 1993). In such circumstances it may be advisable to consider other arrangements.

Even in situations where carers have drifted into their role some people, when faced with the realization that things will not improve, may be reluctant to 'take it on', as in this case of a wife caring for her husband with early Alzheimer's disease:

> Our relationship has always been bad, no, worse than that, dreadful. I mean he was away all the time and even when he came home he acted as if he never wanted to be here. I began to dread him coming home and I only put up with it for the sake of the children. They kept us together. You see I got used to leading my own life and since this started (the dementia) he's around the house all the time relying on me for things, like finding out the times of the bus or demanding to know where I've hidden his car keys. Well I just don't want to do anything for him but he is ill, forgetful and that. Everyone would expect me to be there for him but he was never there for me. I feel so trapped and on my own.

Alternatively when previous relationships have been good there is no such reticence and there is a willingness, indeed often a strong desire, to take on the caring role, as this 82-year-old man, caring for his wife with Alzheimer's disease, attests:

> We've been married over 60 years. I took her on for life and we made vows to each other. That means everything to me and no one is going to take her away from me. I would have to be dead first. I'll put up with all this because I love her and she's my wife. I take everything day by day and I thank God for every day we are alive. As long as I get someone to help me with a bath for her, I don't need anything else. Ever.

In certain circumstances, tensions between professionals and family carers become apparent during the 'taking it on' stage, especially where the carer wishes to take a relative home and is advised not to, or doubts are expressed by the carer when the professional perceives there to be no real problem. These tensions often arise and are exacerbated by the view of caring that professionals hold. Therefore in cases of high physical dependency, potential carers may be advised not to take a relative home even when they wish to do so. This can evoke a variety of responses. Some carers appreciate being given the option but elect to take their relative home anyway. Others consider that professionals, and doctors in particular, are overstepping the mark and interfering in decisions that are not their's to make: 'This consultant chap told me that I couldn't take her [his wife] home and that I'd have to put her in a nursing home. I said who the bloody hell do you think you are? I've been married to her for 44 years and you're not going to tell me where's the best place for her.'

Fundamentally, the most crucial aspect of 'taking it on' is therefore the nature of the decision-making process; we would agree with Opie (1994) that all carers should actively be encouraged to explore their decision and the implications of it. In circumstances where there has been a poor previous relationship or carers voice doubts about their abilities, then questions must be asked about the advisability of initiating a caring situation. For those carers who are willing to 'take it on', reasonable boundaries and expectations should be established including setting limits on care (Bell *et al.* 1987; Pratt *et al.* 1987; Fotrell 1988; Bell and Gibbons 1989; Beach 1993; Nolan *et al.* 1994).

Elsewhere (Nolan *et al.* 1994) the tenets of an informed choice have been described in the following way:

- Sufficient information on the illness/disease, its progress and treatment, should be available for carers to be able to form a realistic picture of the likely future, even if this is only to know that it is uncertain.
- On the basis of this information, carers will have a better idea of what is likely to happen. They should also be informed of what they can expect to receive in the way of support and services.
- There should be a full exploration of what it is reasonable to achieve in terms of caring. Discussion of the fact that there may well be times of emotional turmoil, anger and frustration, and that these are normal re-actions, is useful. Furthermore, achievable standards for caring should be considered. Many carers set their own standards too high, leading to potential disappointment and failure.
- The limits and burdens of care should be discussed, as should carers' rights to some time to themselves. Even at this early stage, it is appropriate to discuss situations in which alternatives to home care might be considered and what the alternatives are. Once again, setting realistic limits can do much to ease future decision-making.

The stage of 'taking it on' should be seen as a priority in terms of professional intervention and support. It was recognized some time ago that the 'beginning' stage of care is a fertile period for instituting help (Bell and Gibbons 1989) and recently a number of authors have reaffirmed this contention (Motenko 1989; Braithwaite 1990; Given and Given 1991; Archbold *et al.* 1992; Beach 1993; Jivanjee 1993; Langer 1993).

A key concept here is that of 'preparedness' (Archbold *et al.* 1992), which is the extent to which carers feel able and competent to take on their role. High levels of preparedness, in terms of having the necessary knowledge, skills and emotional support, are associated with reduced levels of depression (Archbold *et al.* 1992; Harvath *et al.* 1994). Conversely in circumstances where carers feel ill-prepared for their role, considering they have much to learn and are faced with an unpredictable situation, then levels of burden are higher (Braithwaite 1990). Langer (1993) suggests that the critical question becomes, how can carers navigate the passage of time with a reasonable sense of competence? Certainly most carers do not initially have such a sense of competence and usually acquire their skills by a process of trial and error (Stewart *et al.* 1993; Harvath *et al.* 1994; Lea 1994); this has been described as 'flailing about' (Stewart et al. 1993). Taraborrelli (1993) argues that most carers 'take it on' in a state of 'initial innocence' in which they have very little information and advice and are generally ignorant of both the extent and the nature of the care they will be expected to deliver. This is by no means uncommon (Allen et al. 1983; Lewis and Meredith 1988a,b; Bell and Gibbons 1989; Pitkeathley 1990; Nolan and Grant 1992a). Moreover, there appears to be little professional input at this time, and the limited support that is offered is confined to the physical aspects of care (Stewart et al. 1993).

Those studies which have focused on the transition to care suggest that 'new' carers who have previous experience, either of caring or of having worked in a 'caring' profession are more likely to adapt quickly and successfully (Stewart et al. 1993; Taraborrelli 1993). The remainder operate in the trial-and-error mode, although eventually many do become 'experts'. This is consistent with the model of skill acquisition outlined earlier (Benner 1984; Dreyfus and Dreyfus 1986), because those with no previous background of caring will operate initially as a novice and are in need of some broad principles and guidelines to follow. Those with some prior experience are more likely to be at the level of advanced beginner or even competence, and although still in need of help, may need different support than 'novice' carers.

A simple but persuasive argument is offered by Braithwaite (1990) when she states that there is probably more to be learned about becoming a carer than there is about becoming a parent, yet we do not have the equivalent of antenatal classes for carers. This represents a lost opportunity that needs to be made good at the stage of 'taking it on'; Brodatey et al. (1994) argue that it is here that generic training in caregiving is the most useful.

Working through it

This stage is comparable with the 'going through it' stage identified by Wilson (1989a,b), but we feel that 'working through it' is much more appropriate. 'Going through it' denotes a certain passivity which is inconsistent with the very active role that the majority of carers in our studies adopted. The chapter on coping clearly indicated the proactive stance that many carers take and the range of strategies that they develop. In this context we do not use the term 'work' to indicate that carers treat their role like a job, although a number do. Rather 'work' is indicative of the active nature of caring during this stage.

The metaphor of work was adopted by Corbin and Strauss (1988, 1992) to convey the trajectory of chronic illness. They take 'work' to mean the day-to-day struggle of people with chronic illness and their carers to give balance and meaning to their situation. They describe a number of types of work and their associated tasks. Such work includes biographical work (defining and maintaining an identity), occupational work, marital work and so on. The manner and type of work varies according to the illness trajectory (Corbin and Strauss 1988, 1992). Our own typology of care and the varying stages of the caring trajectory follow a similar logic. In the 'working through it' stage carers are in fact providing instrumental care but anticipatory, protective, preservative, (re)constructive and reciprocal care are also much in evidence.

The primary purpose in working through it is to maximize the positive elements whilst seeking to minimize the negative. As we illustrated in the previous chapter, it is by achieving this that carers gain many of their satisfactions. So for instance providing simple pleasures, maintaining dignity and ensuring that needs are tended to are all integral to the successful delivery of care.

During the process of 'working through it' carers themselves become experts, particularly in the day-to-day aspects of their role. In terms of coping they develop routines and try differing tactics in a constant endeavour to maximize the positive aspects of care. As has been noted in the literature, the longer caring continues, the less stressful it may become (Motenko 1989); and the more competent carers feel in their role, the less likely they are to be stressed or burdened (Archbold et al. 1992; Jivanjee 1993; Harvath et al. 1994):

> As Mum's been getting worse I've tried all sorts of things over the years, like putting a baby-listening system in her room, tying a bell to her door so that when she opens it at night I will know she's up and about. I've even spent night after night in her bed so that she feels safe and knows someone's there. She doesn't recognize me now but I know she's my mother. It gets hard sometimes but, as it has gone on, it has also got easier in some ways. Things aren't so much of a surprise anymore and I feel I have been through the worst.

> We know she has Alzheimer's disease. She knows it and I know it. We take it one day at a time and plan our day out well in advance. Shopping in the morning and lunch at midday. We always used to eat later but we find it works better for us this way. Tea at 5 and supper at 8. We take our supper to bed and watch TV together. Mind you, she does not always follow it [both laugh]. It may not be life to some, but it's everything to us.

Many carers have their first contact with formal services during this period, and it is clearly very important that due account is taken of the carer's perspective. Yet as we have highlighted earlier, services often fail to do this and may inhibit or even obstruct carers from reaching their goals. This is not an isolated finding, as many other studies have demonstrated how services can ride roughshod over carers carefully planned routines (Lewis and Meredith 1988a,b; Braithwaite 1990). Even if advice is seemingly accepted it is in fact often ignored by carers, who carry on with what they believe is best:

> I only really got help towards the end. No one would take me seriously before that. I was always fobbed off with excuses at the surgery about how busy they were. So I didn't bother them after a while. It was when he got ill with his breathing that they came to see me. That was only last year. We had a social worker visit us then to give me advice and support. She would come here and tell me to try this and that with him . . . like make a list of things to do every day. If only she knew! I'd done that for years but didn't say anything. I just tolerated them to be honest and after they had gone I just got on with my own thing.

> Just where are they? I mean, I only want a bit of help with mum in the evenings to put her to bed. Sometimes they come [social services support staff] and sometimes they don't. Even when they do come it's at their own convenience, not mine. It's hardly ever the same person twice. I've no idea why. Mum's been in bed at 7 o'clock before now just because no one could be found to come later.

Yet well planned and carefully tailored advice and support can be very helpful, especially in situations where stressors are ambiguous (Boss 1988, 1993) or unpredictable (Archbold *et al.* 1992). It is here that the balance between what Harvath *et al.* (1994) term local knowledge and cosmopolitan knowledge is important. These authors argue that carers have local knowledge, expertise in their particular circumstances, particularly in the way that the person they are caring for responds to their illness. It has been suggested that carers have three primary types of local knowledge: knowledge of the cared-for person's illness or disability; knowledge of the cared-for person's normal behaviour; and biographical knowledge of past and present interests, likes, hopes and aspirations (Nolan and Grant 1992a). These form the basis of carers' efforts at (re)constructive care.

Cosmopolitan knowledge, on the other hand, is more global and generic. It is not concerned with the specifics of a situation but the generalities. Harvath *et al.* (1994) suggest that it is the skilful blending of these differing types of knowledge that will result in the most profitable interactions between carers and service providers. Despite the suggestion that service providers can assist carers by bringing to bear a wide range of knowledge and theoretical perspectives and applying them with judgement and skill (Hughes 1993), others have argued that one of the ways in which professionals assert their power is via controlling access to services (Bond 1992; Ellis 1993). Nikkonen (1994), in an analysis of expert power, suggests that an expert's position of authority is based on the belief that the knowledge they have is not available to 'all and sundry'. This has led some to conclude that professionals can be overly paternalistic and seek to keep their expertise to themselves (Triantafillou and Meshenesco 1994). In overcoming this tendency these authors argue that trust between professional and family carers is essential. However, they recognize that in order to facilitate trust, professional carers need additional training and experience in working with family carers. Training alone, however, is likely to be insufficient unless it is accompanied by a cognitive shift so that professionals are more willing to relinquish their authority and both share their knowledge with carers and learn from them (Schultz *et al.* 1993). Fundamentally this means adopting the role of facilitator and enabler rather than doer or provider. Paradoxically, if carers are seen to be coping, the services are often withdrawn. However, it is frequently not with the physical tasks of caring that carers most value support:

> I get tired now, but it's mainly from being up at all hours and being the only person in her life. She depends on me for everything now. Shopping, making the food, tidying the house, paying the bills, giving her a wash, putting on her clothes, taking her to the toilet. You name it and I have done it. But I feel I know what I'm doing now. I didn't at first. She was always losing her purse and hiding things that came through the letter box . . . and she would leave the gas on and burn the pans when trying to make us dinner. I was always 'interfering' then. Now the only thing I really miss is someone to talk to – anyone really. They [home care staff] stopped coming when they saw I was managing. I never really wanted them here but I miss their company. I haven't seen anyone for the past year.

As Brody (1995) notes, there is a marked tendency for services to focus on elements of care that are tangible and easy to describe because the emotional elements such as conflict, guilt, anxiety and depression are too slippery. It is not until we try and grasp such slippery elements that policy and practice will begin to respond adequately to the needs of many carers.

The 'working through it' phase provides the ideal opportunity for professional carers to assist family carers to develop and refine their coping strategies, as described earlier. One of the key roles that professionals can play here is, as appropriate, to assist carers to prepare for 'reaching the end'.

Reaching the end: the final phase or another transition?

Although the majority of carers wish to continue in their role for as long as possible, there comes a point when for many it is not in either their best interests, or those of the cared-for person. In describing this as 'reaching the end' we are not necessarily suggesting that carers cease to care. Rather, that the end of instrumental care is reached and generally, at least as far as service providers in the community are concerned, carers are seen no longer to need their support. The stage of instrumental care may end in a number of ways, for example when a child with learning difficulties leaves home, or an elderly disabled parent is admitted to a nursing home. This does not mean that family carers no longer care, rather that another form of care is substituted.

Although carers are often poorly served in the 'taking it on' and 'working through it' stages, current limitations are brought into the most stark relief during 'reaching the end'. We will illustrate this using admission to residential or nursing home care as an example, and will identify deficits during three sub-phases: making the decision; finding a home; and living with the consequences.

Maintaining the cared-for person in the community and keeping them out of an institution is of central importance to family carers (Davies 1980; Hirschfield 1981, 1983; Nolan and Grant 1992a); it provides one of the primary motivations for and a major satisfaction of caregiving. In circumstances where this is no longer possible the potential guilt is enormous, though events precipitating admission are usually a consequence of the carer's failing health rather than a lack of commitment (Hunter *et al.* 1993). Reaching the decision to place a relative in a care home is therefore extremely difficult and is a period of considerable emotional turmoil. This is exacerbated by the fact that most admissions to care are made at a time of crisis, usually following an acute episode of ill-health (Willcocks *et al.* 1987; Challis and Bartlett 1988; Neill 1989; Allen *et al.* 1992; Gair and Hartery 1994; Dellasega and Mastrian 1995). The suddenness with which decisions are often made belies the fact that many admissions are predictable, inasmuch as there are 'warning signs' apparent for some time prior to the actual final crisis (Hunter *et al.* 1993). In principle this allows time for forward planning.

Unfortunately such opportunities are mostly wasted as there is little open discussion amongst families about the role and value of institutional care. Indeed, such topics are often studiously avoided because of the largely negative and dysfunctional image of institutional care (Victor 1992; Higham 1994), admission to which has been described as one of the most pervasive sources of anxiety marking later life (Biedenham and Normoyle 1991). Consequently, both older people and their carers refuse to contemplate the possibility of admission until the last minute (Lawrence *et al.* 1987; Willcocks *et al.* 1987; Allen *et al.* 1992; Hunter *et al.* 1993).

Describing the results of a number of studies looking at the manner in which older people entered nursing and residential care, Nolan *et al.* (1996) note the invidious position in which many carers are placed, particularly when admission follows a period of hospitalization. Because the older person is often too frail or too sick to be an active participant in the admission process, the onus is placed on the carer to be the prime mover. Indeed, pressure is often exerted by the older person, professionals or both. Owing to the 'taboo' nature of residential care, most carers have not discussed wishes and preferences with the older person in anticipation of a possible admission, nor do they have any clear criteria of their own on which to base a judgement. Moreover, because many professionals, particularly doctors seek swift discharge from hospital, carers feel additional pressure to make decisions hurriedly.

With few exceptions carers received minimal help at this difficult period and generally considered that they were left to 'sink or swim'. A range of emotional reactions were described including guilt, anger, relief and help-lessness. Although the long-term effects of having to make this decision cannot be judged on the basis of the work conducted by Nolan *et al.* (1996), the literature suggests that many carers are left with a legacy of guilt and continued stress (Allen *et al.* 1992; Zarit and Whitlach 1992; Ade-Ridder and Kaplan 1993; Dellasega and Mastrian 1995).

Our own work over a number of years would support such a conclu-sion, with carers often describing persistent guilt, unabated with the passage of time. There are obvious deficits in current practice in the way that older people and their carers are assisted to make decisions about entry to resi-dential or nursing home care.

Making the decision, however, is only the first step; there are equally important choices to be made, especially concerning the type of home to be selected. Finding a home therefore poses another dilemma for both carer and cared-for person. The concept of choice would dictate that in ideal circumstances a home could be selected from a range of options according to a list of preferred criteria. In reality such a selection process is rarely achievable. First, as indicated before, older people and their carers do not usually have criteria upon which to make a selection, as little prior thought has been given to the prospect of entering a nursing home. Second, because entry to care often occurs at a time of crisis, there is relatively little time to engage in a thorough search. Third, even if a home is selected there is no guarantee that a place is available. These factors are exacerbated if the move follows a period of hospitalization.

There is considerable evidence that hospital discharge of elderly people is poorly handled (Young *et al.* 1991; Neill and Williams 1992; Tierney *et al.* 1993), thereby making choice a notional concept. The United Kingdom Central Council for Nursing Midwifery and Health Visiting (UKCC), the statutory body for these professions, recently considered it necessary to issue a series of research-based recommendations on hospital discharge 'directed at managers and policy-makers at all levels' (UKCC 1995). Similarly the Relatives Association, a national lobbying organization for the relatives and friends of older people in homes, conclude that far from being given the necessary time to make the 'momentous decisions' needed prior to selecting future care options for older people, 'families are made to feel uncomfort-able, even bullied, if they do not accept the date [for discharge] by which the consultant wants the bed' (Relatives Association 1994).

To exacerbate these matters, the levels of frailty amongst many older people discharged from hospital effectively precludes them from an active role in choosing a home. This again is often left to their relative.

For family carers, choosing a home is often a cause of considerable stress because they have rarely been given advice or guidance and are poorly informed about what to look for when making a selection (Roberts *et al.* 1991; Allen *et al.* 1992; Zarit and Whitlach 1992; Hunter *et al.* 1993; Dellasega and Mastrian 1995). For example, Nolan *et al.* (1996) found that none of the carers in their studies had been given information about the inspection reports produced by local social services inspection units even though such reports have been in the public domain for some time. The process of choosing a home was noted to cause considerable unease and added further stress at an already difficult period. Even those carers for whom it might have been anticipated that choice would pose few problems experienced considerable difficulties. Financial matters in particular were a major cause for concern, with one businessman who was successfully running a large enterprise admitting that he was totally baffled by the financial arrangements.

Adequate and sensitive professional input at this time can, however, ease the situation considerably, and a number of instances of 'best practice' were observed in the above studies (Nolan *et al.* 1996). It has been suggested that discussing the possibility of admission to care should be raised before crises occur (Hunter *et al.* 1993; Nolan *et al.* 1994); Beach (1993) believes that it needs to be raised during the early stages of caring. However, if difficult decisions have to be made at a time of crisis and under the additional pressure of time constraints, then older people and carers need greater assistance. Nolan *et al.* (1996) describe a typology of admissions ranging from the positive choice through the rationalized alternative and discredited option to the *fait accompli*. They argue that the positive choice represents the ideal but that the *fait accompli* is becoming increasingly prevalent. Four sets of processes interact to produce a positive choice, these being anticipation (the degree of prior thought that has been given to the move); participation (the degree of active involvement achieved by older people and their carers); information (how much advice has been offered); and exploration (of alternatives to admission, of feelings about admission and of a range of possible homes). The literature would suggest that such considerations rarely apply.

Due to the sudden nature of the admission, older people themselves are often not involved in the decision-making process and are frequently not even consulted (Neill 1989; Sinclair 1990; Reinhardy 1992; Booth 1993), with the decision either being instigated or made by others, sometimes by family members, but more typically professionals, usually doctors (Chenitz 1983; Willcocks *et al.* 1987; Challis and Bartlett 1988; Sinclair 1990; Allen *et al.* 1992; Bland *et al.* 1992; Porter and Clinton 1992; Gair and Hartery 1994; Johnson *et al.* 1994; Dellasega and Mastrian 1995). Furthermore, despite the putative introduction of consumer choice, older people may enter care without alternatives having been discussed (Sinclair 1990; Roberts *et al.* 1991; Allen *et al.* 1992; Bland *et al.* 1992; Hunter *et al.* 1993).

Willcocks *et al.* (1987) believe that decisions about institutional care cannot adequately be taken alone because they are alien, different and distanced from all other experiences which people accumulate over a lifetime.

In these circumstances even 'expert' carers return to the role of novice (Benner 1984; Dreyfus and Dreyfus 1986) and rely on rule-based judgements. Clearly there is scope for greater support during the process of making the decision to enter care and subsequently choosing a home.

After having selected a home, carers also have to 'live with the consequences'. Lewis and Meredith (1989) described the grief, guilt and loss experienced by many family carers following admission to a residential or nursing home but noted that professional carers tended to treat them as if their problems were over. It is now more widely recognized that, contrary to popular opinion, entry to care does not necessarily mark the end of caregiving for the family member but rather signals a different but still potentially stressful involvement (Bowers 1988; Zarit and Whitlach 1992; Ade-Ridder and Kaplan 1993; McCullough *et al.* 1993; Dellasega and Mastrian 1995). Bowers (1988) suggests that family carers wish to maintain an active involvement, which includes ensuring that staff have the relevant information to provide good care. More recently, it has been demonstrated that nine out of ten carers continue to provide input beyond simply visiting (Kane and Penrod 1995), and that professional carers at this time should seek to sustain agreed caregiving relationships whilst not forcing any non-agreed ones. This requires close collaboration between family carers and those working in residential and nursing homes. It seems that when this occurs there is improved understanding, and a better quality of care emerges (Anderson *et al.* 1992).

Over and above this, carers also need support to deal with the conflicting emotions that many still feel. Without this it is difficult to move on to a 'new beginning'. To move on successfully, family carers have to create a balanced perception of what they have achieved during caring, to recognize the value of their efforts over several years and to come to the realization that the choice to place the cared-for person in alternative care was the right and the best one. As one son caring for his father said, 'I knew Dad had to go somewhere. I've tried to balance work, family and care for the last six years. I love him but it's time to move on. I wish I could go on but it's come to the end. Someone else will have to do it now.'

Moving on for most carers does not mean forgetting what has passed but rather 'building on the past', the start of caring, to create a 'new beginning', and so the wheel of caring turns full circle:

> I knew I couldn't go on when my health began to go down. I've cared for him at home for the last nine years. I've done it all you know, everything. Haven't relied on anybody for anything so I've got to be pleased about that, haven't I? They've sorted a place out for him close to the village and I'll be able to see him as much as I want. He's going there in the next few days, poor thing. I'll miss him. I might go there myself if things get worse with me.
>
> (81-year-old wife)

After she went into the home I spent the first two years thinking about it all. I would go and see her, of course I would, but I would also think about what I had done. I felt very guilty about putting her there but when I see her now I know I couldn't have managed. I dream about her a lot you know; not how she is now, but years ago when we were much younger. I used to get upset at first about the dreams but I like them now.

(80-year-old husband)

The above accounts confine reaching the end largely, although not entirely, to the fairly short period of time leading up to entry to care. This is often characteristic of spousal or child–parent caregiving relationships. In parent–child relationships, however, other quite differing considerations may apply (Grant 1989, 1990). Here parents are more likely to be actively contemplating 'reaching the end' throughout the caring history, especially in terms of how their child will manage when they are no longer able to provide care. This process of 'letting go' (Grant 1989) is a difficult, lengthy and stressful one, that can become more acute as parents age (Grant 1990). In such situations the stage of reaching the end is shaped by quite different factors and operates within broader parameters than that which we have described above. This signals the need for further theoretical elaboration and empirical testing of our model in other caregiving contexts.

Creating a new beginning is difficult for most of us at the best of times, but for a family carer, particularly one who may have done little else for several years and for whom caring may have constituted both a role and a sense of identity, it can be virtually impossible. Withdrawing professional support at such a time in the belief that 'problems are all over' (Lewis and Meredith 1989) is simply not sanctionable. McLaughlin and Ritchie (1994) argue that most carers are ill-prepared for a life after caring, and that this is exacerbated for those who have been caring for the longest period.

Perhaps one of the most pernicious after-effects of care is the long-term financial disadvantage that is often its legacy. This is usually ignored (McLaughlin and Ritchie 1994). In a sample of 1000 ex-carers from a representative group of 3500 people aged 55–69 ('The Retirement Survey'), Hancock and Jarvis (1994) provide an overview of some of the long-term effects of caring. They suggest a number of common themes. The first is that looking at large samples *en masse* masks differences and suggests that there is little to discriminate non-carers and ex-carers. They argue that generalizations are therefore of little help and may actually be counterproductive. They note that it is the longer-term carers who are more likely to suffer lower incomes and have poorer pensions, these differences being particularly stark for women. Clearly there are important policy issues here that transcend caring and concern the extent to which women and men can combine work and family. Acknowledging the limitations of their study, Hancock and Jarvis suggest the need for further research into the long-term effects of caring on a range of policy issues. They contend that when carers cease to be 'carers' they are not transformed overnight into 'non-carers' (p. 79).

We would suggest that such a transformation is not possible or meaningful. Certainly one might be a 'non-carer' in the sense of no longer providing instrumental care but other forms of care – preservative, (re)constructive and reciprocal – continue. Even after the death of a cared-for person it is possible to speculate that what might be termed 'retrospective' care continues, in that carers frequently reflect upon what they have done in order to make sense of events. A legacy of guilt at the end of caring (in the instrumental sense) does not provide a sound platform upon which to build a new beginning.

Having outlined here a temporal model of caring and described the various processes that occur, largely from a carer's perspective, attention is now given to the way in which the perspectives of the carer and cared-for person can be integrated.

6

INTEGRATING PERSPECTIVES

[A]s research on caregiving has come of age, it has been
confronted with both conceptual limitations and lack of empirical
support for a unidimensional view.

(Kahana and Young 1990: 76)

In selecting a title for this book we chose to emphasize the multidimensional
nature of family caring because we believe, as did Kahana and Young (1990),
that a unidimensional approach is simply inadequate. In an important contribution to the caregiving literature, Kahana and Young outlined a number
of potential caregiving models, the relative emphasis of which varied depending upon whether they centred on the caregiver, cared-for person or
both (asymmetrical or symmetrical models), and whether they were static
or dynamic. The authors suggested the need for 'clarification of several
components of the caregiving paradigm' (p. 87), particularly the concept of
dependency; the motivations for caregiving; and the similarities and differences in paradigms of informal (family) and formal caregiving relationships,
when considered from a temporal perspective.

At various points in this book we have attempted to address some of
these issues. We are conscious, however, that although reference has been
made to the perception of the cared-for person, the main focus has been on
the carer. This has been deliberate, not from any desire to accord one perspective priority or hegemony on the basis of merit but because we consider that
the data we have drawn upon allow us to have some confidence in our as-
sertions about carers – less so about cared-for persons. Hence in this chapter
attention is turned to the perspectives of the cared-for person and the manner
in which these might be integrated with those of other key stakeholders.

We will address our arguments largely to a dyadic relationship, but we
will also make reference to a family systems model and the need to incorporate the views of professional carers.

The concept of negotiation is one that figures prominently in the literature both on ordinary family life (Finch and Mason 1993) and on caregiving (Opie 1994; Gubrium 1995; Wenger *et al.* 1996). Opie (1994) argues that caring is a highly particularistic activity heavily influenced by individual life history and biography, and that as such it is a lived and negotiated experience. On this basis it has been contended that caring is 'fuzzy' because negotiations and changes occur daily (Gubrium 1995). As we have illustrated throughout this book, such negotiations may be open and overt, but they are often subtle and implicit, even covert. Whatever form they take they range from mundane day-to-day events to complex and delicate issues, thereby underpinning much of what we conceive as caring.

Negotiation is necessarily a shared activity, it takes at least two people; for although we may talk to ourselves, negotiating with ourselves is meaningless. Moreover, whilst it is possible to negotiate with a relative stranger, in the present context, negotiation, like caring, occurs within an established relationship. A meaningful dialogue about caring therefore cannot be complete without addressing the perspective of the cared-for person. Space only permits us to outline a number of key concepts here which may act as analytic levers for further discourse.

Cicarelli (1992) examines the nature of decision-making in family caregiving and identifies autonomy as one of the main tensions. He argues that 'personal autonomy is a central and complex value of our society' (p. vii) yet it is essentially compromised in caregiving situations, where there is an inherent risk of paternalism. He suggests that in any dyadic relationship, but in caregiving particularly, a balance has to be struck between individual views and those held by significant others. A congruence of views, or at least the willingness to compromise to achieve a degree of congruence, is important to good caring relationships (Phillips and Rempusheski 1986; Kahana and Young 1990; Nolan 1993). We believe that in many respects there is a congruence between the needs and wishes of cared-for people and those who care for them; we will draw upon the literature on chronic illness to illustrate this.

Achieving congruence: implications for chronic illnesses

We suggested earlier that one of the main purposes behind many caregiving actions was to (re)construct the identity of the cared-for person and to provide them with a means of maintaining a reciprocal relationship. We identified one of the principal barriers as the instrumental focus of most definitions of care, and a similar orientation amongst the services and interventions offered to carers. We would contend that such considerations apply to the needs of individuals with chronic illness or disability.

A number of authors (Asvoll 1992; Corbin and Strauss 1992; Kaplun

1992; McBride 1993) have noted that chronic illness represents one of the major challenges facing the health and welfare systems of the developed world, and yet our knowledge of such conditions is sparse and underdeveloped. Service responses have been inhibited by the inappropriate application of models designed primarily for use in acute illness (Pott 1992). In particular there has been a tendency to treat chronic conditions in a homogeneous fashion (Corbin and Strauss 1988, 1992; Rolland 1988, 1994). This denies the diversity, multiplicity and complexity of the situation facing individuals with a chronic illness or disability and their carers. Verbrugge and Jette (1994) contend that most people have to live with rather than die from a chronic illness; the challenge for services therefore becomes how to help people get the most from their life. This of course is the main aim of most family caregivers, for whom chronic illnesses present their own challenges:

> it is very likely that dyadic interactions between patient and caregiver will differ greatly for the Alzheimer's patient and his or her caregiver from that of the elderly victim of a heart attack. In the first case, the patient's trajectory is almost certain, taking an erratic but ultimately predictable course downward . . . In the case of the elderly heart attack patient, there are far more divergent courses taken by the illness, and outcomes may also vary greatly.
>
> (Kahana and Young 1990: 92)

These are issues that we will address shortly using the model suggested by Rolland (1988, 1994) as a device to achieve integration.

Informed debate about the perspective of the cared-for person (for the purpose of our argument we are assuming they have a chronic illness or disability) is inhibited because the literature lacks well-developed concepts in this connection. There is a 'bedlam' vocabulary in which terms have been invented and defined in numerous, often conflicting ways, according to Verbrugge and Jette 1994, who believe that there is a need to develop a conceptual scheme providing at least the basic architecture on which research, policy and clinical care can be built.

We would reiterate our belief that this will not happen, at least in a way that is congruent with the perspectives of disabled people, until there is a fundamental shift away from the focus on physical functioning. This is well illustrated if one considers the care of older people within the health and social care system. It has long been recognized that frail older people often fall between two stools and have trouble claiming legitimate attention from either the health or the social services (Williams 1980). Whilst older people are acutely ill they are seen as the responsibility of the Health Service. When returned to health and in need of social support, then there is little argument as to where they obtain such assistance. However, frail older people have always posed a problem for service systems. This is well illustrated when considering the evaluation of medical services for older people.

Early in its genesis, geriatric medicine, in an effort both to facilitate discharge and provide a focus for 'therapeutic' interventions, substituted a functional model of health for a medical one (Wilkin and Hughes 1986). Rehabilitation, specified in terms of a return to optimal physical functioning, became the defining criterion. However, the success of rehabilitation measured by functional criteria is open to serious question because it is now apparent that professional notions of 'success' do not equate with those of older people themselves (Clark 1995; Koch et al. 1995; Porter 1995). As Porter (1995: 38) cogently notes: 'What is real about lived experience is quite different from the reality circumscribed by ADL tools and by the independent performance of ADL tasks.'

In tracing the replacement of the 'heroic model' of geriatric medicine with a more holistic one focusing on individual quality of life, Clarke (1995) notes two disturbing trends in the way such a concept has been defined. First, there is the assumption that quality of life is closely aligned to independence and autonomy, which Clark (1995) contends neglects the values of community, collectiveness and interdependence which are equally important. Second, the definition of quality of life is a slippery one, and in order to escape this conundrum the concept of functional ability has been employed as a proxy measure. Both these trends, according to Clark, need to be countered, and alternative models developed which centre upon 'the unique individual and his or her experience of illness and frailty'. Such a focus on the individual experience of illness is consistent with the literature on caregiving; ultimately, however, this needs to be broadened to include other perspectives as well.

Identifying quality of life as a key notion for service provision is helpful but still begs the question as to what constitutes a good quality of life. Without a framework within which to consider important concepts, the quality of life of disabled people and their carers cannot be enhanced; nor is it possible to give a thorough consideration as to how to create a meaningful and satisfying work environment for those paid individuals providing care. The unclear or taken-for-granted manner in which the parameters of good care have been defined effectively inhibits achieving acceptable standards. For example, whilst concepts such as privacy, dignity, independence, choice, rights and fulfilment (DoH/SSI 1989) are presented as benchmarks of good care, what such ideas really mean and how they can be achieved in the context of very high levels of physical and mental frailty is far from clear. As Kellaher and Peace (1990) suggest, simply using ideas with increasing frequency does not ensure greater clarity of meaning. Gilloran et al. (1993) argue that it is simplistic and misleading to use 'buzzwords' such as autonomy and individuality without agreement about their definition. Regarding the quality of care provided for dependent older people they note: 'measuring the concept of quality is like a dog's favourite slipper, well chewed, continuously worried, yet remaining undefeated' (p. 269).

One of the most consistent themes to emerge from the literature on chronic illness is that objective reality and subjective perceptions are not necessarily congruent. In terms of making sense of their lives, people with chronic illness and disability rely primarily on subjective frames of reference (Bury 1982; Charmaz 1983, 1987; Corbin and Strauss 1988; Benner and Wruebel 1989; Clark 1995; Koch *et al.* 1995; Porter 1995). This point is so simple and yet so frequently overlooked by professionals delivering care that Clark (1995) argues that there is a major conceptual gap between professional and lay people in the meanings they ascribe to health and health-related problems. Benner and Wruebel (1989: 190) argue that 'If health care providers are to understand when and where interventions are needed, they must first understand a person's meanings in that person's own terms.'

This is even more important with respect to chronic illness, where the patient, rather than the professional, is the expert regarding their own condition (Corbin and Strauss 1988; Benner and Wruebel 1989; Clark 1995). Yet the frames of reference brought to bear by professionals are often not only inconsistent with each other but also at variance with those of the patient (Benner and Wruebel 1989; Ellis 1993; Clark 1995). Clark (1995) suggests that the 'value maps' held by older individuals are more likely to be concerned with issues of 'self-identity' than physical and mental health, and that interventions must focus more closely on the meanings that people give to their lives rather than simply assuring survival and postponing institutionalization.

Similarly, some of the major theoretical contributions to an understanding of chronic illness (Bury 1982; Charmaz 1983, 1987; Corbin and Strauss 1988, 1992) have highlighted the importance of 'biographical work' in terms of the struggle to find 'valued lives and selves' (Charmaz 1987) and to 'define and maintain an identity' (Corbin and Strauss 1988). Charmaz (1987) for example outlines four 'types' of identity that might be construed: 'the supernormal' (better than deemed possible); 'the restored' (the return to former self); 'the contingent' (that seen as possible but doubtful); and 'the salvaged' (that which retains at least some positive links with the past). She argues that acceptance of one of these images both by the disabled person and others is essential, even if by conventional standards the disabled person may no longer be productive or useful. Corbin and Strauss (1988) likewise describe four biographical processes – although these are sequential rather than mutually exclusive – seen to be important to successful adaptation: contextualizing (putting the present situation into perspective); coming to terms (being able to visualize a future biography); reconstituting identity (seeing themselves as a person with a purpose in life); and restoring biography (seeing new directions for future growth and development).

If younger individuals with chronic illness find these – the major tasks – a challenge, how much more difficult is it for individuals who have the 'double jeopardy' of being both very old *and* very frail, individuals for whom the possibility of continued growth and development is generally not even considered a possibility (Koch *et al.* 1995). Certainly the needs of very frail

older individuals are not given serious consideration in our currently fragmented system of health and social care, where the role and purpose of
services, such as day hospitals for example, have been redefined so as to be
explicitly consistent with professional values even when it is acknowledged
that these are contrary to the wishes of many patients (Nolan and Scott
1993). Yet the tailoring of services to the needs of very frail individuals is
even more important as they are maintained in the community for longer
periods, and levels of dependency increase.

This point is well illustrated in a recent – and possibly the first – paper
to attempt to quantify how very frail older people spend their time at home.
Lawton *et al.* (1995) studied a group of highly impaired older people living
with a family carer and discovered that they were passive for 81 per cent
of their waking day; only 7 per cent of their time was spent in what they
termed 'potentially enriching activity'. Based on these results the authors
question whether in fact such individuals might not have been better off in
institutional care. They argue that the challenge for the future is to identify
how to provide meaningful stimulation for highly dependent older people
in all care settings, whether in the community or an institution.

They suggest that the quality of life for such people would be enhanced by opportunities to demonstrate everyday competence and to engage in some form of cognitively challenging activity. Lawton and colleagues
argue that service providers need to be creative and imaginative, and to see
the provision of such activities as an integral part of their work rather than
as simply a diversion. They believe that: 'For even the lowest levels of
competence there is a range within which increased demands made by the
environment are capable of enhancing function and subjective well-being'
(p. 169).

Hughes (1995) implicitly adopts such ideas when she identifies the
values that should underpin community care for older people as being
'personhood' (the older person should be seen as a person first and old
second); 'citizenship' (the older person should be valued and seen to be
important as a member of society); and 'celebration' (a recognition of the
diversity in old people and the fact that old age is an authentic period in life,
valued in its own right). Building on these she sees empowerment, participation, choice and integration as the benchmarks of quality, but recognizes
the difficulty of translating some of these into practice.

As laudable as these ideals may be their utility with respect to extremely frail older people needs to be questioned. This is not to denigrate
such concepts, rather it is to recognize that the challenge becomes how do
we achieve these aims at the more extreme ends of frailty where, for example, most personal care may be carried out by another individual and
personal space is frequently invaded. It seems clear from most of the recent
literature that the key to quality hinges largely on the nature of interpersonal relationships and the recognition that the dependent person, no matter
how frail, has the status of a human being.

On the basis of the above it is reasonable to suggest that for those disabled individuals who remain cognitively able, the prime focus of interventions must be to help them construct and sustain a sense of biography, of self and of person. As a review of several years work (Brandstädter 1995) has demonstrated, the majority of older people are able to maintain a positive self-image in the face of the many changes and losses at physical, psychological and social levels that ageing brings. This requires a balanced perspective which incorporates both assimilative activities and accommodative activities. The aim of the former is to maintain current interests, skills and abilities for as long as possible, whilst the latter seeks to develop equally valued outlets when maintaining existing ones is no longer possible. Older people who are able to achieve this balance adjust to ageing more satisfactorily.

For those who are cognitively frail, the aims of formal care are even less clear, and consequently the reduction of stress and burden in carers is often used as a proxy measure. Yet as Miesen (1995) argues, to exclude people with dementia from active participation in their care is to 'metaphorically decapitate' them. Certainly in the early stages of dementia, recent work has indicated that sufferers are often very proactive in managing their symptoms (Keady and Nolan 1995b,c) and utilize a range of coping strategies both to maintain competence and to keep the true extent of their failing abilities from those around them. This is an area in which much further work is required.

Whilst of necessity somewhat cursory, the above brief review has demonstrated the congruence that exists between carers and cared-for persons in terms of the outcomes of care. We would argue that the concepts of (re)constructive and reciprocal care in particular provide a meaningful context for further debate. Specifically, they highlight the interdependent and dynamic nature of caregiving and care receiving, such that in the best situations neither party is seen as dependent on the other but that both continue to contribute to a valued relationship. However, within this congruence there is also diversity, both in terms of individual biographies and the challenges posed by the heterogeneous nature of chronic illness.

Chronic illness: accounting for heterogeneity

An appreciation of chronic illness and its impact on those suffering it and their carers cannot be fully obtained without recognizing the diverse nature of the conditions that go under this broad umbrella term (Corbin and Strauss 1988, 1992; Rolland 1988, 1994; Benner and Wruebel 1989; Biegel *et al.* 1991). We have found (Nolan and Grant 1992a; Nolan *et al.* 1994; Nolan and Caldock 1996) one of the most useful frameworks for assisting our thinking in this area to be that of Rolland (1988, 1994); this is particularly appropriate in the present context as Rolland has named his 1994 approach an 'integrative treatment model'. Although at first sight his model may appear to offer a primarily medical view, this is not the case, as it fully acknowledges the importance of social factors, whilst also stressing the role of personal perspectives, beliefs and value systems.

Rolland's model centres around a typology of chronic illness. It was devised as a means to assist both practitioners and researchers to better understand the nature of chronic illness and its impact on sufferers and their families. He argues that chronic illness and disability form the interface between the biological and psycho-social worlds; his typology recognizes both the diverse and common elements of various conditions, in addition to accounting for qualitative and quantitative variation over time.

He contends that his approach has several implications for practice, particularly in terms of providing a framework for assessment and intervention. He believes that it offers a way 'to think longitudinally and to reach a fuller understanding of chronic illness as an ongoing process with landmarks, transition points and changing demands . . . taken together, the typology and the time phases provide a context to integrate other aspects of a comprehensive assessment' (Rolland 1988: 36). Such characteristics could not be more relevant to our present purpose.

As noted, the model is based upon a typology of chronic illness which differentiates conditions upon four main dimensions: onset, course, outcome and incapacity.

In terms of *onset*, a disease may manifest itself in either an actual or gradual fashion. An acute onset condition such as a heart attack is usually unexpected and unanticipated, and sudden changes and adaptations are required. This necessitates the rapid mobilization of resources and skills by both carer and cared-for person. Families cope best if they are able to manage highly charged situations; move between roles in a flexible way; and problem solve and make maximum use of outside resources.

For example, in a family where traditional gender roles still exist, a sudden illness in the husband may require his partner to manage the financial affairs. At such a time, people need to be able to make decisions and solve problems, whilst at the same time adapting to and accepting the interventions of relative strangers in highly personal matters. Not all individuals and families have either the skills or the ability to cope at such times. Alternatively, a disease which develops gradually and which may provide more time for adjustment also generates the potential for more anticipatory anxiety, especially prior to diagnosis. This can create a more prolonged period of uncertainty and doubt. Indeed, as Corbin and Strauss (1988) suggest, the diagnostic limbo is a particularly stressful period for both the person awaiting the diagnosis and their family. At this time 'information work' is seen to be particularly important in order to try and reduce uncertainty.

Disease may also run differing *courses*, broadly characterized by Rolland (1988, 1994) as progressive, constant or relapsing/episodic. In progressive conditions, the carer and cared-for person have to deal with symptoms which may manifest in a stepwise or progressive deterioration. This provides minimal relief whilst also requiring constant adaptation and role change, a combination which may soon lead to exhaustion. Moreover, progression may be rapid or slow. In contrast, constant conditions are usually characterized by an initial crisis and period of adjustment, followed by a long period of stability with a greater or lesser degree of disability. Relapsing conditions, on the other hand, have stable periods of varying length but require frequent movement between being symptomatic and symptom-free, with the uncertainty this can cause. Carers are particularly likely to feel 'on-call', and to have to respond rapidly to demands with little warning. The marked contrast between periods of 'normal life' and a crisis phase can be particularly taxing for both carer and cared-for person.

The *outcome* of a disease, according to Rolland, is a crucial feature that has a profound impact relating primarily to the expectation of death. Certain conditions have a very low expectation, for example osteoarthritis, whereas others, for example AIDS, are almost invariably fatal. Many illnesses fit into the intermediate category and are usually associated with a shortening of the lifespan and an increased possibility of sudden death, for example, cardiovascular disease and recurrent myocardial infarction. This latter group causes particular problems with the constant awareness that 'it might happen any time', which may result in overprotection of the cared-for person. They may be 'wrapped in cotton wool', and their independence and potential contribution may be reduced as a consequence. The similarities between this sort of reaction and protective care (Bowers 1987) are obvious. This reinforces Cicarelli's (1992) contention that there is a delicate balance to be achieved in caring between seeking to maintain an element of autonomy for the cared-for person and acting in a paternalistic way.

Alternatively, some cared-for people may find paternalism desirable and relinquish responsibilities that they are capable of fulfilling. Once again, the boundary between this sort of reaction and being seen as manipulative and overly demanding is tenuous. It is in circumstances such as these that congruence of beliefs and expectations between carer and cared-for person are important. As Phillips and Rempusheski (1986) point out, in situations where beliefs and behaviours are congruent then caregiving relationships are usually good. Alternatively, if there is a marked divergence between beliefs and behaviours then caring becomes increasingly fraught and poor and abusive situations may arise (Phillips and Rempusheski 1986; Nolan 1993).

For carers, diseases in which there is a high element of uncertainty about the outcome can cause considerable tension between the desire for a period of increased intimacy whilst simultaneously feeling the need to disengage so that emotional separation is less painful.

The final dimension on which diseases may be differentiated is that of *incapacity*. Rolland outlines five areas of incapacity: cognitive; sensory; mobility; energy and stigma. Each of these requires differing adjustments which are, however, crucially influenced by the families' expectations of the cared-for person. Those who tend to foster autonomy generally limit incapacity, whereas those who take over from the cared-for person increase incapacity. As has been illustrated, situations are particularly fraught when the carer and cared-for person have differing expectations of autonomy and independence, that is, differing beliefs about roles and responsibilities in the caring situation. The extent of incapacity varies considerably according to the illness or disability in question, and Rolland suggests that this poses particular stresses for families. So, for example, acute onset conditions such as stroke usually result in maximum incapacity at the start of caring, whereas for progressive diseases, the prospect of ever increasing but uncertain degrees of incapacity are faced on a regular basis. However, as Rolland points out, this does give more time for preparation and allows the cared-for person to make a greater contribution to planning their future.

The four dimensions of disease processes (onset, course, outcome and incapacity) are united by what Rolland terms the 'meta characteristic', which is *predictability*. Thus a disease may be more or less predictable on any or all of the above dimensions or, alternatively, it may be quite unpredictable. As was identified in the chapter on coping, stresses or demands that are ambiguous (Boss 1988, 1993) or unpredictable (Archbold *et al.* 1992, 1995) are considered to be particularly difficult to handle. Therefore conditions which have a relapsing course, for instance multiple sclerosis, present unpredictable demands. Others, such as Alzheimer's disease, are ambiguous because, according to Boss *et al.* (1988) and Boss (1993), the cared-for person is physically present but psychologically absent.

As well as onset, course, outcome and incapacity, the *time* phase of the disease is an important consideration. Rolland contends that in psychosocial terms, there are three major time phases to consider: crisis, chronic and terminal, each of which require distinct tasks and resources. The *crisis* phase relates to the symptomatic but prediagnostic period and brings a set of practical and existential tasks. So, at a practical level, there may be adjustments to pain, incapacity or other symptoms, together with adaptations to diagnostic and treatment procedures whilst establishing relationships with health personnel for both carer and cared-for. At an existential level, there is a requirement to create meaning out of the situation whilst maintaining a sense of control over events. This may be coupled with the need to move towards an uncertain future. The *chronic* phase spans that period between initial crisis and the terminal stage. The time-scale may vary tremendously but is often called the 'long haul'.

If the time-scale is short, Rolland likens it to 'living in limbo', whilst a lengthy chronic phase may lead to the feeling that there is 'no light at the end of the tunnel'. There are critical transition periods between all these phases, with various 'business' that needs to be transacted before progress can be made. For example, in a crisis phase, one has to acquire an understanding of the nature of the disease and accept a diagnosis before the task of entering and coping with the chronic phase can be properly begun. Rolland feels that moving from the crisis to the chronic phase is a new period of socialization for both the carer and cared-for person.

The notion of business or work in chronic illness is mirrored in the writings of Corbin and Strauss (1988, 1992). They believe that whilst illnesses are partly determined by characteristics such as those suggested by Rolland (1988, 1994), they can also be *shaped*. This is a psychological process whereby the course of the illness is perceived in different terms, depending upon the understanding that the person has. Shaping is largely determined by the amount of information available. It is during the diagnostic work that professional carers (usually doctors) and those with chronic illness and their carers first come into contact. Corbin and Strauss (1988) suggest that the main difference in perception at this stage, and indeed throughout the trajectory of the illness, is the importance professional and lay people attach to various components of the disease. Therefore for the sufferer and carer the biographical impact is the most important, whereas the professional is more concerned with the biomedical.

In terms of their biographical impact, chronic diseases – especially those which are uncertain and unpredictable – tend to isolate the past from the present, and present from the future, so biography and identity are rendered discontinuous (Corbin and Strauss 1988). Therefore an 'accommodation' is needed to try and restore a sense of control, balance, continuity and meaning. In order to 'put life back together', new definitions must be sought and discovered. These processes, described earlier are: contextualizing; coming to terms; reconstituting identity and recasting biography (Corbin and Strauss 1988).

Such processes and also those suggested by Rolland (1988, 1994) have clear conceptual similarities with some of the stages in our own temporal model of caring. Therefore 'recognizing the need' is likely to coincide with 'contextualizing', which, according to Corbin and Strauss (1988), begins in earnest when the implications of symptoms in terms of biography are realized. 'Coming to terms', on the other hand, will probably be concurrent with 'taking it on' and the early stage of 'working through it'. Reconstituting identity and restoring biography are not so much stages as processes that occur iteratively throughout the illness course, a constant process of defining and redefining identity to construct a meaningful future. Corbin and Strauss consider that help from other people is important at this stage, particularly in terms of 'engineering performances' that allow the cared-for person to achieve a sense of mastery and control. We would see such engineering as being consistent with certain types of (re)constructive care. We would fully endorse their suggestion that practitioners need to be sensitive to the trajectory of a person's illness and aware of the stage of his or her biographical work.

Rolland's work (1988, 1994) presents an overarching model which was developed primarily from clinical experience and a synthesis of the literature rather than research-based empirical work *per se*. Corbin and Strauss

(1988) base their conclusions on a series of detailed interviews with couples dealing with chronic illness, and they present a perspective which relates mainly to the cared-for person, although they do recognize the valuable role of the carer throughout. Our own temporal model is based mainly on a series of interviews with dementia carers, although we draw on several years of data studying many hundreds of carers in applying the model to differing circumstances. Although the terminology within these conceptualizations is different, there is nevertheless consistency in many of the key emergent themes; this suggests that an integration of perspectives is possible. However, we are as yet only at the stage of 'beginning knowledge' (Wilson 1989a) and there is considerable scope for further, more detailed work.

Moving beyond dyadic interactions

Caring and being cared-for (or about) are of course to do with much more than illness or disability. Whilst illness may have occasioned the need for care, and the nature of the illness remains important, this provides the backcloth in most circumstances. In periods of relapse or acute exacerbation the illness will figure more prominently, but for most of the time there are more important considerations. For the person with chronic illness, the critical issue is about maintaining a sense of self (Charmaz 1983, 1987), whereas one of the main purposes of caring is to assist in this process. In the meantime, both carer and cared-for person have to be getting on with other work, such as occupational work, marital work, child-care work and domestic work (Corbin and Strauss 1988). It is here that family systems perspectives are of relevance.

On the basis of our description so far, it would be easy to see Rolland's model (1988, 1994) as a primarily medicalized approach with some window-dressing of social and psychological components – a kind of wolf in sheep's clothing. This would be well wide of the mark, however, for he also provides considerable illustrative detail about the role of family belief systems, the family life-cycle and the interface of these factors with the illness trajectory. Space does not permit a discussion of these here, but for Rolland they form a crucial component of work with families where one member has a chronic condition. Other authors have also highlighted the importance of extending the unit of analysis to include the family (Boss 1988, 1993; Boss *et al.* 1988; Thompson *et al.* 1993; Litwak *et al.* 1994). Indeed, we would suggest that there are a number of trajectories that need to be considered, and the impact of one upon the other identified. These might include: the caregiving trajectory; the illness trajectory; the family life-cycle trajectory; and, for those individuals who are in receipt of services for several years, a service trajectory. An integration and synthesis of these at a conceptual level and the empirical testing of their consequences remains a significant challenge for all those interested in family caregiving.

Rolland (1988) terms his model the 'therapeutic quadrangle', three corners of which are represented by the carer, the cared-for person and the illness or disability. Located at the fourth corner is the perspective of the practitioner or formal caring system. This is an essential addition, because any attempt at integration would be incomplete without reference to such systems. This is certainly true in the UK where, despite the rhetoric of the NHS and Community Care Act (DoH 1990) and its reference to empowerment and involvement, services are still required to be consistent with local agency policy. To exacerbate matters, the distinction between a range of terms such as 'involvement' and 'empowerment' – which are often used interchangeably – remain to be drawn (Grant 1996). As we have illustrated frequently throughout this text, there is often considerable mismatch between the perceptions of those assessing for or providing services and those being assessed for or receiving them. The essential basis of this mismatch is the persistent way in which both services and the eligibility criteria for them define need largely in terms of physical or mental dependency. This is tellingly illustrated in a recent review of measures to determine the outcomes of community services for people with dementia (Ramsey *et al.* 1995). Whilst scholarly and comprehensive, the review focuses almost exclusively on quantifiable measures and assesses them in terms of pyschometric properties such as validity, reliability and similar parameters. Although there may be a role of such benchmarks in epidemiological work, as the mainstay of outcome evaluation in community care they are severely limited.

It is simply not meaningful to carers and cared-for persons to reduce their efforts to a statistically significant change in a depression inventory or an ADL scale. Neither is it meaningful to base an assessment of their need for support on similar measures. Until this conceptual leap is made, the interface between family carers and professional carers will remain 'contested territory' (Lewis and Meredith 1989). Moreover, services will continue to inhibit or obstruct carers' efforts rather than facilitate them.

The road to improved services for carers does not lie in the search for powerful and enduring predictors of stress, burden or need; it lies, in good individual assessments (Harper *et al.* 1993) linked to a multidimensional approach (Levesque *et al.* 1995) that recognizes the dynamic nature of caregiving and the complex and subtle interactions between carer and cared-for person. The ramifications of achieving such an aim and the implications for theory, policy and practice in family caregiving are considered in the concluding chapter.

7

REACHING THE END OR A NEW BEGINNING?

Finally, we all know there's no simple or single solution. There will always be some strains and some pain. Benevolently intended programs have limitations, and societal provisions cannot solve all problems. But as a society, we are not doing our best right now. True, we do not know all we need to know. But surely we know enough to make a start.

(Brody 1995: 28)

Writing of the future prospects for caregiving, Brody (1995) argues that if services are to be effective then they must be able to respond to the change, continuity and diversity that characterizes family care. Her observation raises important points. For there is indeed no simple or single solution, and caregiving will always necessarily have difficult and onerous elements. On the other hand, in this book we have striven to bring together a number of differing perspectives that might better illuminate some of the less explored dimensions of family care. Whilst acknowledging the difficulties of caring, we have attempted to debunk the myth that caring is 'hardly reciprocal and only rarely rewarding'. Applying a transactional paradigm, we have explored the change, continuity and diversity that is family care. In so doing, the proactive and resourceful nature of the coping strategies carers employ has become evident, and some taken-for-granted assumptions have been questioned. Similarly, the diverse and pervasive range of satisfactions that carers experience has emerged as central to a more complete understanding of caregiving. We have located this experience within a temporal model of care and begun the task of integrating a range of differing perspectives. Most fundamentally of all, in our view, we have taken heed of Gubrium's (1995) advice, gone back to basics and posed the question 'what is this thing some call caregiving?'. We are under no illusions about having provided complete or definitive answers, but our purpose will have been served if we have removed a few conceptual blinkers and put another nail (unfortunately not the last, we suspect) in the coffin of the belief that family caring can be understood primarily in terms of its instrumental components.

In this concluding chapter we will address some of the implications of our work for theory, method, policy and practice in family caring.

Theoretical and methodological considerations

As we noted earlier, our intention in applying a transactional perspective was not to dwell on the pathologizing aspects of family care but to recognize the interactive, dynamic and contextual nature of caring. We feel that as a heuristic device it has proved more than adequate, but as with anything that brings knowledge into the open it has left a range of questions unanswered. It can be no other way. Moreover, in taking a fairly catholic perspective on family care we have probably answered fewer questions than we have raised. This, however, is not necessarily a bad thing if it paves the way for a new and better understanding. Below are some of the many areas that we feel merit further exploration.

One of the central elements of family care to emerge was its reciprocal nature. This is by no means a new conclusion. However, the analysis of the satisfactions of care offered in this book provides, we believe, new insights which serve further to highlight the diffuse, generalized and often hypothetical nature of exchange in intimate relationships. Certainly the notion of 'altruism as reciprocity' gained strong empirical support, and the act of giving to the cared-for person with no expectation of any tangible return was seen to underpin many of the satisfactions of carers. This itself raises some interesting issues. Even if a carer is happy to give (and gain at least some form of psychic return) in this way, this may still leave the cared-for person feeling indebted. As individuals become increasingly frail, one of the challenges they face is how to maintain a perception of reciprocity. Hirschfield (1981, 1983) suggested that in dementia caregiving, the best relationships were those in which the person with dementia was seen to reciprocate 'by virtue of their existence'. In other words the carer expected no return other than the satisfaction gained from knowing that their efforts helped to maintain the cared-for person's quality of life. Many of the sources of satisfaction in our studies, for example maintaining the dignity of the cared-for person, seeing that their needs were well tended to, and giving the best possible care, are of a similar nature. However, for the physically frail but cognitively intact person this may still leave them in a position of perceived indebtedness. A number of authors have suggested that one of the principal motivations in family interactions is to maintain a sense of balance so that one party does not feel constantly beholden to the other (Bulmer 1987; Antonucci and Jackson 1989; Finch and Mason 1993). Whilst some cared-for people may not feel indebted, perhaps because of the earlier help that they provided for the carer, the 'bank balance' (Antonucci and Jackson 1989) of many others may soon run into the red.

On the other hand, as Kahana and Young (1990) argue, the contribution of, for example, many frail older people has been relatively ignored. They suggest that an older person may be a marvellous raconteur or a good listener, or, as in our studies, the provider of advice. A major deficit in most caregiving research is a failure to explore the perspective of the cared-for person. How do such individuals feel about being the recipients of care, how do they maintain a sense of balance and interdependence, what strategies do they have to sustain a perception of equitable exchange? Cicarelli (1992) raises a number of similar arguments with regard to autonomy. He suggests that the concept of autonomy requires much fuller exploration because if it is interpreted in a literal sense, someone who is highly dependent cannot be autonomous. Building on the work of Collopy (1988), he differentiates between 'decisional' and 'executional' autonomy. The former is the opportunity to make decisions and the latter the ability to execute consequent actions. Cicarelli (1992) contends that decisional autonomy is possible even in situations when executional autonomy is not. He goes on to suggest a continuum of autonomy: direct autonomy; consultative autonomy; joint autonomy; delegated autonomy; surrogate autonomy. At one end (direct autonomy), a person retains total control whereas at the other, having passed through various degrees of shared autonomy, the decisions are all made by a third party in what is believed to be the best interests of the other person. Cicarelli suggests that in the complex society in which we live, direct autonomy is notional at best and that other forms are more relevant. Certainly in advanced frailty, joint or delegated autonomy may be more realistic. Similar considerations may be applied to reciprocity; we need to explore further the range and meanings of this concept, particularly in situations where exchange becomes highly abstract.

Although this book has been primarily about family care, the concept of reciprocity is equally – possibly more – important in professional care. Most family caregiving relationships are built upon a long history where repayment of past services, hypothetical exchange or simply loving and valuing the other person are often sufficient to keep a relationship reciprocal. This is not the case in professional care. If community care is successful and people are maintained in their own homes for longer periods, those who do eventually need admission to some alternative form of care will be increasingly frail, both cognitively and physically. What then are the sources of job satisfaction for those providing care? We noted earlier that good professional care, as with good family care, depends on the cared-for person somehow 'mattering' (Radsma 1994; Fealy 1995; Scott 1995). This is perhaps best illustrated with regard to the care of frail older people in institutional settings.

It seems clear from most of the recent literature that the key to quality of care in such settings hinges largely on the nature of interpersonal relationships and the recognition that the older person, no matter how frail, has the status of a human being. It is therefore essential that older people are seen to have the potential for continued growth and development, something which remains conspicuous by its absence in many care settings (Koch *et al.* 1995). Kadner (1994) suggests that intimacy is the essence of a therapeutic interaction, and that to achieve this requires the self-disclosure of personal information. Therefore as Scott (1995) highlights, constructive care requires that staff perceive themselves as an instrument of care and that they have a personal investment in the people they are caring for. Scott recognizes that this is a profoundly demanding role in terms of energy, imagination, time and emotion but as Kayser-Jones (1981: 49) notes, 'A personal relationship between staff and the elderly in long-term care institutions is desirable and essential.' Developing and nurturing such relationships is not, however, simply a matter of intuition and being a 'good' person, for as Goodwin (1992) points out, tender loving care without proper knowledge and skills is potentially disastrous.

If staff are therefore to invest the levels of energy, imagination and emotion required to provide good care, they must perceive some reciprocal element to the relationship. Indeed, the ability to sustain what has been termed 'therapeutic reciprocity' (Marck 1990; Nolan and Grant 1993) is seen as essential to the maintenance of acceptable care for frail older people. Yet this is very difficult to achieve in situations where a meaningful context for exchange cannot be construed.

It seems to us that an increasingly important characteristic of the genuinely 'expert' carer (whether family or professional) will be the ability to create a sense of interdependence in relationships with frail individuals. If this is to be achieved, a deeper and more thorough exploration of the nature of reciprocity as perceived by both carers and cared-for persons is required.

Expertise was another concept that we brought to bear on our data; this again provided a fruitful avenue which requires further probing. That many carers have a sense of expertise is beyond doubt, and perceiving oneself as a competent carer is clearly an important consideration. However, the manner in which such expertise is gained, how carers acquire their role and its associated knowledge and skills, requires more detailed empirical study. The same applies to the potential for enhancing the process by which carers gain expertise and to methods for sharing such knowledge between family and professional carers. Each has a lot to learn from the other.

Maintaining a sense of competence in the cared-for person is equally important, especially as levels of frailty rise. Lawton *et al.* (1995) raise crucial questions about the quality of life of very frail older people in the community, suggesting that, above a certain level of frailty, people may be better off in institutional care. Their work suggests that those living in the community may find the opportunities for potentially 'enriching' activities extremely limited; they argue that one of the challenges for the future is to determine how the lives of very frail older people can be enriched. They believe that maintaining a sense of competence is one such way, but this begs the question as to competence in what? Further conceptual and empirical work is required in this area as Lawton and colleagues' study was limited methodologically, relying solely on accounts from family carers.

Carers in our studies sought to maintain levels of competence in the cared-for person for as long as possible using a variety of subtle strategies that formed the basis of protective, preservative and (re)constructive care. Other studies have reached similar conclusions about the desire of carers to maintain a sense of normality (Bowers 1987; Clarke 1995), yet services often overlook this.

Although we feel that we have shed further light on the coping strategies that carers employ and the satisfactions that they experience, this is only the first step. The methodological limitations of the survey techniques we employed are apparent. These are compounded by the fact that we did not explore the nature of difficulties, coping and satisfactions with the same carers. We can therefore say nothing about how they interact. For whilst we may now be more aware that carers employ a diverse range of coping strategies and that they perceive many of them to be helpful, we do not know whether they are able to target these strategies in the most effective way. It is conceivable that an individual may have a range of strategies at their disposal but use them inappropriately, for example a problem-solving approach may be applied to an irresolvable problem. Similarly, we do not know how satisfactions and difficulties may mutually reinforce one another. Certainly we can hypothesize; for example an absence of appreciation is a well-recognized stressor and the presence of appreciation a perceived reward. Similarly, manipulative and demanding behaviour from the cared-for person is stressful, whereas caring for someone who, despite their problems, does not grumble and moan is seen as satisfying. But it is unlikely that the interrelationship between difficulties, satisfactions and coping will be as straightforward as this, and studies considering these dynamics would no doubt provide further valuable insights.

We think it is likely that satisfactions may protect carer well-being, and that the absence of satisfactions can be used as an indicator of risk both for poor carer health and poor (possibly abusive) caring relationships, but this remains speculation. Given the potentially powerful role of satisfactions as mediating factors, studies are needed that allow us to do more than speculate. We also need to explore further the potential variations in satisfactions and coping amongst differing carers by gender, race, kinship relationships or other variables. The survey samples we have drawn upon here were confined largely to spouses or children caring for parents. One might anticipate differing forms of satisfactions, and possibly coping, amongst parents caring for children.

The extended version of Bowers's (1987, 1988) typology of care that we elaborated and the longitudinal model that is published for the first time here are intended to offer differing perspectives on the caring experience. They are well grounded in our empirical data but should be seen as initial formulations only. We are satisfied that the broad parameters are adequate, but there is considerable scope to probe the nuances and variations in greater depth as these will provide further, possibly more interesting, dimensions.

Methodologically, as noted by others (Opie 1994; Brody 1995; Gubrium 1995), we welcome the return (or at least the re-emergence) of the qualitative study. We would not totally eschew quantitative approaches, as they are important to identify the commonalties upon which to base rational policy, but we see deterministic, causal models as having had their day. Such models are useful to the extent that they provide 'sensitizing concepts' and they are powerful in that statistical data may help persuade policy-makers. For example, a small qualitative study that suggests that subjective perceptions are more important than the objective circumstances of care in determining burden is unlikely to have a significant impact upon the policy-making machine. However, large quantitative studies that reach a similar conclusion are more difficult to ignore. The other striking methodological message, although it is certainly not new and may even sound trite, is the need for longitudinal studies of the caring experience that incorporate the perspectives of the carer and cared-for person.

Until we can gather prospective data, our theoretical formulations will remain relatively impoverished. Widening horizons must also involve far greater efforts to move beyond the caregiving dyad and include, where appropriate, the whole family unit, and the type of integration and synthesis of differing trajectories to which we referred in the last chapter.

Our intention in this section has not been to provide a comprehensive consideration of all the possible theoretical issues that require elaboration but to highlight what for us are some of the more interesting. This is obviously a partial view and others may well have identified a differing set of concerns. Nevertheless we feel it adds weight to Kahana _et al._'s (1994) contention that only a small corner of the potential field of study in family care has yet been addressed.

Policy considerations

The absence of a coherent policy for family care has been noted both in the UK (Twigg and Atkin 1994) and the USA (Kane and Penrod 1995). Some of the reasons for this in the UK have been explored by Twigg and Atkin, and we do not intend to rehearse these arguments again. We believe, however, that an adequate policy for carers cannot be considered without reference both to community care policies and those relating to long-term care.

Twigg and Atkin contend that carers are no longer the 'Cinderellas' of the policy arena. Whilst it is true that they have figured far more prominently on policy agendas recently, we see relatively little that gives other than cautious grounds for optimism that their actual situation will improve. In a sense it might be better if carers _were_ like Cinderella, because eventually she gets to go to the ball, whereas the longer-term prospects for carers are often bleak, certainly on a range of financial parameters (Hancock and Jarvis

1994). Clearly adequate recompense for carers and some means of providing at least an element of long-term financial security is needed. This has even been recognized by the British Medical Association (BMA 1995) who, in a series of recommendations premised largely on a view of carers as resources, suggest that there is a need for 'improved financial support for carers, including the introduction of a carers allowance to act as an adequate earnings replacement benefit and to compensate for the time spent caring' (p. 8). They also advise that the government should consider introducing the range of other financial benefits recommended by Glendinning and McLaughlin (1993), so that Britain is brought more in line with other European countries. They add a caveat that such benefits should be targeted at those groups most heavily involved in care.

Interestingly, debates about financial recompense for carers also figure on European (Evers 1995) and American agendas (Linsk *et al.* 1995). Evers (1995) notes the diversity of financial support available in Europe, both in terms of direct financial payments and social security benefits, but he adds a further important dimension that enables carers to remain in the labour market. He suggests that whilst adequate recompense is essential to all carers, the manner in which it is most appropriately targeted may vary. For an elderly spouse caring for their partner, direct recompense and/or better benefits might be the most appropriate. But for a son, or more likely a daughter, then strategies to allow them to remain in employment (if they so wish) and still continue to provide care and support are needed. Evers argues that this will require far more public debate about the binding (or otherwise) nature of the norms relating to family responsibilities.

In terms of a philosophical basis for a policy of family care, Evers suggests that governments must move towards a system of complementary and supplementary services rather than substitutive ones. This is consistent with our concept of facilitative interventions which seek to build upon rather than replace (or obstruct) the efforts of family carers. There will always be a role for some substitutive services, but even these will need to complement carers' existing strategies. Therefore the suggestion that carers should have a right to at least two weeks respite a year (BMA 1995) is a step in the right direction, but is unlikely to be beneficial until the nature and purpose of respite care is construed in a much more holistic fashion (Nolan and Grant 1992a; Montgomery 1995).

Turning his attention specifically to the UK, Evers (1995) suggests that there are currently two conflicting movements emerging, the one towards consumerism and a free market approach, and the other towards case (care) management, where a professional is responsible for putting together a broad service package. Although this package is putatively based on an assessment of need, Evers takes the view that in reality it is driven by administrative and professional perspectives and the need to ration scarce resources. Recent evaluations of assessment practice in the UK would seem to confirm this (Ellis 1993; Manthorpe and Twigg 1995; Nolan and Caldock 1996).

As a solution to these two conflicting trends, Evers (1995) offers the concept of modified care management. This was developed in the Netherlands, where there is an attempt for care managers to combine subtly both the role of advocate and assessor of need. This creates a 'care triangle' (Knipscheer 1992) which facilitates the involvement of users and carers but differs from a consumerist model in that it provides a greater role for professionals. However, there is also the potential for conflict in situations where professionals attempt to combine the role of advocate with that of assessing the need for care. Issues such as these require clarification before more meaningful partnerships can be created. For example, service delivery models do exist and have been empirically tested, especially in the field of learning difficulties (see, for example, Dunst and Trivette 1988; Dunst *et al.* 1989). The extent to which such approaches can be applied to differing caregiving contexts requires further consideration. On the other hand, the concept of a care triangle is consistent with the idea of a partnership arrangement operating within a 'therapeutic quadrangle' (Rolland 1988, 1994), in which the role of the professional is as a consultant and adviser and rarely as a direct provider of care. This clearly has implications for education and practice for work with carers, which will be addressed shortly.

The NHS and Community Care Act 1990 advocated far greater involvement and participation for carers, but largely overturned any meaningful contribution by relegating carers' viewpoints to those of the user and the assessor (Nolan *et al.* 1994). The implementation of the Carers (Recognition and Services) Act 1995 provides the opportunity to redress the balance. Unfortunately it seems that this potential may not be realized. On the basis of the policy guidance and the principles of the Act itself, carer involvement is immediately inhibited by two striking limitations. First, the Act itself is 'concerned with carers who are either providing or intending to provide regular and substantial care'. Second, carers are only entitled to an assessment if the cared-for person is also receiving one. These factors effectively render the Act impotent with regard to many carers who may be most in need. To exacerbate matters, the interpretation of 'regular and substantial' is left to local authorities. Although there may be a faint glimmer of hope that some enlightened authorities will take a more holistic interpretation, the glimmer is faint indeed in the glare of the financial limitations already inhibiting innovation in terms of assessment of need (Manthorpe and Twigg 1995). If lessons learned from the evaluations of assessment practice in community care provide any indication, authorities will focus on the instrumental acts of care, largely utilizing ADL scales (Caldock 1994a,b; Nolan and Caldock 1996).

We think that a policy for carers cannot be fully developed outside of the context of both community care policy and long-term care policy. In fact it seems to us that the distinction between community care and long-term care is becoming blurred and increasingly meaningless. Whilst the primary aim of community care is to keep people at home for as long as possible, given the prevailing demography the need to maintain institutional alternatives is inescapable (Bond and Bond 1992; Victor 1992; Higham 1994). As Ebrahim *et al.* (1993) contend, long-term care (LTC) in the UK has been conceptualized almost exclusively in terms of institutional provision, a tendency also apparent in the US (Phillips-Harris and Farnale 1995). However, others have suggested a more encompassing definition (Kane and Kane 1991; Cicarelli 1992; Kane and Penrod 1995) in which LTC refers to the whole range of services and interventions that assist people in need of support to lead meaningful lives, irrespective of the environment of care. Within this scenario institutional care represents one amongst a number of options rather than being viewed as an inherently inferior alternative (Victor 1992; Higham 1994).

This is important because our data, consistent with several studies (Davies 1980; Hirschfield 1981, 1983; Allen *et al.* 1992; Dellasega and Mastrian 1995), indicate that family carers do not, by and large, see institutional care as an acceptable alternative. It is only considered as a last resort. Community care policies are likely to reinforce such a perception. There needs to be a more constructive debate about the role and value of institutional provision as one form of LTC.

As Willcocks (1986) argues, the case against institutional care is incomplete and is based more on historical failure than a realistic assessment of current potential. Indeed, Lawrence *et al.* (1987) suggest that it was only during the 1980s that we were 'helped to discover' that living at home was good for us. In a lucid and well-argued paper, Baldwin *et al.* (1993) detail the sustained attack against institutional care but contend that such critiques have been both unidimensional and unidirectional and are guilty of presenting a static view which projects residents 'devoid of their pasts and denied their futures' (p. 70). Developing their arguments further, they suggest that there has been a dearth of comparative studies with similarly frail populations in community settings and a consequent uncritical acceptance of the supposed superiority of community care. They pose the question – what quality of life do frail older people really achieve at home? – and they note: 'Many older people at home cope without the benefit of regular care. In such circumstances depersonalisation, loneliness, withdrawal and depression may be common and might in other contexts be described as institutionalisation' (p. 75).

Although it is probably true that given the choice, most older people would prefer to live in their own homes, this is not universally so, especially as levels of frailty increase (Allen *et al.* 1992; Johnson *et al.* 1994). The inherent risk of a slavish adherence to community care policies, which after all have yet to demonstrate their efficacy (Wistow 1995), is that institutional provision will become yet further maligned. Indeed, the promulgation of community care has served to reinforce an already largely negative image of residential and nursing homes, which are increasingly viewed as being universally 'dysfunctional' (Higham 1994). If such a perception is to be countered and entry to care be seen as a positive choice (Wagner 1988), then there is a need for further, more informed debate about the nature of what constitutes LTC and what are the options available.

The interface between acute and LTC (including community care) also needs further exploration. Wistow (1995) argues that although the parallel developments of the NHS and community care reforms were putatively coordinated, in reality they occurred with little thought as to the impact of one upon the other. Therefore in a Health Service which is increasingly orientated towards acute care and the very rapid throughput of patients from expensive hospital beds, hospital discharge has once again surfaced as the arena in which tensions between acute and LTC come to the forefront. This has serious implications for carers and cared-for persons. First, as many carers take on their role following an acute health crisis, the push for ever shorter lengths of hospital stay provides very little time to make an informed choice about caregiving, or to receive adequate preparation for the role. As we have indicated at various points throughout this book, the perception of an informed choice and adequate preparation for caregiving are precursors of both better care and less burden. Moreover, in the absence of a thorough assessment of prior relationships, caring circumstances may be created that are far from ideal. Second, as admission to care may also follow hospitalization, this leaves little time to make what may be one of the most crucial of life's decisions (Allen *et al.* 1992). We would agree with Brody (1995: 28) that there is an urgent need to address 'the chaos of hospital discharge process and the process of admission to nursing homes'.

Practice considerations

At various stages we have made reference to what we consider to be the practice implications of our results. A brief synthesis is given below.

As Parker and Lawton (1994) point out there are currently few services with the explicit aim of helping carers, and even those which are targeted primarily at carers, such as respite care, take a rather narrow view as to their purpose (Nolan and Grant 1992a; Montgomery 1995). We think that present services are inherently reductionist, reducing carers' problems mainly to the physical aspects of care (Ellis 1993; Twigg and Atkin 1994; Liston *et al.* 1995; Montgomery 1995), often breaking caring down into discrete tasks (Schultz *et al.* 1993; Greene and Coleman 1995). This fragments the caring experience and does little to permit a holistic picture to emerge.

This reductionist approach is compounded by a lack of professional experience and expertise in working with family carers, and a failure to clarify both the role and purpose of interventions and the relationship between professional and family carers. Some commentators have suggested that working with family carers is a new and difficult role for professionals

(Lewis and Meredith 1989) and that there is no real tradition of practice in this area (Twigg and Atkin 1994). Twigg and Atkin suggest that the relationship between family and professional carers can be conceptualized in terms of four models: carers as resources; carers as co-workers; carers as co-clients, and the superseded carer. Whilst these may well represent the current situation, we believe that none of these models is in fact appropriate. Carers as resources, whilst undeniably the most prevalent (albeit implicit) perception, is essentially exploitative and is not supportable on moral, ethical or even pragmatic grounds. Carers as co-workers is possibly the most appropriate; but as this is still basically motivated by instrumental aims, Twigg and Atkin suggest, we feel that the requisite balance is not achieved. Carers as co-clients and the superseded carer may be appropriate in certain circumstances, but we believe that neither model is adequate as the primary basis for determining relationships between family and professional carers.

We would suggest that a more explicit partnership is required and that *carers as experts* should constitute the primary model for work with family caregivers. Here the explicit purpose is to increase carers' competency, to move them as rapidly as possible from 'novice' to 'expert' and to sustain them in the expert role throughout the various stages of the caregiving trajectory. Abrams (1985) asserted some time ago that competency is a prerequisite of care and that enabling this was an essential but badly neglected process. Little would seem to have changed in the intervening decade. We believe that a 'carer as expert' model provides a meaningful framework which could result in a substantial improvement to practice.

However, for such a model to become operational a number of criteria need to be met:

- There has to be an individual assessment of caregiver need that moves beyond the instrumental and takes a multidimensional approach (Given and Given 1991; Sharp 1992; Jerrom *et al.* 1993; Thompson *et al.* 1993; Levesque *et al.* 1995), including where appropriate, the family unit and the influence of varying trajectories.
- Carers need to be empowered so that they see their own needs as legitimate and have a sense of 'entitlement' with regard to services (Schultz *et al.* 1993; Fisher 1994; Triantafillou and Mestheneos 1994; Twigg and Atkin 1994).
- A far more comprehensive range of services needs to be available. These must match the problems carers experience and be sufficiently flexible to respond to changes in the caring trajectory (Braithwaite 1990; Smith *et al.* 1991; Thompson *et al.* 1993; Brodatey *et al.* 1994; Kane and Penrod 1995). Kane and Penrod (1995) suggest a pharmacological metaphor for services so that we talk in terms of what are the indications and contradictions for services, what is the dosage and duration of treatment, what may be the possible side-effects and so on.
- Whilst recognizing that there will always be a need for help with physical

aspects of care and that in certain circumstances substitutive services are appropriate, there needs to be a cognitive shift towards a *modus operandi* in which professionals become facilitators rather than doers. We are not referring here to a care management approach underpinned by the role of broker, but rather to the sort of comprehensive educative/supportive model advocated some years ago by Zipple and Spaniol (1987). The primary aim of interventions here is to enhance the skills, competence and expertise of family carers (Spaniol and Jung 1987; Zipple and Spaniol 1987; Dunst and Trivette 1988; Dunst *et al.* 1989; Ellis 1993; Schulz *et al.* 1993; Triantafillou and Mestheneos 1994; Archbold *et al.* 1995; Levesque *et al.* 1995).

- If this is to be achieved there has to be a 'paradigmatic leap' in the professional psyche. This will require considerable training and support (Ellis 1993; Triantafillou and Meitheneos 1994; Archbold *et al.* 1995).
- In considering the 'success' of interventions, there needs to be a move away from global measures such as a reduction in burden or psychological distress towards a more individualized approach that determines what works for a carer in their particular circumstances (Smith *et al.* 1991; Harper *et al.* 1993; Thompson *et al.* 1993; Levesque *et al.* 1995).

A number of studies exemplify the extent and nature of change that is required. Smith *et al.* (1991) address the need for support amongst daughters and daughters-in-law providing care for ageing parents. They argue that current interventions are too global and outcome measures too general, and that improvements would not occur until the focus for interventions is defined by carers themselves. In looking at the needs of female child carers, they consider that no single problem is dominant and that service inputs have to account for this diversity. However, a number of factors do emerge as significant (in a personal rather than a statistical sense) and these are: to develop improved coping skills, especially in time management and the ability to see personal time as legitimate; dealing with family issues, particularly negotiating private time with spouses and considering the impact of caring on their own children; being able to respond to the older person's needs; the quality of the relationship with the older person; how to elicit formal and informal support; dealing with guilt and feelings of inadequacy; long-term planning, particularly what to do if institutional care is needed. On the basis of their study, Smith *et al.* (1991) conclude that services must be flexible and personalized and that problems cannot be determined by *a priori* means.

Dunst *et al.* (1989) outline a model for the delivery of services to parents of children with learning difficulties using the acronym SHaRE (sources of help received and exchanged). This model is based on enabling and empowering families to identify their own needs and strengths in order to help them mobilize resources, thereby becoming more self-sufficient and interdependent.

Underpinning SHaRE is the notion of competence and the assumption that individuals have the capacity to achieve competence, providing that the social systems in which they operate are supportive and they are given opportunities to deploy their competence in a way that allows them to acquire a sense of control over their lives. The roles of staff within this model are considered to be different to those typically described and include the role of empathetic listener; resource; consultant; mobilizer; enabler; and mediator. Dunst *et al.* (1989) argue that whilst not without its difficulties, the model provides a way to redefine the purpose and rationale behind interventions with family carers.

The work of Archbold and colleagues in North America (Archbold *et al.* 1992, 1995) provides another elegant practice model developed for work with family carers of older people. Although a nursing model and geared towards the health care system operating in the US, we believe that it could successfully be transposed to other contexts, both professionally and geographically. The model is given the acronym PREP, standing for preparedness, enrichment and predictability. It has three principal aims:

- to increase the preparedness and competence of family carers providing home care to disabled relatives;
- to enrich and enhance the caregiving experience in order to maximize the satisfactions of both carer and cared-for person;
- to make the unpredictable aspects of caring more predictable by improving carers' coping skills and their ability to anticipate future care needs.

In order to achieve these aims a fourfold strategy is advocated, including direct support, interventions and teaching; a carer advice line; a Keep in Touch (KIT) system of regular follow-ups; and, when appropriate, a conclusion of interventions that specifically focuses on the positive aspects of caregiving, highlighting what the carer has achieved. Underpinning the model is the need for a systematic assessment of the entire family system (where appropriate) in which there is family/practitioner collaboration. The intention is to blend local and cosmopolitan knowledge in order to produce an individual plan. The model has been subjected to a pilot test, and this suggests that it has the potential not only to achieve its aims but to do so in a cost-effective manner.

Such an approach brings together many of the elements required to achieve better service support for carers, and merits close attention. Indeed we can see immediate application for some of our own indices, although clearly other tools may also be appropriate. A programme could be devised as follows:

- Increasing preparedness – the extent to which carers can be adequately prepared for their role depends in part on the stage in the caregiving trajectory at which they first come into contact with services. If this is in the early or novice stages then the tenets we suggested in the previous chapter during the 'recognizing the need/taking it on' stages would apply. If carers do not come into contact until the 'working through it' stage, then there is a need for a thorough assessment of the range of difficulties they face, and their existing level of knowledge and expertise. The Carers Assessment of Difficulties Index (CADI) (Nolan and Grant 1992a) was designed for this express purpose and provides a mechanism for identifying both the most prevalent difficulties in a particular caring situation and those which are perceived as the most stressful. This lays the platform for an individualized intervention plan.

- Enriching caring – as discussed in depth in Chapter 4, the satisfactions of caring form an important but neglected dimension. Working with carers to identify sources of satisfaction whilst simultaneously addressing perceived difficulties has the potential to increase the effectiveness of support. In instances where there are few, if any satisfactions, then this can signal the need for an in-depth consideration of future caring arrangements. The Carers Assessment of Satisfactions Index (CASI) (Nolan and Grant 1992a) provides a basis for discussion in this area.

- Increasing predictability – working with carers to make their situation more predictable requires knowledge not only of their circumstances (for example the stage in the caring trajectory, the nature of illness or disability that the cared-for person has, the stage in the family life-cycle and so on) but also the range of coping strategies that carers employ, and whether or not these are the most appropriate ones for the difficulties they face. The Carers Assessment of Managing Index (CAMI) (Nolan and Grant 1995b) was designed for this purpose.

Irrespective of the mechanism of assessment, however – and our indices offer only one approach – we believe that the rationale and logic underlying such models as SHaRE and PREP provide a vehicle to define better the interactions between family and professional carers, bringing together in a coherent way many of the disparate elements of the caregiving situation. To be effective, however, they will require that professionals develop a fundamentally different approach to the way that carers are perceived. We feel that the 'carer as expert' model provides a potentially fruitful way forward.

Envoi

The title of this book reflects our belief that there is a need to 'break the mould' of the way that caregiving is conceptualized. In following Gubrium's (1995) advice, and questioning some of the taken-for-granted assumptions about what constitutes family care, we are conscious that this process has only just started. There is a need to follow new theoretical, methodological and empirical routes to a better, more holistic, understanding. On the road to expertise we consider that we ourselves are currently advanced beginners at best. We look forward to learning more from family carers who so willingly share their rich and diverse experiences in the hope that one day we may reach competence.

Appendix 1

CHARACTERISTICS OF SAMPLE FOR POSTAL SURVEYS

Coping sample (n = 260)

Gender of cared-for person M 41%   Gender of carer M 29%
                            F 58%   F 70%

Relationship of carer to cared-for person   Length of time caring
Child   41%   Less than 5 years   64%
Wife   27%   5–10 years   26%
Husband   23%   10 years +   10%
Other relative   6%
Friend   3%

Live in same household   Yes 86%   No 14%

	Age of cared-for person	Age of carer
40 or below	5%	16%
41–60	7%	23%
61–70	18%	24%
71–80	37%	26%
81+	33%	11%

Satisfactions sample (n = 200)

Gender of cared-for person   M 32%   Gender of carer   M 31%
                             F 68%   F 68%

Relationship of carer to cared-for person   Length of time caring
Child   39%   Less than 5 years   52%
Wife   25%   5–10 years   35%
Husband   26%   10 years +   13%
Other relative   7%
Friend   3%

Live in same household   Yes 84%   No 16%

	Age of cared-for person	Age of carer
40 or below	2%	11%
41–60	10%	17%
61–70	16%	32%
71–80	31%	23%
81+	40%	17%

Appendix 2

Satisfactions derived from interpersonal dynamic (n = 200)

	A great deal of satisfaction %	Quite a lot of satisfaction %	No real satisfaction %	This does not apply to me %
Cared-for person as main beneficiary				
Maintaining the dignity of the person I care for is important	81	15	3	2
I get pleasure from seeing the person I care for happy	73	15	4	9
It's nice when something I do gives the person I care for pleasure	66	21	3	10
Shared benefit				
Caring is one way of expressing my love for the person I care for	74	15	7	5
Caring has brought me closer to the person I care for	32	17	18	34
Caring has strengthened close family ties and relationships	26	13	13	47
Carer as main beneficiary				
The person I care for is appreciative of what I do	34	25	18	24
It's nice to feel appreciated by those family and friends I value	37	19	14	31
Despite all their problems the person I care for does not grumble or moan	32	14	16	38

Satisfactions derived from interpersonal dynamic (n = 200)

	A great deal of satisfaction %	Quite a lot of satisfaction %	No real satisfaction %	This does not apply to me %
Carer as main beneficiary				
Caring enables me to fulfil my sense of duty	42	25	11	22
Caring makes me feel needed and wanted	39	14	17	31
Caring provides a challenge	30	18	19	34
I am able to test myself and overcome difficulties	26	19	20	35
Caring has helped me to grow and develop as a person	23	20	11	46
It helps to stop me from feeling guilty	21	10	11	58
Caring has provided a purpose in my life that I did not have before	13	12	13	62
Shared benefit				
At the end of the day I know I will have done the best I could	68	22	6	4
I feel that if the situation were reversed, the person I care for would do the same for me	66	13	6	16
I am the sort of person who enjoys helping people	43	35	8	15
I am able to repay their past acts of kindness	45	21	10	25
Caring is one way of showing my faith	37	18	8	37
Cared-for person as main beneficiary				
It is nice to see the person I care for clean, comfortable and well turned out	69	23	3	6
I am able to ensure that the person I care for has their needs tended to	77	18	2	3

Satisfactions derived from interpersonal dynamic (n = 200)

	A great deal of satisfaction %	Quite a lot of satisfaction %	No real satisfaction %	This does not apply to me %
Cared-for person as main beneficiary				
I am able to keep the person I care for out of an institution	68	12	5	15
Knowing the person I care for the way I do, means I can give better care than anyone else	60	18	10	11
It's good to help the person I care for overcome difficulties and problems	58	17	10	15
It's good to see small improvements in their condition	34	14	10	42
I am able to help the person I care for reach their full potential	30	15	15	41
Carer as main beneficiary				
Caring has allowed me to develop new skills and abilities	21	21	18	39
Caring has given me the chance to widen my interests and contacts	18	12	9	62

REFERENCES

Abrams, P. (1985) (Edited by Bulmer, M.) Policies to promote informal care: some reflections on voluntary action, neighbourhood involvement and neighbourhood care, *Ageing and Society*, 5: 1–18.

Ade-Ridder, L. and Kaplan, L. (1993) Marriage, spousal caregiving and a husband's move to a nursing home: a changing role for the wife? *Journal of Gerontological Nursing*, 19(10): 12–23.

Alber, J. (1993) Health and social services, in A. Walker, J. Alber and A.M. Guillemard (eds) *Older People in Europe: Social and Economic Policies: the 1993 Report of the European Observatory*. Brussels: Commission of the European Communities.

Aldous, J. (1994) Someone to watch over me: family responsibilities and their realization across family lives, in E. Kahana, D.E. Biegel and M.L. Wykle (eds) *Family Caregiving Across the Lifespan*. Thousand Oaks, CA: Sage.

Allen, I., Hogg, D. and Peace, S. (1992) *Elderly People: Choice, Participation and Satisfaction*. London: Policy Studies Institute.

Allen, I., Levin, E., Siddell, M. and Vetter, N. (1983) The elderly and their informal carers, in Elderly People in the Community: Their Service Needs. London: HMSO.

Anderson, K.H., Hobson, A., Steiner, R. and Rodel, B. (1992) Patients with dementia: involving families to maximise nursing care, *Journal of Gerontological Nursing*, 18(7): 19–25.

Antonovsky, A. (1987) *Unravelling the Mystery of Health*. San Francisco, CA: Jossey Bass.

Antonucci, T. and Jackson, J. (1989) Successful ageing and life course reciprocity, in A.W. Warnes (ed.) *Human Ageing and Later Life: Multidisciplinary Perspectives*. London: Edward Arnold.

Anwar, S. and Hill, P. (1994a) Contract culture, *Care Weekly*, 11 August: 11.

Anwar, S. and Hill, P. (1994b) *Making Contact: a Report on Methods of Consultation with Carers from Ethnic Communities*. Oldham: Oldham Disability Alliance.

Arber, S. and Ginn, J. (1990) The meaning of informal care: gender and the contribution of elderly people, *Ageing and Society*, 10: 429–54.

Arber, S. and Ginn, J. (1995) Gender differences in informal caring, *Health and Social Care in the Community*, 3: 19–31.

Archbold, P.G., Stewart, B.J., Greenlick, M.R. and Harvath, T.A. (1992) The clinical assessment of mutuality and preparedness in family caregivers of frail older people, in S.G. Funk, E.M.T. Tornquist, S.T. Champagne and R.A. Wiese (eds) *Key Aspects of Elder Care: Managing Falls, Incontinence and Cognitive Impairment*. New York: Springer.

Archbold, P.G., Stewart, B.J., Miller, L.L., Harvath, T.A., Greenlick, M.R., Van Buren, L., Kirschling, J.M., Valanis, B.G., Brody, K.K., Schook, J.E. and Hagan, J.M. (1995) The PREP system of nursing interventions: a pilot test with families caring for older members, *Research in Nursing Health*, 18: 1–16.

Askham, J., Henshaw, L. and Tarpey, M. (1995) *Social and Health Authority Services for Elderly People from Black and Minority Ethnic Communities*. Age Concern Institute of Gerontology. London: HMSO.

Asvoll, J.E. (1992) Foreword, in A. Kaplun (ed.) *Health Promotion and Chronic Illness: Discovering a New Quality of Health*. Copenhagen: WHO (Europe).

Atkin, K. and Rollings, J. (1992) Informal care in Asian and Afro-Caribbean communities: a literature review, *British Journal of Social Work*, 22: 405–18.

Atkin, K. and Rollings, J. (1993) *Community Care in Multi-Racial Britain: a Critical Review of the Literature*. London: HMSO.

Atkin, K., Cameron, E., Badger, F. and Evers, H. (1989) Asian elders' knowledge and future use of community social and health services, *New Community*, 15(2): 439–46.

Baldwin, N., Harris, J. and Kelly, D. (1993) Institutionalisation: why blame the institutions? *Ageing and Society*, 13: 69–81.

Bandura, A. (1982) Self-efficacy in human agency, *American Psychologist*, 37: 122–47.

Barrera, M. and Ainlay, S.L. (1983) The structure of social support: a conceptual and empirical analysis, *American Journal of Community Psychology*, 11: 133–43.

Bayley, M. (1973) *Mental Handicap and Community Care*. London: Routledge and Kegan Paul.

Beach, D.L. (1993) Gerontological caregiving: analysis of family experience, *Journal of Gerontological Nursing*, 19(12): 35–41.

Begum, N. (1992) Doubly disabled, *Community Care*, 24 September, Supplement: iii–iv.

Begum, N. (1995) *Care Management and Assessment from an Anti-racist Perspective*. York: Joseph Rowntree Foundation.

Bell, R. and Gibbons, S. (1989) *Working with Carers: Information and Training for Work with Informal Carers of Elderly People*. London: Health Education Authority.

Bell, R., Gibbons, R. and Pinchen, I. (1987) *Action Research with Informal Carers: Patterns and Processes in Carers Lives*, report on phase two. Cambridge: Health Promotion Service.

Benner, P. (1984) *From Novice to Expert: Excellence and Power in Clinical Nursing*. Menlo Park, CA: Addison Wesley.

Benner, P. and Wruebel, J. (1989) *The Primacy of Caring: Stress and Coping in Health and Illness*. Menlo Park, CA: Addison Wesley.

Beresford, B. (1994) *Positively Parents: Caring for a Severely Disabled Child*. London: HMSO.

Bewley, C. and Glendinning, C. (1994) Representing the views of disabled people in community care planning, *Disability and Society*, 9(3): 301–14.

Bhalla, A. and Blakemore, K. (1981) *Elders of the Ethnic Minority Groups*. Birmingham: All Faiths for One Race.

Biedenham, P.J. and Normoyle, J.B. (1991) Elderly community residents reactions to the nursing home: an analysis of nursing home related beliefs, *The Gerontologist*, 31(1): 107–15.

Biegel, D.E., Sales, E. and Schulz, K. (1991) *Family Caregiving in Chronic Illness*. Newbury Park, CA: Sage.

Biegel, D.E., Song, L. and Chakravarthy, V. (1994) Predictors of caregiver burden among support group members of persons with chronic mental illness, in E. Kahana, D.E. Biegel and M.L. Wykle (eds) *Family Caregiving Across the Lifespan*. Thousand Oaks, CA: Sage.

Birchwood, M. and Smith, J. (1987) Schizophrenia and the family, in J. Orford (ed.) *Coping with Disorder in the Family*. London: Croom Helm.

Blakemore, K. and Boneham, M. (1993) *Age, Race and Ethnicity: a Comparative Approach*. Buckingham: Open University Press.

Bland, R., Bland, R., Cheetham, J., Lapsley, I. and Revellon, S. (1992) Residential Care for Elderly People: their Costs and Quality. Edinburgh: HMSO.

Bond, J. (1992) The politics of caregiving: the professionalisation of informal care, *Ageing and Society*, 12: 5–21.

Bond, S. and Bond, J. (1992) *Evaluating Continuing Care Accommodation: an Overview of Nursing Staff Survey, Report no. 60*. University of Newcastle-upon-Tyne: Centre for Health Services Research.

Booth, T. (1993) Obstacles to the development of user centred services, in J. Johnson and R. Slater (eds) *Ageing and Later Life*. London: Sage.

Boss, P. (1988) *Family Stress Management*. Newbury Park, CA: Sage.

Boss, P. (1993) Boundary ambiguity: a block to cognitive coping, in A.P. Turnbull, J.M. Patterson, S.K. Behr, D.L. Murphy, J.G. Marquis and M.J. Blue-Banning (eds) *Cognitive Coping, Families and Disability*. Baltimore, MD: Paul H. Brookes.

Boss, P., Caron, W. and Horbol, J. (1988) Alzheimer's disease and ambiguous loss, in C.S. Chilman, F.M. Cox and E.W. Nunnelly (eds) *Chronic Illness and Disability*. Newbury Park, CA: Sage.

Bowers, B.J. (1987) Inter-generational caregiving: adult caregivers and their ageing parents, *Advances in Nursing Science*, 9(2): 20–31.

Bowers, B.J. (1988) Family perceptions of care in a nursing home, *The Gerontologist*, 28(3): 361–7.

Bradshaw, J. and Lawton, D. (1978) Tracing the causes of stress in families with handicapped children, *British Journal of Social Work*, 8: 181–92.

Braithwaite, V.A. (1990) *Bound to Care*. Sydney: Allen and Unwin.

Brandstädter, J. (1995) Maintaining a sense of control and self-esteem in later life: protective mechanisms. Paper presented at III European Congress of Gerontology, Amsterdam, 30 August–2 September 1995.

British Medical Association (1995) *Taking Care of the Carers*. London: BMA.

Brodatey, H., Roberts, K. and Peters, K. (1994) Quasi-experimental evaluation of an educational model for dementia caregivers, *International Journal of Geriatric Psychiatry*, 9: 195–204.

Brody, E.M. (1995) Prospects for family caregiving: response to change, continuity and diversity, in R.A. Kane and J.D. Penrod (eds) *Family Caregiving in an Ageing Society*. Thousand Oaks, CA: Sage.

Bronfenbrenner, U. (1979) *The Ecology of Human Development: Experiments by Nature and Design*. Cambridge, MA: Harvard University Press.

Brown, C. (1984) *Black and White Britain: the Third PSI Survey*. London: Heinemann.

Brown, J. (1993) Coping with stress: the beneficial role of positive illusions, in A.P. Turnbull, J.M. Patterson, S.K. Behr, D.L. Murphy, J.G. Marquis and M.J. Blue-Banning (eds) *Cognitive Coping, Families and Disability*. Baltimore, MD: Paul H. Brookes.

Buchman, F. (1947) *Remaking the World*. Publisher unknown.

Bulmer, M. (1987) *The Social Basis of Community Care*. London: Allen and Unwin.

Burden, R.L. (1980) Measuring the effects of stress on mothers of handicapped infants: must depression always follow? *Child Care, Health and Development*, 6: 111–25.

Burr, W.R., Klein, S.R. and associates (1994) *Re-examining Family Stress: New Theory and Research*. Thousand Oaks, CA: Sage.

Bury, M. (1982) Chronic illness as biographical disruption, *Sociology of Health and Illness*, 4(2): 167–82.

Caldock, K. (1994a) Policy and practice, fundamental contradictions in the conceptualisation of community care for elderly people, *Health and Social Care in the Community*, 2: 133–41.

Caldock, K. (1994b) The new assessment: moving towards holism or new road to fragmentation, in B. Challis, B. Davies and K. Traske (eds) *Community Care: New Agendas and Challenges from the UK and Overseas*. BSG/PSSRN Arena: Aldershot.

Cantor, M.H. (1983) Strain among caregivers: a study of experience in the United States, *The Gerontologist*, 23: 597–604.

Carlisle, D. (1994) Facing up to race, *Nursing Times*, 29 June: 14–15.

Carlson, K.W. and Robertson, S.E. (1993) Husbands and wives of dementia patients: burden and social support, *Canadian Journal of Rehabilitation*, 3: 163–73.

Carson, J., Fagin, L. and Ritter, S. (1995) *Stress and Coping in Mental Health Nursing*. London: Chapman Hall.

Cartwright, J.C., Archbold, P.G., Stewart, B.J. and Limandri, B. (1994) Enrichment processes in family caregiving to frail elders, *Advances in Nursing Science*, 17(1): 31–43.

Challis, L. and Bartlett, H. (1988) *Old and Ill: Private Nursing Homes for Elderly People*, Age Concern Institute of Gerontology, research paper no. 1. London: ACE Books.

Chappell, N.L., Penning, M.J. and Sorensen, S. (1995) *Informal Caregivers to Adults in British Columbia*. Victoria, British Columbia Centre on Aging, University of Victoria and Caregivers Association of British Columbia.

Charmaz, K. (1983) Loss of self: a fundamental form of suffering in the chronically ill, *Sociology of Health and Illness*, 5(2): 168–95.

Charmaz, K. (1987) Struggling for self: identity levels of the chronically ill, *Research in the Sociology of Health Care*, 6: 283–321.

Cheng, P. and Tang, S. (1995) Coping and psychological distress of Chinese parents of children with Down Syndrome, *Mental Retardation*, 33(1): 10–20.

Chenitz, W.C. (1983) Entry to a nursing home as status passage: a theory to guide nursing practice, *Geriatric Nursing*, March/April 1983, 92–7.

Cicarelli, V.G. (1992) *Family Caregiving: Autonomous and Paternalistic Decision Making*. Newbury Park, CA: Sage.

Clark, C.L. (1995) Quality of life, values and teamwork in geriatric care: do we communicate what we mean? *The Gerontologist*, 35(3): 402–11.

Clarke, P.G. (1995) Care of elderly people suffering from dementia and their co-resident informal carers, in B. Heyman (ed.) *Researching User Perspectives on Community Health Care*. London: Chapman and Hall.

Clifford, D. (1990) *The Social Costs and Rewards of Care*. Aldershot: Avebury.

Coe, R.M., Miller, D.K. and Flaterty, J. (1992) Sense of coherence and perception of caregiver burden, *Behaviour, Health and Ageing*, 2(2): 93–9.

Cohen, C.A., Pushkar Gold, D., Shulman, K.I. and Zucchero, C.A. (1994) Positive aspects in caregiving: an overlooked variable in research, *Canadian Journal on Aging*, 13(3): 378–91.

Coleman, C.K., Piles, L.L. and Poggenpoel, M. (1994) Influence of caregiving on families of older adults, *Journal of Gerontological Nursing*, November 1994: 40–9.

Collopy, B.J. (1988) Autonomy in long-term care: some crucial distinctions, *The Gerontologist*, 28(supplement): 10–17.

Conway-Turner, K. and Karasik, R. (1993) Adult daughters' anticipation of caregiving responsibilities, *Journal of Women and Aging*, 5(2): 99–114.

Corbin, J.M. and Strauss, A. (1988) *Unending Work and Care: Managing Chronic Illness at Home*. San Francisco, CA: Jossey Bass.

Corbin, J.M. and Strauss, A. (1992) A nursing model for chronic illness management based upon the trajectory framework, in P. Woog (ed.) *The Chronic Illness Trajectory Framework*. New York: Springer.

Cotterill, L. (1994) *The Social Integration of People with Schizophrenia*. Aldershot: Avebury.

Cox, C. (1995) Comparing the experiences of black and white caregivers of dementia patients, *Social Work*, 40(3): 343–9.

Crittenden, P.M. (1985) Social networks, quality of child rearing and child development, *Child Development*, 56: 1299–313.

Crookston, E.M. (1989) *Informal Caring: the Carer's View*. Middlesborough: Cleveland County Council Research and Intelligence Unit.

Cunningham, C. and Jupp, S. (1991) *Parents Deserve Better: a Review of Early Counselling in Wales*. Cardiff: Standing Conference on Voluntary Organisations.

Dalley, G. (1988) *Ideologies and Caring: Rethinking Community and Collectivism*. London: Macmillan.

Davies, A.J. (1980) Disability, home-care and the care-taking role in family life, *Journal of Advanced Nursing*, 5: 475–84.

Davies, B. (1995) The reform of community and long term care of elderly persons: an international perspective, in T. Scharf and G.C. Wenger (eds) *International Perspectives on Community Care for Older People*. Aldershot: Avebury.

Dayson, D. (1992) The TAPS project 15: the social networks of two group settings – a pilot study, *Journal of Mental Health*, 1: 99–106.

Dellasega, C. and Mastrian, K. (1995) The process and consequences of institutionalising an elder, *Western Journal of Nursing Research*, 17(2): 123–40.

Department of Health (1990a) *Caring for People: Community Care in the Next Decade and Beyond: Policy Guidance*. London: HMSO.

Department of Health (1990b) *The National Health Service and Community Care Act: A Brief Guide*. London: DoH.

Department of Health (1996) *Carers (Recognition and Services) Act: Policy Guidance*. London: DoH.

Department of Health/Social Services Inspectorate (1991) *Care Management and Assessment: Practitioners' Guide*. London: HMSO.

Department of Health/Social Services Inspectorate (1989) *Homes Are for Living in*. London: HMSO.

Dill, D. and Feld, E. (1982) The challenge of coping, in D. Belle (ed.) *Lives in Stress: Women and Depression*. Beverly Hills, CA: Sage.

Dohrenwend, B.S. and Dohrenwend, B.P. (1974) *Stressful Life Events: Their Nature and Effects*. New York: Wiley.

Dooghe, G. (1992) Informal caregiving of elderly people: a European review, *Ageing and Society*, 12: 369–80.

Dreyfus, H.L. and Dreyfuss, S.E. (1986) *Mind over Machine: the Power of Human Intuition and Expertise in the Era of the Computer*. Oxford: Basil Blackwell.

Dunn, M., O'Driscoll, C., Dayson, D., Wills, W. and Leff, J. (1990) The TAPS Project 4: an observational study of the social life of long-stay patients, *British Journal of Psychiatry*, 157: 842–8.

Dunst, C.J. and Trivette, C.M. (1980) Toward experimental evaluation of the family, infant and preschool program, in H.B. Weiss and F.A. Jacobs (eds) *Evaluating Family Programs*. New York: Aldine de Gruyher.

Dunst, C.J., Trivette, C. and Deal, A. (1988) *Enabling and Empowering Parents*. Cambridge, MA: Brookline Books.

Dunst, C.J., Trivette, C.M., Gordon, N.J. and Pletcher, L.L. (1989) Building and mobilizing informal family support networks, in G.H.S. Singer and L.K. Irvin (eds) *Support for Caregiving Families: Enabling Positive Adaptation to Disability*. Baltimore, MD: Paul H. Brookes.

Ebrahim, S., Wallis, C., Brittis, S., Harwood, R. and Graham, N. (1993) Long term care for elderly people, *Quality in Health Care*, 2: 198–203.

Edwards, J.R. and Cooper, C.L. (1988) Research in stress, coping and health: theoretical and methodological issues, *Psychological Medicine*, 18: 15–20.

Ell, K. (1996) Social networks, social support and coping with serious illness: the family connection, *Social Science and Medicine*, 42(2): 173–83.

Ellis, K. (1993) *Squaring the Circle: User and Carer Participation in Needs Assessment*. York: Joseph Rowntree Foundation.

Equal Opportunities Commission (1982) *Who Cares for the Carers? Opportunities for Those Caring for the Elderly and Handicapped*. Manchester: EOC.

Eraut, M. (1994) *Developing Professional Knowledge and Competence*. London: Falmer Press.

Eribo, L. (1991) *The Support You Need: Information for Carers of Afro-Caribbean Elderly People*. London: Kings Fund Centre.

Evandrou, M. (1993) The health, employment and income status of informal carers in Britain. Paper given at BSG Annual Conference, University of East Anglia, Norwich, September.

Evers, A. (1995) The future of elderly care in Europe: limits and aspirations, in F. Scharf and G.C. Wenger (eds) *International Perspectives on Community Care for Older People*. Aldershot: Avebury.

Farooqi, S. (1994) Ethnic differences in infant care practices and in the incidence of sudden infant death syndrome in Birmingham, *Early Human Development*, 38(3): 209–13.

Farran, C.J., Keane-Hogarely, E., Salloway, S., Kupferer, S. and Wilkin, C.S. (1991) Finding meaning: an alternative paradigm for Alzheimer's disease family caregivers, *The Gerontologist*, 31(4): 483–9.

Fatimilehin, I. and Nadirshaw, Z. (1994) A cross-cultural study of parental attitudes and beliefs about learning disability, *Mental Handicap Research*, 7(3): 202–7.

Fealy, G.M. (1995) Professional caring: the moral dimension, *Journal of Advanced Nursing*, 22(6): 135–40.

Fengler, A.P. and Goodrich, N. (1979) Wives of disabled men: the hidden patients, *The Gerontologist*, 26(3): 248–52.

Fenton, S. (1987) *Ageing Minorities: Black People as They Grow Old in Britain*. London: Commission for Racial Equality.

Finch, J. and Groves, D. (1983) *A Labour of Love: Women, Work and Caring*. London: Routledge and Kegan Paul.

Finch, J. and Mason, J. (1990) Filial obligations and kin support for elderly people, *Ageing and Society*, 10: 151–75.

Finch, J. and Mason, J. (1993) *Negotiating Family Responsibilities*. London: Routledge.

Fisher, M. (1990) Care management and social work: working with carers, *Practice*, 4(4): 242–52.

Fisher, M. (1994) Man-made care: community care and older male carers, *British Journal of Social Work*, 24(6): 659–80.

Fisher, J.D., Nadler, A. and dePaulo, B.M. (eds) (1983) *New Directions in Helping: Recipient Reactions to Aid*. New York: Academic Free Press.

Fitting, M., Rabins, P., Lucas, M.J. and Eastham, J. (1986) Caregivers for dementia patients: a comparison of husbands and wives, *The Gerontologist*, 26: 248–52.

Folkman, S. and Lazarus, R.S. (1985) If it changes it must be a process: a study of emotion and coping during three stages of a college examination, *Journal of Personality and Social Psychology*, 48: 150–70.

Forrester-Jones, R. and Grant, G. (1995) Social networks and lives of people with long-term mental health problems, in C. Crosby and M. Barry (eds) *Community Care: Evaluation of the Provision of Mental Health Services*. Aldershot: Avebury.

Fotrell, E. (1988) Why good respite care is so difficult to provide, *Geriatric Medicine*, 18(10): 71.

Gair, G. and Hartery, T. (1994) Old peoples' homes: residents views, *Baseline (Journal of the British Association for Services to the Elderly)*, 54: 24–7.

Gallagher, T.J., Wagenfeld, M.O., Baro, F. and Haepers, K. (1994) Sense of coherence, coping and caregiver role overload, *Social Science and Medicine*, 39(12): 1615–22.

George, L.K. (1986) Caregiver burden: conflict between norms of reciprocity and solidarity, in K.A. Pillemar and R.S. Wolf (eds) *Elder Abuse: Conflict in the Family*. Dover, MA: Auburn House.

George, L.K. (1994) Caregiver burden and well-being: an elusive distinction, *The Gerontologist*, 34(1): 6–7.

George, L.K. and Gwyther, L.P. (1986) Caregiver well-being: multidimensional examination of family caregivers of demented adults, *The Gerontologist*, 26: 253–9.

Gilhooly, M.L.M. (1984) The impact of caregiving on caregivers: factors associated with the psychological well-being of people supporting a dementing relative in the community, *British Journal of Medical Psychology*, 57: 35–44.

Gilloran, A.J., McGlew, T., McKee, K., Robertson, A. and Wight, D. (1993) Measuring the quality of care on psychogeriatric wards, *Journal of Advanced Nursing*, 18: 269–75.

Given, B.A. and Given, C.W. (1991) Family caregivers for the elderly, in J. Fitzpatrick, R. Tauton and A. Jacox (eds) *Annual Review of Nursing Research*, vol. 9. New York: Springer.

Glendinning, C. and McLaughlin, E. (1993) *Paying for Care: Lessons from Europe*, Social Security Advisory Committee research paper 5. London: HMSO.

Goodwin, S. (1992) Freedom to Care, *Nursing Times*, 88(34): 34–9.

Gottlieb, B. (ed.) (1981) *Social Networks and Social Support*. Beverly Hills, CA: Sage.

Gourash, N. (1978) Help seeking: a review of the literature, *American Journal of Community Psychology*, 6(5): 413–23.

Grant, G. (1986) Older carers, interdependence and the care of mentally handicapped adults, *Ageing and Society*, 6, 333–51.

Grant, G. (1989) Letting go: decision-making among family carers of people with a mental handicap, *Australia and New Zealand Journal of Developmental Disabilities*, 15(3 & 4): 189–200.

Grant, G. (1990) Elderly parents with handicapped children: anticipating the future, *Journal of Aging Studies*, 4(4): 359–74.

Grant, G. (in press) Consulting to involve or consulting to empower? in P. Ramcharan, G. Roberts, G. Grant and J. Borland (eds) *Empowerment in Everyday Life: Learning Disability*. London: Jessica Kingsley.

Grant, G. and Nolan, M. (1993) Informal carers: sources and concomitants of satisfaction, *Health and Social Care in the Community*, 1(3): 147–59.

Grant, G. and Wenger, G.C. (1993) Dynamics of support networks: differences and similarities between vulnerable groups, *Irish Journal of Psychology*, 14(1): 79–98.

Grant, G., Nolan, M. and Ellis, N. (1990) A reappraisal of the Malaise Inventory, *Social Psychiatry and Psychiatric Epidemiology*, 25: 170–8.

Grant, G., McGrath, M. and Ramcharan, P. (1994) How family and informal supporters appraise service quality, *International Journal of Disability, Development and Education*, 41(2): 127–41.

Grant, G., McGrath, M. and Ramcharan, P. (1995) Community inclusion of older people with learning disabilities, *Care in Place*, 2(1): 29–44.

Green, H. (1988) *Informal Carers*. General Household Survey 1985 series. GHS No. 15, supplement 16. London: OPCS Social Survey Division.

Greene, V.L. and Coleman, P.D. (1995) Direct services for family caregivers: next steps for public policy, in R.A. Kane and J.D. Penrod (eds) *Family Caregiving in an Ageing Society: Policy Perspectives*. Thousand Oaks, CA: Sage.

Griffin, A.P. (1983) A philosophical analysis of caring in nursing, *Journal of Advanced Nursing*, 8: 189–295.

Gubrium, J. (1995) Taking stock, *Qualitative Health Research*, 5(3): 267–9.

Gunaratnam, Y. (1993) Breaking the silence: Asian carers in Britain, in J. Bornat, C. Pereira, D. Pilgrim and S. Williams (eds) *Community Care – a Reader*. London: Macmillan.

Hackett, L. and Hackett, R.J. (1993) Parental ideas of normal and deviant child behaviour: a comparison of two ethnic groups, *British Journal of Psychiatry*, 162: 353–7.

Hancock, R. and Jarvis, C. (1994) *The Long Term Effects of Being a Carer*, Age Concern Institute of Gerontology. London: HMSO.

Harper, D.J., Manasse, P.R., James, O. and Newton, D.T. (1993) Intervening to reduce distress in caregivers of impaired elderly people: a preliminary evaluation, *International Journal of Geriatric Psychiatry*, 8: 139–45.

Harris, P.B. (1993) The misunderstood caregiver? A qualitative study of the male caregiver of Alzheimer's disease victims, *The Gerontologist*, 33(4): 551–6.

Harvath, T.A. (1994) Interpretation and management of dementia-related behaviour problems, *Clinical Nursing Research*, 3(1): 7–26.

Harvath, T.A., Archbold, P.G., Stewart, B.J., Godow, S., Kirschling, J.M., Miller, L.L., Hogan, J., Brody, K. and Schook, J. (1994) Establishing partnerships with family caregivers: local and cosmopolitan knowledge, *Journal of Gerontological Nursing*, 20(2): 29–35.

Hasselkus, B.R. (1988) Meaning in family caregiving: perspectives on caregiver/professional relationships, *The Gerontologist*, 28(5): 686–91.

Henwood, M. (1992) *Through a Glass Darkly: Community Care and Elderly People*. London: Kings Fund Institute.

Higham, P. (1994) Individualising residential care for older people. Paper given at BSG Annual Conference, University of London, September 1994.

Hinriden, G.A. and Niedireche, G. (1994) Dementia management strategies: adjustment of family members of older patients, *The Gerontologist*, 34: 95–102.

Hirschfield, M.J. (1981) Families living and coping with the cognitively impaired, in L.A. Copp (ed.) *Care of the Ageing*. Edinburgh: Churchill Livingstone.

Hirschfield, M.J. (1983) Home care versus institutionalisation: family caregiving and senile brain disease, *International Journal of Nursing Studies*, 20(1): 23–32.

Hooyman, N.R. and Gonyea, J. (1995) *Feminist Perspectives on Family Care: Policies for Gender Justice*. Thousand Oaks, CA: Sage.

House, J.S., Umberson, D. and Landis, K.R. (1988) Structures and processes of social support, *Annual Review of Sociology*, 14: 293–318.

Hughes, B. (1993) A model for the comprehensive assessment of older people and their carers, *British Journal of Social Work*, 23: 345–80.

Hughes, B.C. (1995) *Older People in Community Care: Critical Theory and Practice*. Buckingham: Open University Press.

Hunter, S., Brace, S. and Buckley, G. (1993) The inter-disciplinary assessment of older people at entry into long-term institutional care: lessons for the new community care arrangements, *Research, Policy and Planning*, 11(1/2): 2–9.

Ingebretsen, R. and Solen, P.E. (1995) Attachment, loss and coping in caring for a dementing spouse. Paper presented at III European Congress of Gerontology, Amsterdam, 30 August–2 September 1995.

James, N. (1992) Care = organisation + physical labour + emotional labour, *Sociology of Health Illness*, 14(4): 488–509.

Jerrom, B., Mian, I., Rukanyake, N.G. and Prattero, D. (1993) Stress on relatives of caregivers of dementia sufferers and predictors of the breakdown of community care, *International Journal of Geriatric Psychiatry*, 8: 331–7.

Jivanjee, P. (1993) Enhancing the well-being of family caregivers to patients with dementia. Paper given at International Mental Health Conference, Institute of Human Ageing, Liverpool.

Johnson, M.L. (1995) Societal dilemmas in ageing societies. III European Congress of Gerontology, Amsterdam, 30 August–2 September 1995.

Johnson, R.A., Schwiebert, V.B. and Rosenmann, P.A. (1994) Factors influencing nursing home placement decisions, *Clinical Nursing Research*, 3(3): 269–81.

Jutras, S. and Veilleux, F. (1991) Informal caregiving: correlates of perceived burden, *Canadian Journal on Aging*, 10(1): 40–55.

Kadner, K. (1994) Therapeutic intimacy in nursing, *Journal of Advanced Nursing*, 19(2): 215–18.

Kahana, E. and Young, R. (1990) Clarifying the caregiving paradigm: challenges for the future, in D.E. Biegel and A. Blum (eds) *Ageing and Caregiving: Theory, Research and Policy*. Newbury Park, CA: Sage.

Kahana, E., Biegel, D.E. and Wykle, M.L. (1994) *Family Caregiving Across the Lifespan*. Thousand Oaks, CA: Sage.

Kahn, R. and Antonucci, T.C. (1980) Convoys over the life course: attachment, roles and social support, in P.B. Baltes and O. Brim (eds) *Life Span Development and Behaviour*. Lexington, MA: Lexington Books.

Kane, R.L. and Kane, R.A. (1991) Special needs of dependent elderly persons, in N.W. Holland *et al.* (eds) *Oxford Textbook of Public Health Medicine*, 2nd edn., vol. 3. New York: Oxford University Press.

Kane, R.A. and Penrod, J.D. (1995) *Family Caregiving in an Aging Society: Policy Perspectives*. Thousand Oaks, CA: Sage.

Kaplun, A. (1992) *Health Promotion and Chronic Illness: Discovering a New Quality of Health*. Copenhagen: WHO (Europe).

Kayser-Jones, J.S. (1981) *Old and Alone, Care of the Aged in the USA and Scotland.* Berkeley, CA: University of California Press.

Keady, J. and Nolan, M.R. (1993a) Coping with dementia: understanding and responding to the needs of informal carers. Paper given at the Royal College of Nursing Research Conference, University of Glasgow, April 1993.

Keady, J. and Nolan, M.R. (1993b) Coping with dementia: towards a comprehensive assessment of the needs of informal carers. Paper given at International Conference on Mental Illness in Old Age, Institute of Human Ageing, Liverpool, June 1993.

Keady, J. and Nolan, M.R. (1994a) Younger Onset Dementia: developing a longitudinal model as the basis for a research agenda and as a guide to interventions with sufferers and carers, *Journal of Advanced Nursing,* 19(4), 659–69.

Keady, J. and Nolan, M.R. (1994b) Working with dementia sufferers and their carers in the community: exploring the nursing role. Paper given at International Nursing Conference, University of Ulster, Coleraine, August 1994.

Keady, J. and Nolan, M.R. (1995a) IMMEL: assessing coping responses in the early stages of dementia, *British Journal of Nursing,* 4(6): 309–14.

Keady, J. and Nolan, M.R. (1995b) IMMEL 2: working to augment coping responses in early dementia, *British Journal of Nursing,* 4(7): 377–80.

Keady, J. and Nolan, M.R. (1995c) A stitch in time: facilitating proactive interventions with dementia caregivers: the role of community practitioners, *Journal of Psychiatric and Mental Health Nursing,* 2: 33–40.

Kellaher, L. and Peace, S. (1990) From respondent to consumer to resident: shifts in quality assurance in the last decade. Paper given at BSG Annual Conference, University of Durham, 1990.

Kiernan, C. and Alborz, A. (1995) *A Different Life,* final report to the Mental Health Foundation on factors influencing the ending of informal care of adults with learning disabilities. Manchester: Hester Adrian Research Centre, University of Manchester.

Kinney, J.M. and Stephens, M.A.P. (1989) Hassles and uplifts of giving care to a family member with dementia, *Psychology and Ageing,* 4: 402–8.

Kitson, A. (1987) A comparative analysis of lay caring and professional (nursing) caring relationships, *International Journal of Nursing Studies,* 24(2): 155–65.

Knipscheer, C. (1992) A triangular model in care for impaired elderly in the Netherlands and its educational implications, in N. Stevens *et al.* (eds) *Education in Gerontology in the 90s. International Perspectives and Developments.* Nijmegen: Department of Psychogerontology.

Knussen, C., Sloper, P., Cunningham, C.C. and Turner, S. (1992) The use of the Ways of Coping (revised) questionnaire with parents of children with Down's syndrome, *Psychological Medicine,* 22: 775–86.

Kobayashi, S., Masaki, H. and Noguchi, M. (1993) Developmental process: family caregivers of demented Japanese, *Journal of Gerontological Nursing,* 22: 775–86.

Koch, T., Webb, C. and Williams, A.M. (1995) Listening to the voices of older patients: an existential-phenomenological approach to quality assurance, *Journal of Clinical Nursing,* 4: 185–93.

Kyle, T.U. (1995) The concept of caring: a literature review, *Journal of Advanced Nursing,* 21(3): 506–14.

Langer, S.R. (1993) Ways of managing the experience of caregiving for elderly relatives, *Western Journal of Nursing Research,* 15(5): 582–94.

Lawrence, S., Walker, A. and Willcocks, D. (1987) *She's Leaving Home: Local Authority*

Policy and Practice Concerning Admissions into Residential Homes for Old People, CESSA research report no. 2. London: Polytechnic of North London.

Lawton, M.P., Kleban, M.H., Moss, M., Rovine, M. and Glicksman, A. (1989) Measuring caregiver appraisal, *Journal of Gerontology*, 44: 61–71.

Lawton, M.P., Moss, M., Kleban, M.H., Glicksman, A. and Rovine, M. (1991) A two factor model of caregiving: appraisal and psychological well-being, *Journal of Gerontology*, 46: 181–9.

Lawton, M.P., Rajagopal, D., Brody, E. and Kleban, M.H. (1992) The dynamics of caregiving for a demented elder among Black and White families, *Journal of Gerontology*, 47(4): 156–64.

Lawton, M.P., Moss, M. and Dunamel, L.M. (1995) The quality of life among elderly care receivers, *Journal of Applied Gerontology*, 14(2): 150–71.

Lazarus, R.S. (1966) *Psychological Stress and the Coping Process*. New York: McGraw Hill.

Lazarus, R.S. (1983) The costs and benefits of denial, in S. Breznitz (ed.) *Denial of Stress*. New York: International Universities Press.

Lazarus, R.S. (1993) Coping theory and research: past, recent and future, *Psychosomatic Medicine*, 55: 234–47.

Lazarus, R.S. and Folkman, S. (1984) *Stress, Appraisal and Coping*. New York: Springer.

Lea, A. (1994) Defining the roles of lay and nursing caring, *Nursing Standard*, 9(5): 32–5.

Levesque, L., Cossette, J. and Laurin, L. (1995) A multidimensional examination of the psychological and social well-being of caregivers of a demented relative, *Research on Aging*, 17(3): 322–60.

Levin, E., Moriarty, J. and Gorbach, P. (1994) *Better for the Break*. London: HMSO.

Lewis, J. and Meredith, B. (1988a) *Daughters Who Care: Daughters Caring for Mothers at Home*. London: Routledge and Kegan Paul.

Lewis, J. and Meredith, B. (1988b) Daughters caring for mothers, *Ageing and Society*, 8(1): 1–21.

Lewis, J. and Meredith, B. (1989) Contested territory in informal care, in M. Jeffreys (ed.) *Growing Old in the Twentieth Century*. London: Routledge.

Linsk, N.L., Keigher, S.M., England, S.E. and Bimon-Rusinowitz, L. (1995) Compensation of family care for the elderly, in R.A. Kane and J.D. Penrod (eds) *Family Caregiving in an Ageing Society: Policy Perspectives*. Thousand Oaks, CA: Sage.

Liston, R., Mann, L. and Banerjee, A. (1995) Stress in informal carers of hospitalised elderly patients, *Journal of the Royal College of Physicians of London*, 29(5): 388–91.

Litwak, E., Jessop, D.J. and Moulton, H.J. (1994) Optimal use of formal and informal systems over the life course, in E. Kahana, D.E. Biegel and M.L. Wykle (eds) *Family Caregiving Across the Lifespan*. Thousand Oaks, CA: Sage.

Local Government Information Unit (1990) *Caring for people – the Government's Plans for Care in the Community*. Special Briefing Paper. London: LGIU.

McBride, A.B. (1993) Managing chronicity: the heart of health care, in S.S. Funk, E.M.T. Tornquist, T. Champagnes and R.A. Wiese (eds) *Key Aspects of Care for the Chronically Ill*. New York: Springer.

McCalman, J.A. (1990) *The Forgotten People: Carers in Three Ethnic Minority Communities in Southwark*. London: Kings Fund Centre.

McCubbin, H.I. and Patterson, J. (1983) Family stress adaptation to crises: a double ABCX model of family behaviour, in H.I. McCubbin, M. Sussman and J. Patterson (eds) *Social Stresses and the Family: Advances and Developments in Family Stress Theory and Research*. New York: Haworth Press.

McCullough, L., Wilson, N., Teasdale, T., Kolpakchi, A. and Skelly, J. (1993) Mapping personal, familial and professional values in long-term care decisions, *The Gerontologist*, 33(3): 324–32.

McKee, K.S., Whittick, J.E., Ballinger, B.B., Gilhooly, M.M.L., Gordon, D.S., Mutch, W.J. and Philp, I. (1994) Coping in family supporters of elderly people with dementia. Paper presented at the British Society of Gerontology Annual Conference, Royal Holloway, September.

McLaughlin, E. and Ritchie, J. (1994) Legacies of caring: the experiences and circumstances of ex-carers, *Health and Social Care in the Community*, 2: 241–53.

Makosky, V.P. (1982) Sources of stress: events or conditions? in D. Belle (ed.) *Lives in Stress: Women and Depression*. Beverly Hills, CA: Sage.

Manthorpe, J. and Twigg, J. (1995) Carers and care management, *Baseline*, 59: 4–17.

Marck, P. (1990) Therapeutic reciprocity: a caring phenomenon, *Advances in Nursing Science*, 13(1): 49–59.

Midlarsky, E. and Kahana, E. (1994) *Altruism in Later Life*. Thousand Oaks, CA: Sage.

Miesen, B. (1995) Awareness in Alzheimer's disease patients: consequences for caregiving research. Paper presented at III European Congress of Gerontology, 30 August–2 September 1995.

Miller, B. and McFall, S. (1992) Caregiver burden and the continuum of care: a longitudinal perspective, *Research on Ageing*, 14(3): 376–98.

Milne, D., Pitt, I. and Sabin, N. (1993) Evaluation of a carer support scheme for elderly people: the importance of 'coping', *British Journal of Social Work*, 23: 157–68.

Mitchell, J.C. (1969) *Social Networks in Urban Situations*. Manchester: Manchester University Press.

Montgomery, R.J.V. (1995) Examining respite care: promises and limitations, in R.A. Kane and J.D. Penrod (eds) *Family Caregiving in an Ageing Society: Policy Perspectives*. Thousand Oaks, CA: Sage.

Morse, J.M., Solberg, S.M., Neander, W.L., Bottroff, J.L. and Johnson, J.L. (1990) Concepts of caring and caring as a concept, *Advances in Nursing Sciences*, 13(1): 1–14.

Motenko, A.K. (1988) Respite care and pride in caregiving: the experience of six older men caring for their disabled wives, in S. Reinharz and G. Rowles (eds) *Qualitative Gerontology*. New York: Springer.

Motenko, A.K. (1989) The frustrations, gratifications and well-being of dementia caregivers, *The Gerontologist*, 29(2): 166–72.

Neill, J. (1989) *Assessing People for Residential Care: a Practical Guide*. London: National Institute of Social Work Research Unit.

Neill, J. and Williams, J. (1992) *Elderly People Leaving Hospital: a Study of Discharge to Community Care*. London: National Institute for Social Work Research Unit.

Nikkonen, M. (1994) Caring from the point of view of a Finnish mental health nurse, *Journal of Advanced Nursing*, 19: 1185–95.

Nolan, M.R. (1986) 'Day care in perspective: a comparative study of two day hospitals for the elderly', MA thesis. University of Wales, Bangor.

Nolan, M.R. (1993) Carer/dependent relationships and the prevention of elder abuse, in P. Decalmer and F. Glendenning (eds) *The Abuse and Neglect of Elderly People: a Handbook*. London: Sage.

Nolan, M.R. and Caldock, K. (1996) Assessment: identifying the barriers to good practice, *Health and Social Care in the Community*, 4(2): 77–85.

Nolan, M.R. and Cunliffe, C. (1991) A study of EMI day services in Gwynedd. Unpublished study conducted for Gwynedd Health Authority, Bangor.

Nolan, M.R. and Grant, G. (1989) Addressing the needs of informal carers: a neglected area of nurses practice, *Journal of Advanced Nursing*, 14: 950–61.

Nolan, M.R. and Grant, G. (1992a) *Regular Respite: an Evaluation of a Hospital Rota Bed Scheme for Elderly People*. London: Age Concern.

Nolan, M.R. and Grant, G. (1992b) Helping new carers of the frail elderly patient: the challenge for nurses in acute care settings, *Journal of Clinical Nursing*, 1: 303–7.

Nolan, M.R. and Grant, G. (1993) Rust out and therapeutic reciprocity: concepts to advance the nursing care of older people, *Journal of Advanced Nursing*, 18: 1305–14.

Nolan, M.R. and Keady, J. (1993) Every cloud has a silver lining: exploring the dimensions of carer satisfaction. British Society of Gerontology Annual Conference on the Experience of Older People – Solidarity Across the Generations, UEA, Norwich, 17–19 September.

Nolan, M.R. and Scott, G. (1993) Audit: an exploration of some tensions and paradoxical expectations, *Journal of Advanced Nursing*, 18: 759–66.

Nolan, M.R., Grant, G. and Ellis, N.C. (1990) Stress is in the eye of the beholder: reconceptualising the measurement of carer burden, *Journal of Advanced Nursing*, 15: 544–55.

Nolan, M.R., Grant, G., Caldock, K. and Keady, J. (1994) *A Framework for Assessing the Needs of Family Carers: a Multi-disciplinary Guide*. Stoke-on-Trent: BASE Publications.

Nolan, M.R., Keady, J. and Grant, G. (1995a) Developing a typology of family care: implications for nurse and other service providers, *Journal of Advanced Nursing*, 21: 256–65.

Nolan, M.R., Keady, J. and Grant, G. (1995b) CAMI: a basis for assessment and support with family carers, *British Journal of Adult/Elderly Care Nursing*, 1(3): 822–6.

Nolan, M.R., Walker, G., Nolan, J., Williams, S., Poland, F., Curran, M. and Kent, B.C. (1996) Entry to care: positive choice or fait accompli? Developing a more proactive nursing response to the needs of older people and their carers, *Journal of Advanced Nursing*, 24: 265–74.

Norman, A. (1985) *Triple Jeopardy: Growing Old in a Second Homeland*. London: Centre for Policy on Ageing.

O'Neill, C. and Sorenson, E.S. (1991) Home care of the elderly: family perspectives, *Advances in Nursing Science*, 13(4): 28–37.

Opie, A. (1994) The instability of the caring body: gender and caregivers of confused older people, *Qualitative Health Research*, 4(1): 31–50.

Orford, J., Rigby, K., Miller, T., Tod, A., Bennett, G. and Velleman, R. (1992) Ways of coping with excessive drug use in the family: a provisional typology based on the accounts of 50 close relatives, *Journal of Community and Applied Social Psychology*, 2: 163–83.

Orr, R.R., Cameron, S.J. and Day, D.M. (1991) Coping with stress in children who have mental retardation: an evaluation of the double ABCX model, *American Journal on Mental Retardation*, 95: 444–50.

Pahl, J. and Quine, L. (1987) Families with mentally handicapped children, in J. Orford (ed.) *Coping with Disorder in the Family*. London: Croom Helm.

Parker, G. and Lawton, D. (1994) *Different Types of Care, Different Types of Carer: Evidence from the General Household Survey*. London: HMSO.

Parker, R. (1981) Tending and social policy, in E.M. Goldberg and S. Hatch (eds) *A New Look at the Personal Social Services*. London: Policy Studies Institute.

Patterson, J.M. (1993) The role of family meanings in adaptation to chronic illness and disability, in A.P. Turnbull, J.M. Patterson, S.K. Behr, D.L. Murphy, J.G. Marquis and M.J. Blue-Banning (eds) *Cognitive Coping, Families and Disability*. Baltimore, MD: Paul H. Brookes.

Pattison, E.M., DeFrancisco, D., Ward, P., Frazier, H. and Crowder, J. (1975) A psychosocial kinship model for family therapy, *American Journal of Psychiatry*, 132: 1246–51.

Pearlin, L.I. and Schooler, C. (1978) The structure of coping, *Journal of Health and Social Behaviour*, 19: 1–21.

Pearlin, L.I., Mullan, J.T., Semple, S.J. and Skaff, M.M. (1990) Caregiving and the stress process: an overview of concepts and their measures, *The Gerontologist*, 30(5): 583–94.

Perkins, R.E. and Moodley, P. (1993) Perceptions of problems in psychiatric inpatients: denial, race and service usage, *Social Psychiatry and Psychiatric Epidemiology*, 28(4): 189–93.

Phillips-Harris, C. and Farnale, J.E. (1995) The acute and long term care interface: integrating a continuum, *Clinics in Geriatric Medicine*, 11(3): 481–96.

Phillips, L.R. and Rempusheski, V.E. (1986) Caring for the frail elderly at home: towards a theoretical explanation of the dynamics of poor quality family care, *Advances in Nursing Science*, 8(4): 62–84.

Pitkeathley, J. (1990) Painful conflicts, *Community Care (Inside)*, 22 February: i–ii.

Porter, E.J. (1995) A phenomenological alternative to the 'ADL research tradition', *Journal of Aging and Health*, 7(1): 24–45.

Porter, E.J. and Clinton, J.F. (1992) Adjusting to the nursing home, *Western Journal of Nursing Research*, 14(4): 464–81.

Pott, E. (1992) Preface, in A. Kaplun (ed.) *Health Promotion and Chronic Illness: Discovering a New Quality of Health*. Copenhagen: WHO (Europe).

Pratt, C., Schmall, V. and Wright, S. (1987) Ethical concerns of family caregiving to dementia patients, *The Gerontologist*, 25(5): 632–8.

Quine, L. and Pahl, J. (1986) Parents with severely mentally handicapped children: marriage and the stress of caring, in. R. Chester and P. Divall (eds) *Mental Health, Illness and Handicap in Marriage*. Rugby: National Marriage Guidance Council.

Quine, L. and Pahl, J. (1991) Stress and coping in mothers caring for a child with severe learning difficulties: a test of Lazarus' transactional model of coping, *Journal of Community and Applied Social Psychology*, 1: 57–70.

Qureshi, H. (1986) Responses to dependency: reciprocity, affect and power in family relationships, in C. Phillipson, M. Bernard and R. Strang (eds) *Dependency and Interdependency in Old Age: Theoretical Perspectives and Policy Alternatives*. London: Croom Helm.

Qureshi, H. and Walker, A. (1989) *The Caring Relationship: Elderly People and Their Families*. Basingstoke: Macmillan.

Radsma, J. (1994) Caring and nursing: a dilemma, *Journal of Advanced Nursing*, 20(3): 444–9.

Ramsey, M., Winget, G. and Higginson, I. (1995) Review: measures to determine the outcome of community services for people with dementia, *Age and Ageing*, 24: 73–83.

Reinhardy, J.R. (1992) Decisional control in moving into a nursing home: post-admission adjustment and well-being, *The Gerontologist*, 32(1): 96–103.

Relatives Association (1994) *Response to the NHS Executive Draft Guidance on NHS Responsibilities for Meeting Long Term Health Care Need*. Relatives Association: London.

Richardson, A. and Ritchie, J. (1986) *Better for the Break: Parents' Views about Adults with a Handicap Leaving the Parental Home.* London: King Edward Hospital Fund for London.

Roberts, S., Steele, J. and Morse, N. (1991) *Finding out about Residential Care: Results of a Survey of Users,* working paper 3. London: Policy Studies Institute.

Robinson, B.C. (1983) Validation of a caregiver strain index, *Journal of Gerontology,* 38(3): 344–8.

Rohde, P., Lewinsohn, P.M., Tilson, M. and Seeley, J.R. (1990) Dimensionality of coping and its relation to depression, *Journal of Personality and Social Psychology,* 58(3): 499–511.

Rolland, J.S. (1988) A conceptual model of chronic and life threatening illness and its impact on families, in C.S. Chilman, E.W. Nunnally and F.M. Cox (eds) *Chronic Illness and Disabilities.* Beverly Hills, CA: Sage.

Rolland, J.S. (1994) *Families, Illness and Disability: an Integrative Treatment Model.* New York: Basic Books.

Rook, K.S. (1992) Detrimental effects of social relationships: taking stock of an emerging literature, in H. Veiel and U. Baumann (eds) *The Meaning and Measurement of Social Support.* New York: Hemisphere.

Schultz, C.L., Smyrnios, K.X., Grbich, C.F. and Schultz, N.C. (1993) Caring for family caregivers in Australia: a model of psychoeducational support, *Ageing and Society,* 13: 1–25.

Schultz, R., Diegal, D., Morycz, R. and Visintairer, P. (1990) Psychological paradigms for understanding caregiving, in E. Light and B.D. Lebowitz (eds) *Alzheimer's Disease: Treatment and Family Stress.* New York: Hemisphere.

Schulz, R. and Williamson, G.M. (1993) Psychological and behavioural dimensions of physical frailty, *Journal of Gerontology,* 48 (special edition): 39–43.

Scott, P.A. (1995) Care, attention and imaginative identification in nursing practice, *Journal of Advanced Nursing,* 21(6): 1196–1200.

Secretaries of State for Health, Social Security, Wales and Scotland (1989) *Caring for People: Community Care in the Next Decade and Beyond,* CM 849. London: HMSO.

Selig, S., Tomlinson, T. and Hickey, T. (1991) Ethical dimensions of intergenerational reciprocity: implications for practice, *The Gerontologist,* 31(5): 624–30.

Seltzer, M.M., Krauss, M.W. and Janicki, M. (1994) *Life Course Perspectives on Adulthood and Old Age.* Washington, DC: American Association on Mental Retardation.

Sharp, T. (1992) Listening to carers, *Nursing Times,* 88(21): 29–30.

Sinclair, J. (1990) Residential care, in I. Sinclair, P. Parker, D. Leat and J. Williams (eds) *The Kaleidoscope of Care: a Review of Research on Welfare Provision for Elderly People.* London: HMSO.

Smith, G.C., Smith, M.F. and Toseland, R.W. (1991) Problems identified by family caregivers in counselling, *The Gerontologist,* 31(1): 15–22.

Social Services Inspectorate (1991) *Care Management and Assessment: Practitioners' Guide.* London: HMSO.

Social Services Inspectorate (1996) *Carers (Recognition and Services) Act: Practice Guide.* London: DoH.

Social Work Services Development Group (1984) *Supporting the Informal Carers: Fifty Styles of Caring. Models of Practice for Planners and Practitioners.* London: DHSS.

Spaniol, L. and Jung, H. (1987) Effective coping: a conceptual model, in A.P. Hatfield and H.P. Lefley (eds) *Families of the Mentally Ill: Coping and Adaptation.* London: Cassell.

Staight, P.A. and Harvey, S.M. (1990) Caregiver burden: a comparison between elderly women as primary and secondary caregivers for their spouses, *Journal of Gerontological Social Work*, 15: 89–104.

Stewart, B.J., Archbold, P.G., Harvath, T.A. and Nkongho, N.O. (1993) Role acquisition in family caregivers of older people who have been discharged from hospital, in S.G. Funk, E.H. Tornquist, M.T. Champagne and R.A. Weise (eds) *Key Aspects of Caring for the Chronically Ill: Hospital and Home*. New York: Springer.

Stoller, E.P. and Pugliesi K.L. (1989) Other roles of caregivers: competing responsibilities or supportive resources? *Journal of Gerontology (Social Sciences)*, 44(5): 231–2.

Stone, A. and Neale, J. (1984) New measure of daily coping: development and preliminary results, *Journal of Personality and Social Psychology*, 46(4): 892–906.

Stone, R., Cafferata, G.L. and Sangl, J. (1987) Caregivers of the frail elderly: a national profile, *The Gerontologist*, 27: 616–27.

Stoneman, Z. and Crapps, J.M. (1988) Correlates of stress, perceived competence and depression among family care providers, *American Journal on Mental Retardation*, 93: 166–73.

Summers, J.A., Behr, S.K. and Turnbull, A.P. (1989) Positive adaptation and coping strength of families who have children with disabilities, in G.H.S. Singer and L.K. Irvin (eds) *Support for Caregiving Families: Enabling Positive Adaptation to Disability*. Baltimore, MD: Paul H. Brookes.

Taraborrelli, P. (1993) Exemplar A: becoming a carer, in N. Gilbert (ed.) *Researching Social Life*. London: Sage.

Taylor, R., Ford, G. and Dunbar, M. (1995) The efforts of caring on health: a community based longitudinal study, *Social Science and Medicine*, 40(10): 1407–15.

Thanki, V. (1994) Ethnic diversity and child protection, *Children and Society*, 8(3): 232–44.

Thompson, E.H., Fellerman, A.M., Gallagher-Thompson, D., Rose, J.M. and Lovett, S.B. (1993) Social support and caregiving burden in family caregivers of frail elderly, *Journal of Gerontology*, 48(5): 245–54.

Thornicroft, G. and Breakey, W.R. (1991) The COSTAR programme: improving social networks of the long-term mentally ill, *British Journal of Psychiatry*, 159: 245–9.

Tierney, A., Closs, S.J., Hunter, H.H. and MacMillan, M.S. (1993) Experiences of elderly patients concerning discharge from hospital, *Journal of Clinical Nursing*, 2: 179–85.

Titterton, M. (1992) Managing threats to welfare: the search for a new paradigm of welfare, *Journal of Social Policy*, 21(1): 1–23.

Tolsdorf, C.C. (1976) Social networks, support and coping: an exploratory study, *Family Process*, 15: 407–17.

Triantafillou, J. and Mestheneos, E. (1994) Professionalising the work of family carers of dependent older people, *Health and Social Care in the Community*, 4(2): 257–60.

Turnbull, A.P. and Turnbull, H.R. (1993) Participatory research in cognitive coping: from concepts to research planning, in A.P. Turnbull, J.M. Patterson, S.K. Behr, D.L. Murphy, J.G. Marquis and M.J. Blue-Banning (eds) *Cognitive Coping, Families and Disability*. Baltimore, MD: Paul H. Brookes.

Twigg, J. and Atkin, K. (1994) *Carers Perceived: Policy and Practice in Informal Care*. Buckingham: Open University Press.

Ungerson, C. (1987) *Policy is Personal: Sex, Gender and Informal Care*. London: Tavistock.

United Kingdom Central Council for Nursing, Midwifery and Health Visiting (1995) Discharge of patients from hospital, Registrars letter 18/1995, UKCC, London.

Verbrugge, L.M. and Jette, A.M. (1994) The disablement process, *Social Science Medicine*, 38(1): 1–14.

Victor, C. (1992) Do we need institutional care? in F. Laczko and C. Victor (eds) *Social Policy and Elderly People*. Aldershot: Gower.

Lady Wagner (Chairman) (1988) *Residential Care: a Positive Choice*, report of the Wagner Committee. HMSO: London.

Walker, A., Alber, J. and Guillemard, A.M. (1993) *Older People in Europe: Social and Economic Policies: the 1993 Report of the European Observatory*. Brussels: Commission of the European Communities.

Walker, A.J., Marlen, S.S.K. and Jones, L.L. (1992) The benefits and costs of caregiving and care receiving for daughters and mothers, *Journal of Gerontology*, 47(3): 5130–9.

Walker, A.S., Skin, H.Y. and Bird, N.D. (1990) Perceptions of relationship change and caregiver satisfaction, *Family Relations*, 39 (April): 147–52.

Warner, N. (1994) *Community Care: Just a Fairy Tale?* London: Carers National Association.

Webb, I. (1987) *People who Care: a Report on Carer Provision in England and Wales*. London: Cooperative Women's Guild.

Wellman, B. (1981) Applying network analysis to the study of support, in G.H. Gottlieb (ed.) *Social Networks and Social Support*. Beverly Hills, CA: Sage.

Wenger, G.C. (1990) Elderly carers: the need for appropriate intervention, *Ageing and Society*, 10: 197–219.

Wenger, G.C. (1994) *Understanding Support Networks and Community Care*. Aldershot: Avebury.

Wenger, G.C. (1996) Social network research in gerontology: how did we get there and where do we go next? in V. Minichiello, N. Chappell, A. Walker and H. Kendig (eds) *Sociology of Ageing*. Melbourne: International Sociological Association.

Wenger, G.C. and Shahtahmasebi, S. (1991) Survivors: support network variation and sources of help in rural communities, *Journal of Cross-Cultural Gerontology*, 6(1): 41–82.

Wenger, G.C., Grant, G. and Nolan, M. (1996) Elderly people as providers and recipients of care, in V. Minichiello, N. Chappell, A. Walker and H. Kendig (eds) *Sociology of Ageing*. Melbourne: International Sociological Association.

Westwood, S. and Bachau, P. (1988) Images and realities, *New Society*, 6 May.

Wikler, L., Wasow, M. and Hatfield, E. (1983) Seeking strengths in families of developmentally delayed children, *Social Work*, July–August, 313–15.

Wilkin, D. and Hughes, B. (1986) The elderly and the health services, in C. Phillipson and A. Walker (eds) *Ageing and Social Policy: a Critical Assessment*. Aldershot: Gower.

Willcocks, D. (1986) Residential care, in C. Phillipson and A. Walker (eds) *Ageing and Social Policy: a Critical Assessment*. Aldershot: Gower.

Willcocks, D., Peace, S. and Kellaher, L. (1987) *Private Lives in Public Places*. London: Tavistock.

Williams, R.G.A. (1980) Innovation in community care and general practice: a study of interpretations in a day hospital, *Social Science and Medicine*, 14: 501–10.

Williams, O., Keady, J. and Nolan, M. (1995) Younger onset Alzheimer's disease: learning from the experience of one spouse carer, *Journal of Clinical Nursing*, 4(1): 31–6.

Willoughby, J. and Keating, N. (1991) Being in control: the process of caring for a relative with Alzheimer's disease, *Qualitative Health Research*, 1(1): 27–50.

Wilson, H.S. (1989a) Family caregivers: the experience of Alzheimer's disease, *Applied Nursing Research*, 2(1): 40–5.

Wilson, H.S. (1989b) Family caregiving for a relative with Alzheimer's dementia: coping with negative choices, *Nursing Research*, 38(2): 94–8.

Winik, L., Zetlin, A.G. and Kaufman, S.Z. (1985) Adult mildly retarded persons and their parents: the relationship between involvement and adjustment, *Applied Research in Mental Retardation*, 6: 409–19.

Wistow, G. (1995) Aspirations and realities: community care at the crossroads, *Health and Social Care in the Community*, 3(4): 227–40.

Wood, J.B. and Parham, I.A. (1990) Coping with perceived burden: ethnic and cultural issues in Alzheimer's family caregiving, *Journal of Applied Gerontology*, 9(3): 325–39.

Woollett, A., Marshall, H., Nicolson, P. and Dosanjh, N. (1994) Asian women's ethnic identity: the impact of gender and context in the accounts of women bringing up children in east London, *Feminism and Psychology*, 4(1): 119–32.

Wright, F.D. (1986) *Left to Care Alone*. Aldershot: Gower.

Wuest, J., Ericson, P.K. and Stern, P.N. (1994) Becoming strangers: the changing family caregiving relationship in Alzheimer's disease, *Journal of Advanced Nursing*, 20: 437–43.

Young, E., Wallace, P. and Victor, C. (1991) *Older People at the Interface: a Study of Provision of Services for Older People within Parkside Health Authority*, occasional paper no. 10. London: Helen Hamblyn Research Unit.

Zarit, S. and Whitlach, C. (1992) Institutional placement: phases of the transition, *Gerontologist*, 32: 665–72.

Zarit, S.H., Reever, K.E. and Bach-Peterson, J. (1980) Relatives of impaired elderly: correlates of feelings of burden, *The Gerontologist*, 20: 649–55.

Zipple, A. and Spaniol, L. (1987) Current education and supportive models of family intervention, in A.B. Hatfield and H.P. Lefley (eds) *Families of the Mentally Ill: Coping and Adaptation*. London: Cassell.

INDEX

CARERS PERCEIVED
POLICY AND PRACTICE IN INFORMAL CARE

Julia Twigg and Karl Atkin

Carers are the bedrock of community care, and yet our understanding of how they do and do not fit into the care system is limited. Concern is often expressed about the need to support carers, but the best way to do this is not always clear.

This book breaks new ground in exploring the reality of how service providers like doctors, social workers, and community nurses respond to carers. It looks at which carers get help and why, analysing how age, relationship, class and gender structure the responses of service providers and carers. It examines the moral and policy issues posed by trying to incorporate carers' interests into service provision. What would services look like if they took the needs of carers seriously? How far can they afford to do so? Is this only achieved at the expense of disabled people? What is the proper relationship between carers and services? Carers pose in acute form many of the central dilemmas of social welfare, and the account presented here has the widest significance for the analysis of community care.

Focusing on the views of carers as well as service providers, the book looks at caring across a variety of relationships and conditions, including people with mental health problems and learning disabilities.

Contents

192pp   0 335 19111 8 (Paperback)   0 335 19112 6 (Hardback)

WITH THIS BODY
CARING AND DISABILITY IN MARRIAGE

Gillian Parker

This book breaks new ground by examining the views both of younger people who become disabled after marriage and of their partners who become involved in helping and supporting them. It explores the giving and receiving of personal care in marriage, and the roles of informal networks, services and income in supporting these couples and their children. It shows how, in the absence of help and support from elsewhere, couples are left in an extremely precarious position – practically, financially, emotionally, and socially. Disabled people argue the need for resources and services that would allow them to be independent of 'informal' help. This book shows that age, class, gender and existing power relations in the marriage affect the experience of both disability and caring and the extent to which 'independence' from informal help is seen by either partner as a legitimate or desirable goal.

Contents
The invisible marriage: disability and caring – Negotiating the boundaries: physical and personal care in marriage – 'They've got their own lives to lead': the role of informal networks – Help from formal services – The economic effect of caring and disability – Disability, caring and marriage – Children, disability and caring – It hurts more inside: being a spouse carer – Conclusions – Appendix – References – Index.

160pp   0 335 09946 7 (Paperback)   0 335 09947 5 (Hardback)

OLDER PEOPLE AND COMMUNITY CARE
CRITICAL THEORY AND PRACTICE

Beverley Hughes

Older People and Community Care sets social and health care practice with older people firmly in the context of the new community care arrangements and the consequent organizational trends towards a market culture. However, it also questions the relative lack of attention given by professionals to issues of structural inequality in old age, compared for example to race and gender. Thus, the book tackles a double agenda:

* How can community care practice be suffused with anti-ageist values and principles?

Addressing this question the book sets out the foundation knowledge and values which must underpin the development of anti-discriminatory community care practice and examines the implications for practitioners in terms of the essential skills and inherent dilemmas which arise.

Older People and Community Care is essential reading for all those working with and managing services to older people, and who aspire to make empowerment for older people a reality.

Contents
Series Editor's Preface – Understanding the NHS and Community Care Act – PART ONE: Knowledge and values – Theories of Ageing – The social condition of older people – Ageism and anti-ageist practice – PART TWO: Skills – Communicating with older people: the professional encounter – Assessment – Implementing and managing care – Direct work with users and carers – Protection – Conclusion: challenges and priorities – Bibliography – Index.

192pp   0 335 19156 8 (Paperback)   0 335 19157 6 (Hardback)